Predict with Trishamsha

Indicator of evil and good

Author

V. P. GOEL

Published by

Performonks Education and Consulting Services LLP

First edition, 2025

ISBN: 978-81-982134-3-3

Published by
Performonks Education and Consulting Services LLP
Gurgaon, Haryana
Email: *rashi@performonks.com*

Books by author

हिंदी में	In English	In Russian
वर्ग कुंडलियों से सटीक फलित	Comprehensive Prediction by Divisional Charts	Comprehensive Prediction by Divisional Charts
योगिनी दशा से फलित	Yogini Dasha for Accurate Prediction	Snapshot Prediction using Yogini Dasha
शोडाषोत्तरी दशा से फलित	Predict Through Shodashottary Dasha	
आयु रहस्य	Unravelling Puzzle of longevity	
	Predict Through Shasti Hayani Dasha	
	Locate Disease Astrologically	Locate Disease Astrologically
जैमिनी ज्योतिष से फलित	Predicting through Jaimini Astrology	Predicting through Jaimini Astrology
नवांश से फलित	Predict with Navamsha	Predict with Navamsha
सप्तांश से फलित	Predict with Saptamsha	Predict with Saptamsha
दशमांश से फलित	Predict with Dashamsha	Predict with Dashamsha
	Predict with Trishamsha	
सरल ज्योतिष 1	Saral Jyotish 1	Saral Jyotish 1
सरल ज्योतिष 2	Saral Jyotish 2	Saral Jyotish 2
सरल ज्योतिष 3	Saral Jyotish 3	Saral Jyotish 3
सरल ज्योतिष 4	Saral Jyotish 4	Saral Jyotish 4
सरल ज्योतिष 5	Saral Jyotish 5	
	Saral Jyotish 6	
सरल षड्बल	Saral Jyotish 7	

Contents

Preface

Trishamsha has been given great importance by Parashara. He includes this divisional chart in Shad Varga – the minimum number of charts that must be analyzed before giving any prediction. This chart is used to indicate the evil effects of the horoscope.

We can outline the importance of Trishamsha as under,

- Apart from Navamsha, for all marriage matters, Trishamsha must be checked for confirmation.
- Trishamsha helps to decide the promise of birth whether it is an evil or good birth. With this we can decide the trend of events of life.
- Trishamsha must be considered for predicting dasa and transit results and the timing of events. No event can happen without confirmation from Trishamsha.

Apart from Parashar Trishamsha, there are other methods of casting Trishamsha, and these have been discussed with their application. These are supported by ample examples.

July 2025

Vinod Prakash Goel
E mail: vpgoel2019@gmail.com
You Tube: saraljyotishbyvpgoel

Chapter 1
Classic

This chart, as the name suggests, is the one thirtieth division of a sign. Maharishi Parashar however divides the sign in five unequal parts ruled by five planets Mars, Saturn, Jupiter, Mercury and Venus. Sun and Moon are not presiding over any part. Sun and Moon are father and mother and as such they cannot cause any miseries. If we see Chaturvimshamsha, all divisions start from Leo or Cancer indicating that they are provider of learning.

Parashar Method

The portion of each planet in any sign is Mars 5°, Saturn 5°, Jupiter 8°, Mercury 7° and Venus 5°. For planets or Lagan in odd signs, the order of ruler ship is as given above. For planets in even sign, the order is reversed. For odd signs the planet occupies the odd sign of the lord of Trimshamsha where for even sign it occupies the even sign of the lord of Trimshamsha.

Table for Odd Sign

Part	Degrees	Lord	Sign in D30	Tatva
1	0° — 5°	Mars	Aries	Fire – Agni
2	5° — 10°	Saturn	Aquarius	Air – Vayu
3	10° — 18	Jupiter	Sagittarius	Ether – Akash
4	18° — 25	Mercury	Gemini	Earth – Prithvi
5	25° —30	Venus	Libra	Water – Jala

Table for Even Sign

Part	Degrees	Lord	Sign in D30	Tatva
1	$0^{\circ}-5^{\circ}$	Venus	Taurus	Water – Jala
2	$5^{\circ}-10^{\circ}$	Mercury	Virgo	Earth – Prithvi
3	$10^{\circ}-18$	Jupiter	Pisces	Ether – Akash
4	$18^{\circ}-25$	Saturn	Capricorn	Air – Vayu
5	$25^{\circ}-30$	Mars	Scorpio	Fire – Agni

Relation of Planet, Tatva and Senses

Planet	Deity	Physical Tatva	Sense
Mars	Agni	Fire	Sight
Saturn	Vayu	Air	Touch
Jupiter	Indra	Ether	Hearing
Mercury	Kubera	Earth	Smell
Venus	Varun	Water	Speech

Remedial action for different planets

D30 Lord	Tatva	Deity	Remedy
Mars	Fire	Sun	Light a lamp
Saturn	Air	Shiva	Pranayama
Jupiter	Ether	Narayan	Meditation
Mercury	Earth	Ganesh	Japa
Venus	Water	Devi	Pooja, Donation

Deities of Parashar Trimshamsha

The presiding deities of Trimshamsha are Agni, Vayu, Indra, Kubera and Varun respectively for odd signs this order is reversed for even sign.

Sun and Moon are not given any lordship in Trimshamsha chart. Thus, no planet can occupy Leo and Cancer in the Parashar Trimshamsha. These two luminaries are higher category planets and do not contribute in the scheme of five Tatva. Five Tatva make up the physical body and are also five senses. Sun is Atma and Moon is mind. We experience problems through the five senses and by the physical body made of five Tatva. Jupiter and Mercury have been given the major share in Trimshamsha.

Similarly, Rahu and Ketu are also left out as they are not given any lordship in Parashar scheme. They represent the purpose of cycle of birth and rebirth. The other five planets show the process of creation and destruction.

Houses of Parashar Trimshamsha

First House – Weakness of self and the miseries i.e. the problems or happiness generated by own doings. Problems acquired in this birth.

Second House – Happiness or miseries due to the family in which you are born. This shows whether you get happiness or sorrows from family.

Third House – Courage to face the miseries of life. Problems arise from neighbors and co born.

Fourth House – The character and the problems due to your behavior at home. It is the house of aggravation or cure of the problems. Problems are due to property.

Fifth House – Good or bad intelligence which can cause happiness or trouble. Perverted thoughts. Trouble from progeny.

Sixth House – It is house of enemy and disease. The diseases of the body with known causes like accident.

Seventh House – Outside world and people at large. The problems arise generally through the society, village etc. These can be through spouse. It shows your public behavior and etiquette.

Eighth House – The congenital miseries which you are born with. The weaknesses which are carried from past karmas.

These are permanent and cannot be remedied. The diseases which cannot be cured and become chronic.

Ninth House – Miseries arising out of disrespect to religion or guru or Gods. One should seek their blessings instead of curses.

Tenth House – Problems due to willful wrong action. The mental attitude which gives happiness or otherwise. The karmas which cause it.

Eleventh House – Greed and the miseries due to greed. The best solution is to avoid greed consciously and get happiness instead of miseries.

Twelfth House – Problems which one faces in foreign country. The place of hospital and sleep.

Examination of D30

1. No human is perfect and is not free from the miseries of life.
2. A strong Lagan and Lagan lord assures problem free life.
3. Malefic planets in the houses are the cause of miseries through the signification of the house.
4. This divisional chart is Tatva based. To alleviate the problems caused by a planet, one should worship the Trimshamsha lord of the planet.
5. We can locate the Trimshamsha lord of sixth lord and eighth lord of birth chart and perform remedial measures. The Trimshamsha lord of the dasha period lord indicates the remedies during its dasha period.
6. Look for a planet which is in Lagan or aspecting Lagan in Rashi chart. Now, if the Lagan of Trimshamsha belongs to that planet, then this planet is the cause of problem. In addition, if the same planet is in Trimshamsha Lagan or aspects it, then it is worst.

7. A malefic sign rising in Trimshamsha and in addition a malefic is associated with Lagan in birth chart gives problems in marriage.
8. The character is seen from fourth house. For good morals, a benefic sign should be there in fourth house and without any malefic association. The fourth house should preferable be vacant. In addition, the fourth house from Lagan lord of D30 should also be vacant.
9. The Trimshamsha lord of Sun indicates the quality of soul (Atma). This is especially true when seen in cyclical, Iyer or Varanasi Trimshamsha.
10. We should look to the placement of sixth lord/and eighth lord of the natal chart to find the source of problem.
11. Placement of planets in three houses of D30 is important and should be examined closely. Planets in Lagan shows the weakness acquired in current birth. The Lagan lord shows the nature of weakness. Planets, especially malefic, show the mental weakness. The Moon sign lord indicates the source of influence on mind under which the action is done. Planets in eighth house are the weakness due to past life. The lord of eighth shows the source of this weakness.
12. The sense governed by the afflicting planet can be used to understand the cause of misfortune.
13. Note the Tatva of birth lagan sign and the Tatva of Trishamsha lagan sign and if they are opposite to each other than there will be lot of problems in life.
14. We can see the Tatva of MD and AD. We can see it in two ways. First is to see the Tatva of Dasha lords. When their Tatva are opposite then the Dasha period brings trouble. We should check them for individual horoscope by the

placement of Dasha lords in sign. We take the Tatva of the sign and decide. For example, we take Saturn and Venus. They are of opposite Tatva of air and water. But if Saturn and Venus occupy ether Tatva then the mutual Dasha period will not be bad. In another situation when Saturn occupy airy sign and Venus is in watery sign then problems will be manifold.

Female horoscope

Many classics have attributed the results of Trishamsha for a female horoscope. These are based on the sign occupied by lagan or Moon in birth horoscope by a planet and its placement in Trishamsha chart. The stronger of lagan and Moon is considered. Why this is attributed to a female horoscope only? Why these cannot be applied to a male horoscope also? Yes, we can apply it to a male horoscope also.

Sign occupied by lagan or Moon in birth of Mars and Trishamsha of Mars.

BPHS: - Aggressive and have premarital sex.

Saravali: - Harlot.

Jatak Parijata: - Ill behaved.

Jatak Bharnam: - Wicked.

Hora Sara: - Give birth to dead child and will not be of good quality.

Kala Prakashika: - Disposed to wickedness and children will die.

Phaldeepika: - Ill behaved

Sign occupied by lagan or Moon in birth of Mars and Trishamsha of Mercury.

BPHS: - Will be involved in conjuration and occultism.

Saravali: - Cunning disposition.

Jatak Parijata: - Corrupt and immoral.

Jatak Bharnam: - Magician.

Hora Sara: - She will be cunning, will follow dirty principles and have few issues.

Kala Prakashika: - Bad character.

Phaldeepika: - Deceitful.

Sign occupied by lagan or Moon in birth of Mars and Trishamsha of Venus.

BPHS: - Adulterous even after marriage.

Saravali: - A female devoid of virtuous history.

Jatak Parijata: - Addicted to a paramour.

Jatak Bharnam: - Wicked._

Hora Sara: - She will beget daughters and will indulge in secret sexual pleasures.

Kala Prakashika: - Indulge in adultery.

Phaldeepika: - Bad character

Sign occupied by lagan or Moon in birth of Mars and Trishamsha of Jupiter._

BPHS: - Saintly and virtuous.

Saravali: - Chaste lady.

Jatak Parijata: - Worthy and virtuous.

Jatak Bharnam: - Sincere to her husband.

Hora Sara: -_Will beget off springs, burdened by expenses galore and dear to her partner.

Kala Prakashika: - Wealthy and will get sons.

Phaldeepika: - Cultured and wealthy.

Sign occupied by lagan or Moon in birth of Mars and Trishamsha of Saturn._

BPHS: - Will be a maid servant or a mistress.

Saravali: - In servitude.

Jatak Parijata: - Menial or slave.

Jatak Bharnam: - Worthy of censure and blame.

Hora Sara: - Will be a servant and vicious in several ways.

Kala Prakashika: - Bad character.

Phaldeepika: - Maid servant.

Sign occupied by lagan or Moon in birth of Mercury and Trishamsha of Mars.

BPHS: - Cunning and guileful.

Saravali: - Female will be cunning.

Jatak Parijata: - Will have sons.

Jatak Bharnam: - Deceitful

Hora Sara: - Will be addicted to another man.

Kala Prakashika: - Few sons.

Phaldeepika: - Deceitful.

Sign occupied by lagan or Moon in birth of Mercury and Trishamsha of Mercury.

BPHS: - Virtuous woman.

Saravali: - A chaste girl.

Jatak Parijata: - Virile, famous and beautiful.

Jatak Bharnam: - Woman of virtues.

Hora Sara: - She will be supreme of the family.

Kala Prakashika: - Woman of good qualities.

Phaldeepika: - Full of good qualities.

Sign occupied by lagan or Moon in birth of Mercury and Trishamsha of Venus.

BPHS: - Lascivious character.

Saravali: - High degree of lust.

Jatak Parijata: - Conspicuous for her elegant attire.

Jatak Bharnam: - Bereft of sexual desire.

Hora Sara: - She will have cattle, wealth and luxuries.

Kala Prakashika: - Happy and wealthy.

Phaldeepika: - Mourning and complaining nature.

Sign occupied by lagan or Moon in birth of Mercury and Trishamsha of Jupiter.

BPHS: - Chaste.

Saravali: - Virtuous housewife.

Jatak Parijata: - Chaste and devoted to her husband.

Jatak Bharnam: - Faithful to her husband.

Hora Sara: - Will be devoted to her husband exclusively and be dear to him.

Kala Prakashika: - Chaste.

Phaldeepika: - Chaste.

Sign occupied by lagan or Moon in birth of Mercury and Trishamsha of Saturn.

BPHS: - She will be hermaphrodite.

Saravali: - Impotent.

Jatak Parijata: - Widow, have her children stillborn or of the form of a eunuch.

Jatak Bharnam: - Husband is impotent.

Hora Sara: - She will equal a neuter, will give birth to dead child (or her children will die) and she will not live with her husband.

Kala Prakashika: - Indulge in adultery and children will die.

Phaldeepika: - Eunuch.

Sign occupied by lagan or Moon in birth of Venus, Trishamsha of Mars.

BPHS: - Will be of wicked nature.

Saravali: - Wicked nature.

Jatak Parijata: - Vicious and quarrelsome.

Jatak Bharnam: - Excessively vicious.

Hora Sara: - She will be wicked, like quarrels, hate her husband and will have a bad history.

Kala Prakashika: - Immoral.

Phaldeepika: - Bad character.

Sign occupied by lagan or Moon in birth of Venus, Trishamsha of Mercury.

BPHS: - She will distinguish herself in various kinds of arts.

Saravali: - Skillful.

Jatak Parijata: - Fond of arts and music.

Jatak Bharnam: - Skillful in arts.

Hora Sara: - She will take pleasure in poetry, arts, singing, playing instruments and she will be beautiful and virtuous.

Kala Prakashika: - Full of virtues.

Phaldeepika: - Learned.

Sign occupied by lagan or Moon in birth of Venus and Trishamsha of Venus.

BPHS: - Will be popular for her good qualities.

Saravali: - Famous for her virtues.

Jatak Parijata: - Fond of wise men, favorite of her husband and liked by people.

Jatak Bharnam: - Prosperous with many qualities.

Hora Sara: - She will have all luxuries, be sharp and dear to all.

Kala Prakashika: - Wealthy and happy.

Phaldeepika: - Famous.

Sign occupied by lagan or Moon in birth of Venus and Trishamsha of Jupiter.

BPHS: - Full of good qualities.

Saravali: - Virtuous.

Jatak Parijata: - Chaste and mother of many children.

Jatak Bharnam: - Many virtues.

Hora Sara: - Bestowed with husband, sons and wealth.

Kala Prakashika: - Chaste and of good nature.

Phaldeepika: - Respected.

Sign occupied by lagan or Moon in birth of Venus and Trishamsha of Saturn.

BPHS: - She will marry for second time.

Saravali: - Given in marriage as second wife.

Jatak Parijata: - Remarriage.

Jatak Bharnam: - She lives in the house of some person other than her husband.

Hora Sara: - She will re marry and beget dead children or loose children and always be sick.

Kala Prakashika: - Children will die and will indulge in prostitution.

Phaldeepika: - Will resort to another husband.

Sign occupied by lagan or Moon in birth of Moon and Trishamsha of Mars.

BPHS: - Will be of independent nature.

Saravali: - Bestows her freedom not as a house wife.

Jatak Parijata: - Endowed with physical strength. When Moon is aspected by malefic, she will take delight in amusement of her paramours.

Jatak Bharnam: - Independent nature.

Hora Sara: - She will be self-willed, sensual and will lose children.

Kala Prakashika: - Independent nature and children will die.

Phaldeepika: - Self-willed and uncontrolled.

Sign occupied by lagan or Moon in birth of Moon and Trishamsha of Mercury.

BPHS: - Will be expert in sculpture art.

Saravali: - Skill in art.

Jatak Parijata: - Will be skilled in arts.

Jatak Bharnam: - expert in sculpture art.

Hora Sara: - Artisan.

Kala Prakashika: - Have knowledge of sculpture and devoted to husband.

Phaldeepika: - Skilled in art.

Sign occupied by lagan or Moon in birth of Moon and Trishamsha of Venus.

BPHS: - Will be characterless.

Saravali: - Will make her unchaste.

Jatak Parijata: - Lustful.

Jatak Bharnam: - Devoted to her husband.

Hora Sara: - She will be either barren or children will die.

Kala Prakashika: - Unchaste and have less children.

Phaldeepika: - Full of virtues.

Sign occupied by lagan or Moon in birth of Moon and Trishamsha of Jupiter.

BPHS: - Endowed with many qualities.

Saravali: - Quite virtuous.

Jatak Parijata: - Short lived and will have few children.

Jatak Bharnam: - Virtues.

Hora Sara: - The issues and longevity is limited.

Kala Prakashika: - Of royal nature.

Phaldeepika: - Endowed with distinguished qualities.

Sign occupied by lagan or Moon in birth of Moon and Trishamsha of Saturn.

BPHS: - Will attain widowhood.

Saravali: - Will betray her husband.

Jatak Parijata: - Will become a widow.

Jatak Bharnam: - Kills her husband.

Hora Sara: - She will be deprived of her husband and will eke out her food with difficulty.

Kala Prakashika: - Live in a foreign country and become a prostitute.

Phaldeepika: - She will kill her husband.

Sign occupied by lagan or Moon in birth of Sun and Trishamsha of Mars.

BPHS: - Will be of talkative nature.

Saravali: - Talkative.

Jatak Parijata: - Have masculine disposition.

Jatak Bharnam: - Independent nature.

Hora Sara: - Very talkative, unchaste, be in distant places and will resemble man in appearance and qualities.

Kala Prakashika: - Wicked.

Phaldeepika: - Will be a wicked wife.

Sign occupied by lagan or Moon in birth of Sun and Trishamsha of Mercury.

BPHS: - Will behave like a man.

Saravali: - Male natured.

Jatak Parijata: - Will be masculine in her ways and vicious.

Jatak Bharnam: - Wicked mind.

Hora Sara: - She will be devoted to her work but not chaste.

Kala Prakashika: - Masculine nature.

Phaldeepika: - Masculine in behavior.

Sign occupied by lagan or Moon in birth of Sun and Trishamsha of Venus.

BPHS: - She will immolate herself.

Saravali: - Chaste.

Jatak Parijata: - Attached to unworthy husband and will suffer from disease.

Jatak Bharnam: - Characterless.

Hora Sara: - Will be dear to king, will not have many issues and always be sick.

Kala Prakashika: - Attached to lower category people.

Phaldeepika: - Attached to a person other than her husband.

Sign occupied by lagan or Moon in birth of Sun and Trishamsha of Jupiter.

BPHS: - She will be a queen.

Saravali: - Queen.

Jatak Parijata: - She will be beloved of a royal husband and endowed with good qualities.

Jatak Bharnam: - Queen of a king.

Hora Sara: - Liked by king.

Kala Prakashika: - Wife of a king.

Phaldeepika: - Wife of a king or landlord.

Sign occupied by lagan or Moon in birth of Sun and Trishamsha of Saturn.

BPHS: - Will go against the family tradition and customs.

Saravali: - Fallen.

Jatak Parijata: - Unchaste and unhappy.

Jatak Bharnam: - Manly behavior.

Hora Sara: - She will be healthy and poor.

Kala Prakashika: - Will be barren.

Phaldeepika: - Without any character.

Sign occupied by lagan or Moon in birth of Jupiter and Trishamsha of Mars.

BPHS: - Will possess many qualities.

Saravali: - Gentle lady with many virtues.

Jatak Parijata: - Will be renowned and have a following.

Jatak Bharnam: - Virtues.

Hora Sara: - Will be a domestic servant and will be famous.

Kala Prakashika: - Good nature and chaste.

Phaldeepika: - Maid servant.

Sign occupied by lagan or Moon in birth of Jupiter and Trishamsha of Mercury.

BPHS: - Will be well acquainted with sciences.

Saravali: - With knowledge.

Jatak Parijata: - Virtuous and highly respected.

Jatak Bharnam: - Endowed with much grandeur.

Hora Sara: - Adored by all.

Kala Prakashika: - Skillful and deviate from religious acts.

Phaldeepika: - Skilled in art.

Sign occupied by lagan or Moon in birth of Jupiter and Trishamsha of Venus.

BPHS: - Will be deviating from good conduct.

Saravali: - Female with evil speech.

Jatak Parijata: - She will possess children, good clothing and ornaments.

Jatak Bharnam: - Faithful to her husband.

Hora Sara: - Will have sons.

Kala Prakashika: - Chaste.

Phaldeepika: - Very chaste.

Sign occupied by lagan or Moon in birth of Jupiter and Trishamsha of Jupiter.

BPHS: - Will have many qualities.

Saravali: - Many virtues.

Jatak Parijata: - Will have abundance of wealth, clothing and ornaments.

Jatak Bharnam: - Famous due to her virtues.

Hora Sara: - Very rich.

Kala Prakashika: - Virtuous and chaste.

Phaldeepika: - Endowed with many good qualities.

Sign occupied by lagan or Moon in birth of Jupiter and Trishamsha of Saturn.

BPHS: - Will be averse to intense sexual relation.

Saravali: - Desiring limited physical union.

Jatak Parijata: - Will be poor.

Jatak Bharnam: - Have a little sexual desire.

Hora Sara: - Will make her poor; beget daughters and independent all times.

Kala Prakashika: - Find pleasure in low caste people.

Phaldeepika: - Madly in love with person other than her husband.

Sign occupied by lagan or Moon in birth of Saturn and Trishamsha of Mars.

BPHS: - Will be a maid servant.

Saravali: - Will be a servant.

Jatak Parijata: - Will be distressed.

Jatak Bharnam: - servant. Slave.

Hora Sara: - She will be a servant, unchaste and will be getting dead children.

Kala Prakashika: - Loss of children.

Phaldeepika: - Maid servant.

Sign occupied by lagan or Moon in birth of Saturn and Trishamsha of Mercury.

BPHS: - Will be of low moral values.

Saravali: - Cruel and devoid of conduct.

Jatak Parijata: - She will know all things but unchaste.

Jatak Bharnam: - Wicked.

Hora Sara: - She will not be loyal to her husband, be unchaste and cunning.

Kala Prakashika: - Bad character.

Phaldeepika: - Unchaste.

Sign occupied by lagan or Moon in birth of Saturn and Trishamsha of Venus.

BPHS: - She will be a learned woman.

Saravali: - Intelligent.

Jatak Parijata: - Barren and spend thrift.

Jatak Bharnam: - Cannot bear children.

Hora Sara: - She will be of lordly disposition, be barren and devoid of good history.

Kala Prakashika: - Barren.

Phaldeepika: - Issueless and poor.

Sign occupied by lagan or Moon in birth of Saturn and Trishamsha of Jupiter.

BPHS: - Will be devoted to her husband.

Saravali: - Chaste lady.

Jatak Parijata: - Will strictly adhere to family customs.

Jatak Bharnam: - Respects husband as God.

Hora Sara: - Dear to her husband, lucky and widely famous.

Kala Prakashika: - Attached to her husband.

Phaldeepika: - Will keep her husband under control.

Sign occupied by lagan or Moon in birth of Saturn and Trishamsha of Saturn.

BPHS: - Will be involved in adultery with low caste persons.

Saravali: - Addicted to a base man.

Jatak Parijata: - Will be disliked by her husband.

Jatak Bharnam: - Have base desires for sex.

Hora Sara: - She will take to bad traditions and will be very unlucky.

Kala Prakashika: - Will follow the religion of lower caste.

Phaldeepika: - She will be in love with person other than her husband.

These dictums are not to be taken literally and should be taken in liberal context. Times have changed and the meanings are bound to change also. These results depend upon the total horoscope and not in isolation.

Example 1 – DOB 19 JUNE 1947, TOB 02.30, POB MUMBAI

Birth Chart

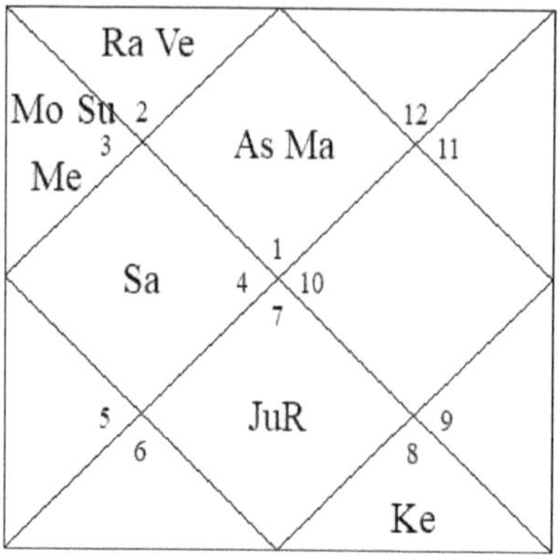

Birth Chart

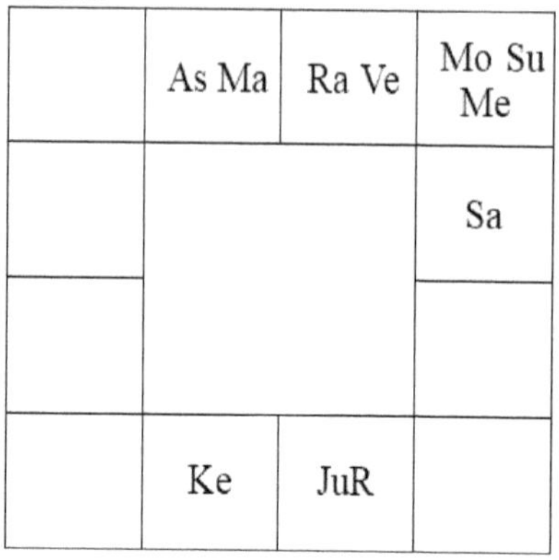

D30

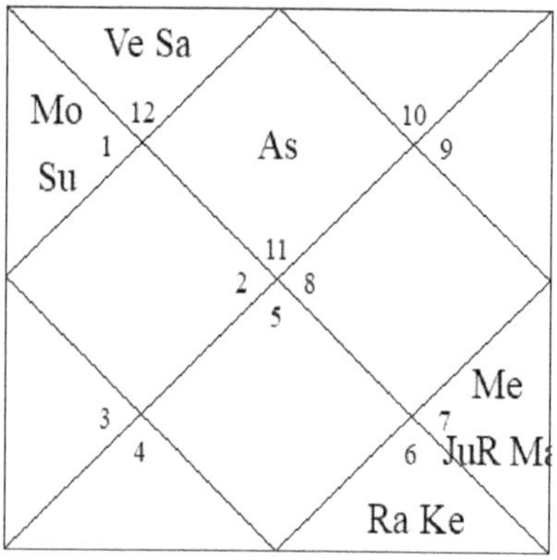

D30

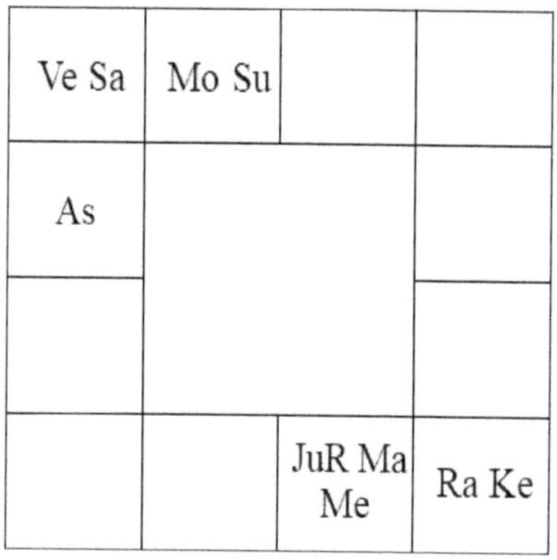

We will examine the placement of lagan and Moon.

Lagan is in the sign of Mars in birth horoscope and is in sign of Saturn in Trishamsha.

Moon is in the sign of Mercury in birth horoscope and is in sign of Mars in Trishamsha.

The results for this placement of lagan and Moon are listed below.

Lagan

BPHS: - Will be a maid servant or a mistress.

Saravali: - In servitude.

Jatak Parijata: - Menial or slave.

Jatak Bharnam: - Worthy of censure and blame.

Hora Sara: - Will be a servant and vicious in several ways.

Kala Prakashika: - Bad character.

Phaldeepika: - Maid servant.

Moon

BPHS: - Cunning and guileful.

Saravali: - Will be cunning.

Jatak Parijata: - Will have sons.

Jatak Bharnam: - Deceitful.

Hora Sara: - Will be addicted to another man.

Kala Prakashika: - Few sons.

Phaldeepika: - Deceitful.

This is a male chart. He had five marriages. Examination of Sun sign in Trishamsha is a good judgment of quality of Atma. In this chart Sun is in sign of Mars and aspected by Mars. Mars gives Tamasic color to Atma.

Example 2 – DOB 28 SEPTEMBER 1929, TOB 22.44.59, POB INDORE

Birth Chart

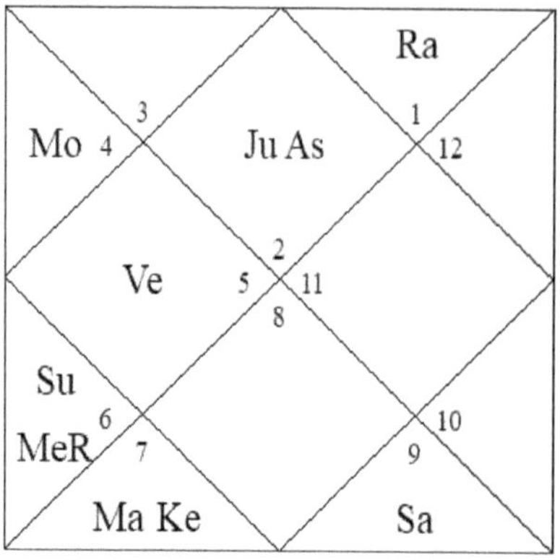

Birth Chart

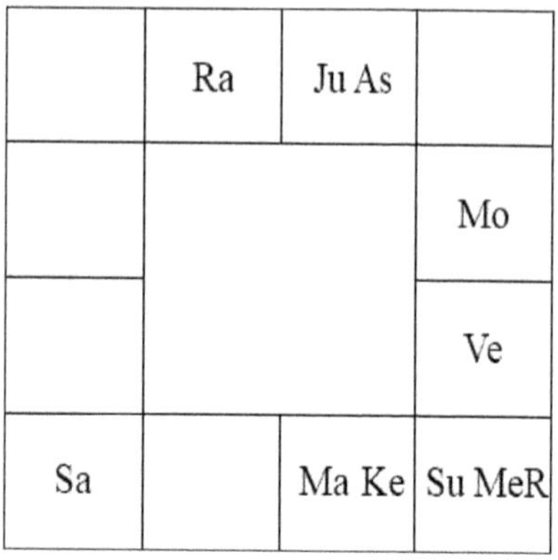

D30

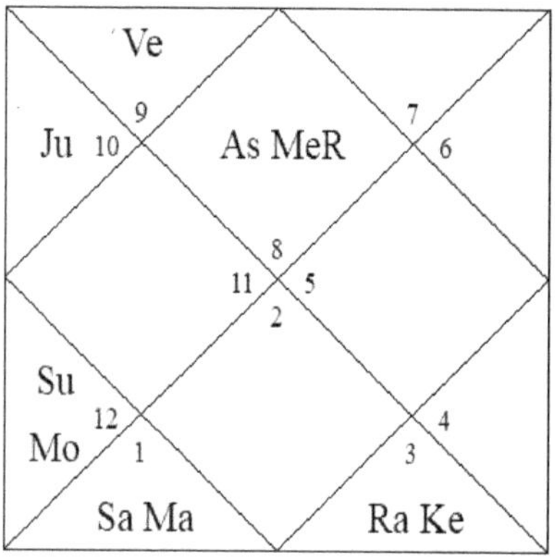

D30

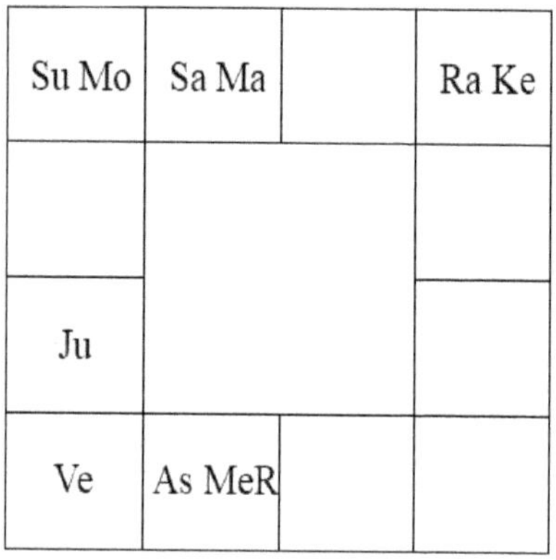

Lagan; Sign occupied by lagan in birth is of Venus and in Trishamsha of Mars.

BPHS: - Will be of wicked nature.

Saravali: - Wicked nature.

Jatak Parijata: - Vicious and quarrelsome.

Jatak Bharnam: - Excessively vicious.

Hora Sara: - She will be wicked, like quarrels, hate her husband and will have a bad history.

Kala Prakashika: - Immoral.

Phaldeepika: - Bad character.

Moon;

Sign occupied by Moon in birth is of Moon and in Trishamsha of Jupiter.

BPHS: - Endowed with many qualities.

Saravali: - Quite virtuous.

Jatak Parijata: - Short lived and will have few children.

Jatak Bharnam: - Virtues.

Hora Sara: - The issues and longevity is limited.

Kala Prakashika: - Of royal nature.

Phaldeepika: - Endowed with distinguished qualities.

She is a famous singer and is not married. Sun is in the sign of Jupiter in Trishamsha. This gives a satwik nature.

Chapter 2
Cyclical Trishamsha

The Parashar Trishamsha divides each sign in five unequal parts. This method leaves out Cancer and Leo. In Trishamsha no planet can occupy these signs. This chart, as the name suggests, should divide each sign in thirty equal parts which results in other types of Trishamsha. There are two methods of casting this type of Trishamsha.

1. **Varanasi Trishamsha**_
2. This Trishamsha is also known as Iyer or cyclical Trishamsha. In this method of casting, each sign is divided in 30 equal parts. Each part or Trishamsha is of 1 degree span. For planets or lagan in odd sign in birth horoscope the counting starts from Aries. For planets or lagan in even sign in birth horoscope the counting starts from Libra. The other Trishamsha follow in direct order. A ready table is given for easy reference.

Table for Varanasi Trishamsha

Part	Degrees	Odd signs	Even signs
1	0 - 1	Aries	Libra
2	1 – 2	Taurus	Scorpio
3	2 – 3	Gemini	Sagittarius
4	3 – 4	Cancer	Capricorn
5	4 – 5	Leo	Aquarius
6	5 – 6	Virgo	Pisces
7	6 – 7	Libra	Aries

Part	Degrees	Odd signs	Even signs
8	7 – 8	Scorpio	Taurus
9	8 – 9	Sagittarius	Gemini
10	9 – 10	Capricorn	Cancer
11	10 – 11	Aquarius	Leo
12	11 – 12	Pisces	Virgo
13	12 – 13	Aries	Libra
14	13 – 14	Taurus	Scorpio
15	14 – 15	Gemini	Sagittarius
16	15 – 16	Cancer	Capricorn
17	16 – 17	Leo	Aquarius
18	17 – 18	Virgo	Pisces
19	18 – 19	Libra	Aries
20	19 – 20	Scorpio	Taurus
21	20 – 21	Sagittarius	Gemini
22	21 – 22	Capricorn	Cancer
23	22 – 23	Aquarius	Leo
24	23 – 24	Pisces	Virgo
25	24 – 25	Aries	Libra
26	25 – 26	Taurus	Scorpio
27	26 – 27	Gemini	Sagittarius
28	27 – 28	Cancer	Capricorn
29	28 – 29	Leo	Aquarius
30	29 – 30	Virgo	Pisces

Example DOB November 1917, TOB 23.11, POB Allahabad

Birth Chart

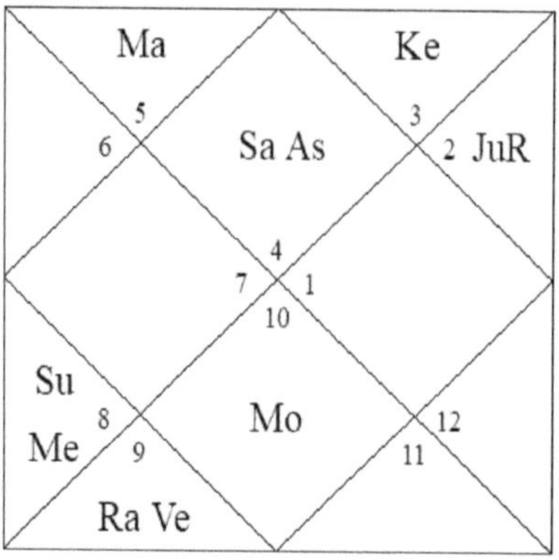

Birth Chart

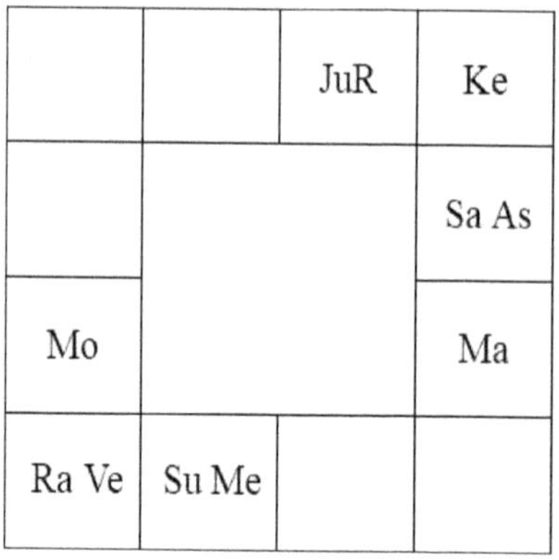

Lagan – Lagan is in 28th Trishamsha in Cancer. Counting will start from Libra. The sign occupied by lagan in Trishamsha will be Capricorn.

Sun – Sun is in 5th Trishamsha in even sign Scorpio. Fifth sign from Libra is Aquarius and Sun goes to Aquarius in Trishamsha.

Moon – Moon is in 6th Trishamsha in Capricorn. Sixth from Libra is Pisces and Moon is placed in Pisces in Trishamsha.

Mars – Mars is in Leo and in 17th Trishamsha. Counting will start from Aries. Leo is 17th sign from Aries and Mars is in Leo in Trishamsha.

Mercury – Mercury is in 14th Trishamsha in even sign Scorpio. Mercury goes to Scorpio in Trishamsha.

Jupiter – Jupiter is in 16th Trishamsha in Taurus. It goes to Capricorn in Trishamsha.

Venus – Venus is in 22nd Trishamsha in Sagittarius. Venus is in Capricorn in Trishamsha.

Saturn – Saturn is also in 22nd Trishamsha in Cancer. Saturn is in Cancer in Trishamsha.

Rahu – Rahu is in 10th Trishamsha in Sagittarius. Rahu occupy Capricorn in Trishamsha.

Ketu – Ketu will always be with Rahu in this Trishamsha. For delineation we should place it opposite to Rahu.

The Trishamsha arrived is as under.

D30 Iyer

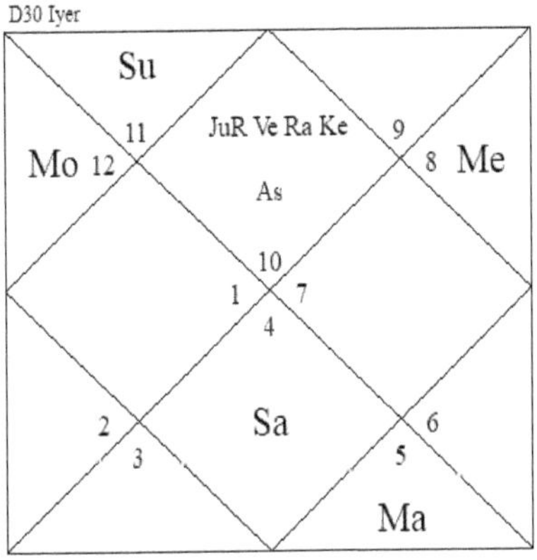

D30 Iyer

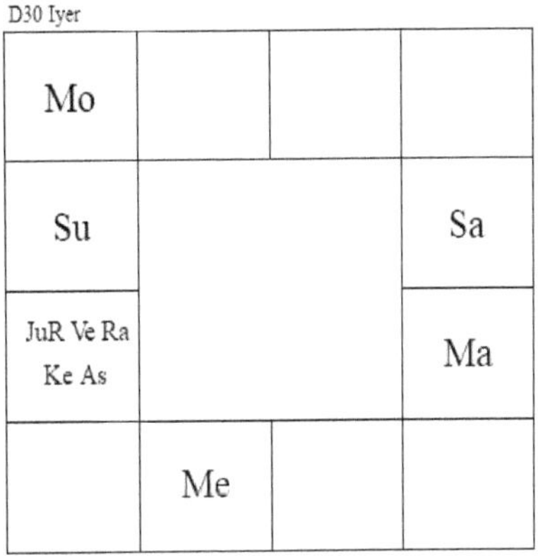

2. Shashtamsha like Trishamsha

This Trishamsha is also known as Venkatesha Trishamsha. In this version of Trishamsha, each sign is divided in 30 equal parts of 1 degree each. The counting is like Shashtamsha. The first part starts from the sign occupied by planet or lagan in birth horoscope. The other parts follow in direct order. A ready table is given.

Table for Shashtamsha like Trishamsha

Sr	Deg.	Ari	Tau	Gem	Can	Leo	Vir	Lib	Sco	Sag	Cap	Aqu	Pis
1	0 - 1	1	2	3	4	5	6	7	8	9	10	11	12
2	1 – 2	2	3	4	5	6	7	8	9	10	11	12	1
3	2 – 3	3	4	5	6	7	8	9	10	11	12	1	2
4	3 – 4	4	5	6	7	8	9	10	11	12	1	2	3
5	4 – 5	5	6	7	8	9	10	11	12	1	2	3	4
6	5 – 6	6	7	8	9	10	11	12	1	2	3	4	5
7	6 – 7	7	8	9	10	11	12	1	2	3	4	5	6
8	7 – 8	8	9	10	11	12	1	2	3	4	5	6	7
9	8 – 9	9	10	11	12	1	2	3	4	5	6	7	8
10	9 – 10	10	11	12	1	2	3	4	5	6	7	8	9
11	10 – 11	11	12	1	2	3	4	5	6	7	8	9	10
12	11 – 12	12	1	2	3	4	5	6	7	8	9	10	11
13	12 – 13	1	2	3	4	5	6	7	8	9	10	11	12
14	13 – 14	2	3	4	5	6	7	8	9	10	11	12	1
15	14 – 15	3	4	5	6	7	8	9	10	11	12	1	2
16	15 – 16	4	5	6	7	8	9	10	11	12	1	2	3
17	16 – 17	5	6	7	8	9	10	11	12	1	2	3	4
18	17 – 18	6	7	8	9	10	11	12	1	2	3	4	5
19	18 – 19	7	8	9	10	11	12	1	2	3	4	5	6
20	19 – 20	8	9	10	11	12	1	2	3	4	5	6	7
21	20 – 21	9	10	11	12	1	2	3	4	5	6	7	8
22	21 – 22	10	11	12	1	2	3	4	5	6	7	8	9
23	22 – 23	11	12	1	2	3	4	5	6	7	8	9	10
24	23 – 24	12	1	2	3	4	5	6	7	8	9	10	11
25	24 – 25	1	2	3	4	5	6	7	8	9	10	11	12
26	25 – 26	2	3	4	5	6	7	8	9	10	11	12	1
27	26 – 27	3	4	5	6	7	8	9	10	11	12	1	2
28	27 – 28	4	5	6	7	8	9	10	11	12	1	2	3
29	28 – 29	5	6	7	8	9	10	11	12	1	2	3	4
30	29 – 30	6	7	8	9	10	11	12	1	2	3	4	5

Example DOB 19 November 1917, TOB 23.11, POB Allahabad

Birth Chart

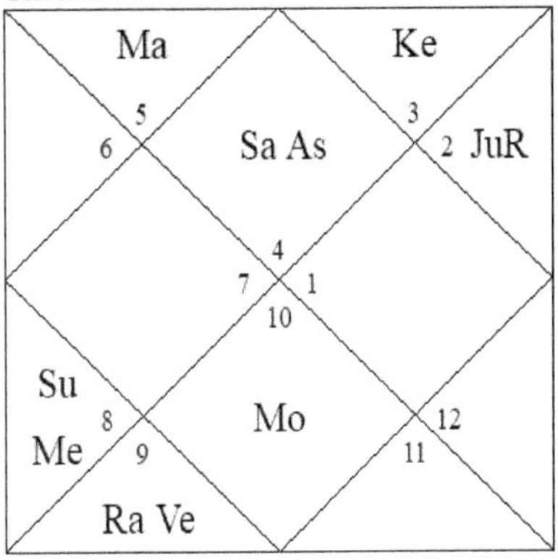

Birth Chart

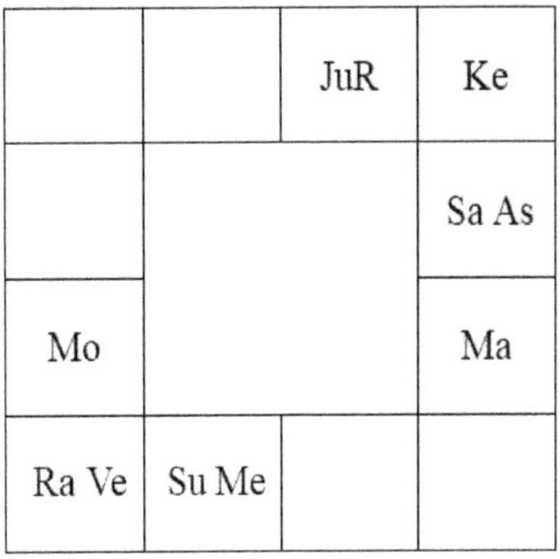

Lagan – Lagan is in 28th Trishamsha in Cancer. Counting will start from Cancer. The sign occupied by lagan in Trishamsha will be Libra.

Sun – Sun is in 5th Trishamsha in even sign Scorpio. Fifth sign from Scorpio is Pisces and Sun goes to Pisces in Trishamsha.

Moon – Moon is in 6th Trishamsha in Capricorn. Sixth from Capricorn is Gemini and Moon is placed in Gemini in Trishamsha.

Mars – Mars is in Leo and in 17th Trishamsha. Counting will start from Leo. Sagittarius is 17th sign from Leo and Mars is in Sagittarius in Trishamsha.

Mercury – Mercury is in 14th Trishamsha in even sign Scorpio. Mercury goes to Sagittarius in Trishamsha.

Jupiter – Jupiter is in 16th Trishamsha in Taurus. It goes to Leo in Trishamsha.

Venus – Venus is in 22nd Trishamsha in Sagittarius. Venus is in Virgo in Trishamsha.

Saturn – Saturn is also in 22nd Trishamsha in Cancer. Saturn is in Aries in Trishamsha.

Rahu – Rahu is in 10th Trishamsha in Sagittarius. Rahu occupy Virgo in Trishamsha.

Ketu – Ketu will always be opposite Rahu in this Trishamsha. Ketu occupy Pisces in Trishamsha.

The Venkatesha Trishamsha for example chart is as under.

D30

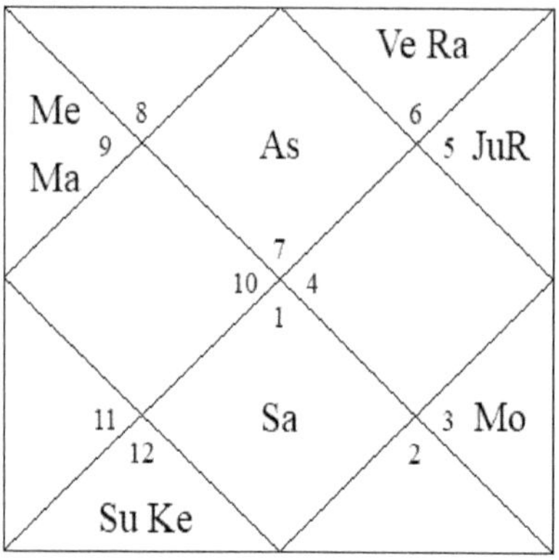

D30

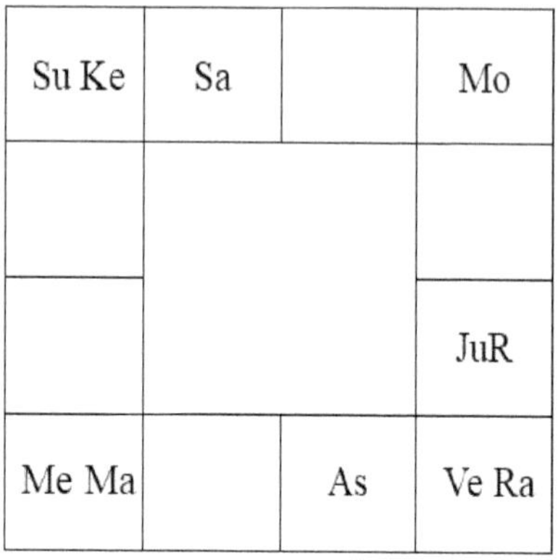

The application of these Trishamsha is given in other chapters.

Chapter 3
Evil or Good

Parashar has said that Trishamsha is seen for "Arista Phalam" or evil effects. Can we use this chart for seeing good effects also? When we refer to fourth house as the house of happiness, we see the unhappiness also. In the same way we can use this chart for indications of good. For this we have to analyze Trishamsha and decide whether it is a chart of good or evil effects. We will name it as favorable or unfavorable chart.

For this assessment, we have to check the lagan of Trishamsha. If the lagan is benefic then it is a chart of favorable effects. The lagan lord is then examined. He should be well placed and well connected. The lagan shows the promise and lagan lord is the action to fulfill the promise. A good lagan lord of a favorable Trishamsha assures good deeds by the person. A good lagan lord of an unfavorable Trishamsha gives deeds which reduce misfortune.

1. The lagan is considered malefic when a sign of malefic rises in lagan, malefic are associated, malefic aspects lagan or lagan is in papa Kartari. There is no association of benefic or lagan lord with lagan by conjunction or aspect. This condition of Trishamsha is considered an unfavorable chart. The person faces lot of problems in life.
2. The lagan is benefic when a sign of benefic rises in lagan, benefic are associated, benefic aspects or lagan is in Subh Kartari. Association of lagan lord by conjunction or aspect is also benefic. There should be no relation of malefic with lagan. This condition is a benefic condition of Trishamsha

and is termed as a favorable chart. This person faces least problems in life.

3. When there is both malefic and benefic influence on Trishamsha lagan then persons have mixture of good and adverse experience in life.
4. Now the manager is examined. When lagan lord is associated with benefic or is in strength it gives insight to fight the adversities. Also, the person will not suffer due to his own actions.
5. When the lagan lord is afflicted and without any benefic association then the person is not able to face the adversities but on the other hand, he creates problems himself and invites them.
6. For a good chart the Kendra and trikona are giver of favorable effects and is reverse for an evil chart.
7. In this world of mortals, it not possible to have a perfect good chart of fortune.
8. We can summaries the combination of lagan and lagan lord.

a. Lagan is benefic without having any malefic relation and lagan lord is also benefic. The person has a fortunate birth and does not create misfortune by self-deeds.
b. Lagan has both benefic and malefic relation and lagan lord is benefic without any malefic relation. The birth is a mix of good and evil and do not create evil effects by self-deeds.
c. Lagan is benefic without having any malefic relation and lagan lord is a mix of benefic and malefic then the person has a good birth and creates evil and good effects by self-deeds.
d. Lagan is malefic without any benefic relation and the lagan lord is fully benefic then the birth is evil but he will not create evil by own deeds.

e. Lagan is malefic without any benefic relation and the lagan lord is also malefic then the birth is evil but he will increase evil by own deeds.
f. These apply to planets and the effects are felt in their dasa.

Example 1 – DOB 23 May 1948, TOB 20.01.45, POB Bareilly

Birth Chart

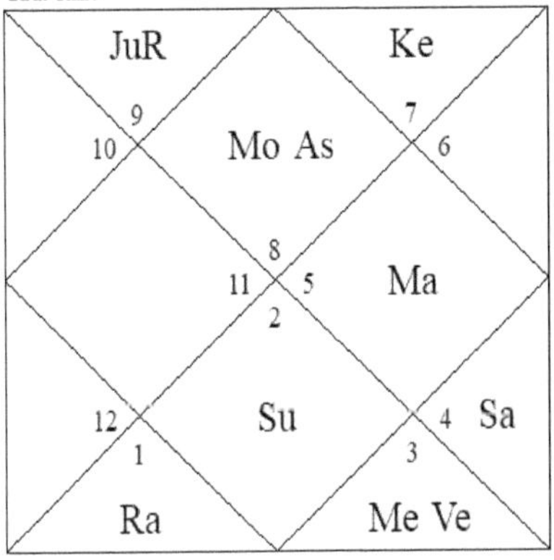

Birth Chart

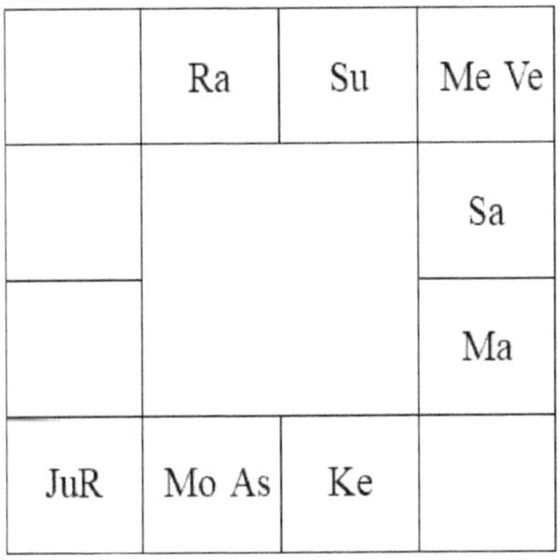

Venkatesha Trishamsha

D30

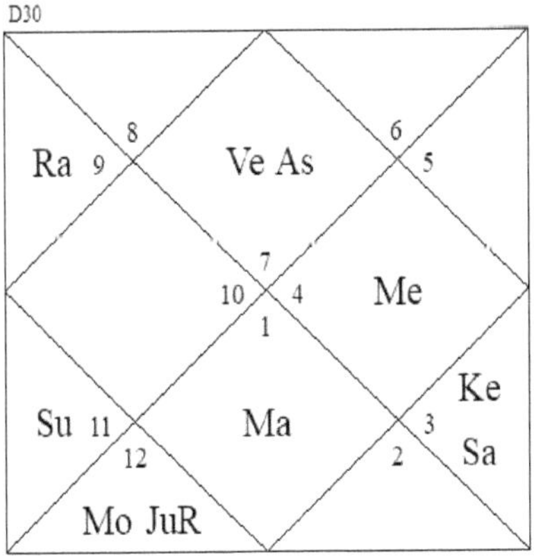

D30

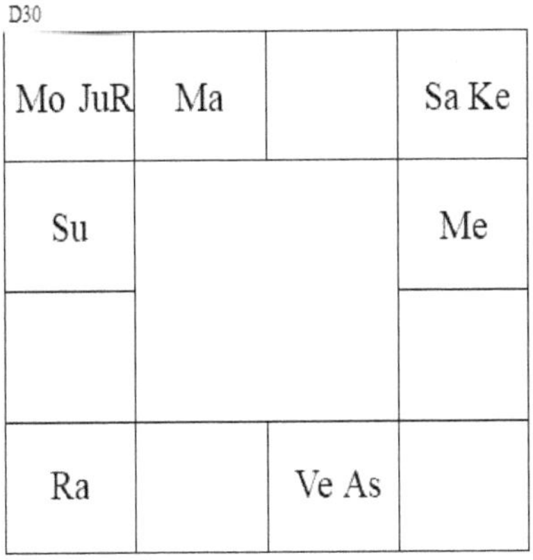

Parashar Trishamsha

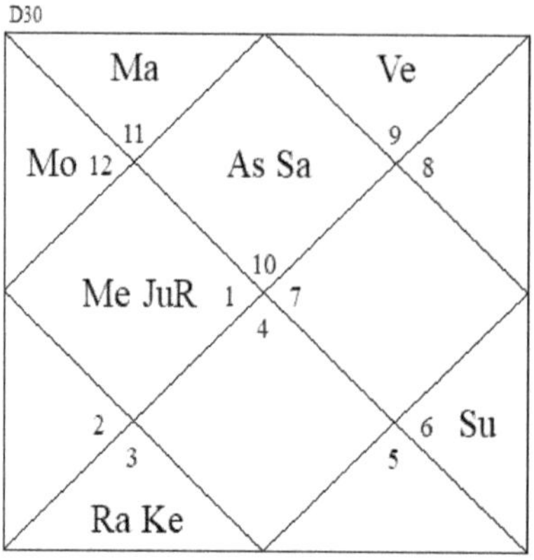

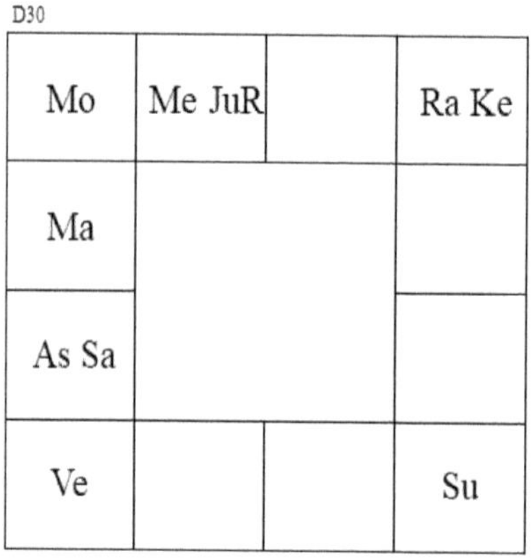

Iyer Trishamsha

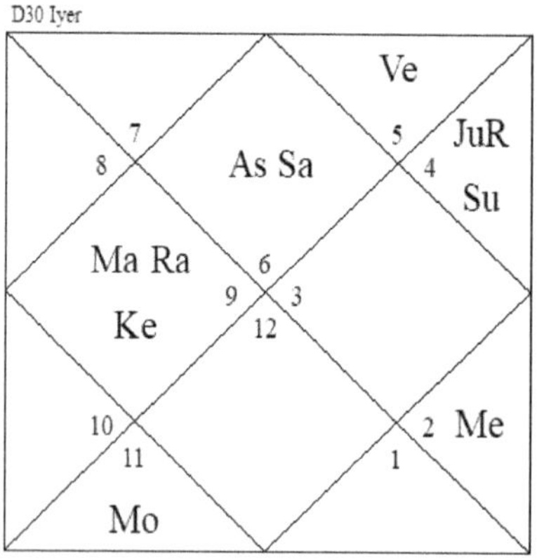

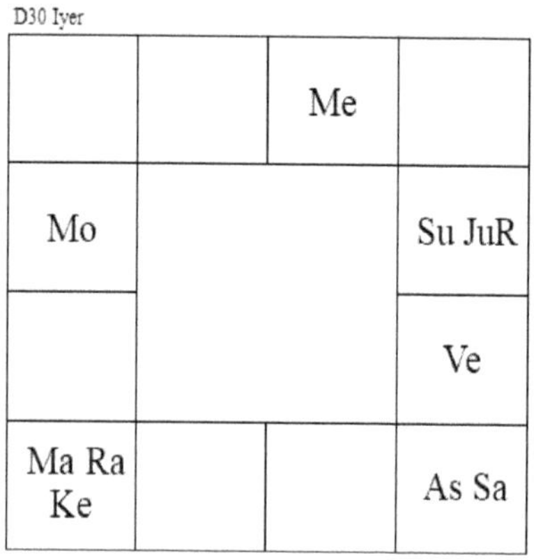

This example is given to illustrate a favorable birth. We will analyze all three Trishamsha charts to verify it.

1. **Venkatesha Trishamsha** – lagan is occupied by lagan lord and is aspected by Mars. Lagan is more towards good. The lagan lord Venus is not afflicted. He is not inviting evil by his actions.
2. **Parashar Trishamsha** – lagan lord is in lagan. Lagan lord Saturn is not afflicted. Lagan is in Kartari with benefic Venus moving towards lagan. No evil is seen.

3. **Iyer Trishamsha** – lagan is again occupied by Saturn and have no aspect. Lagan lord Mercury is in ninth house in a sign of friend.

He is a senior IAS officer and was selected to a cabinet rank assignment. He is still in lime light.

Example 2 – DOB 22 August 1931, TOB 23.08.56, POB Bulandshahr

Birth Chart

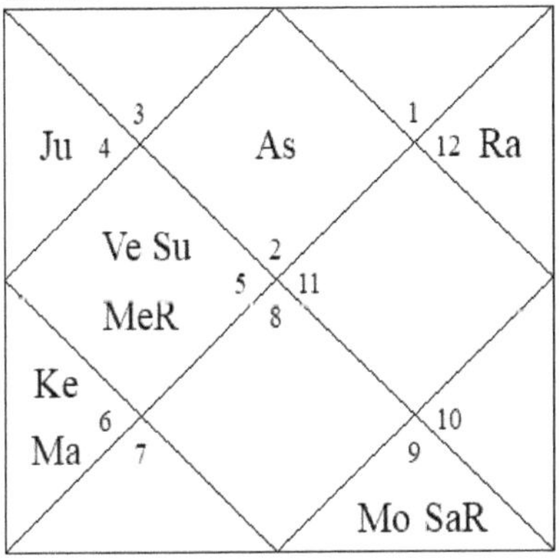

Birth Chart

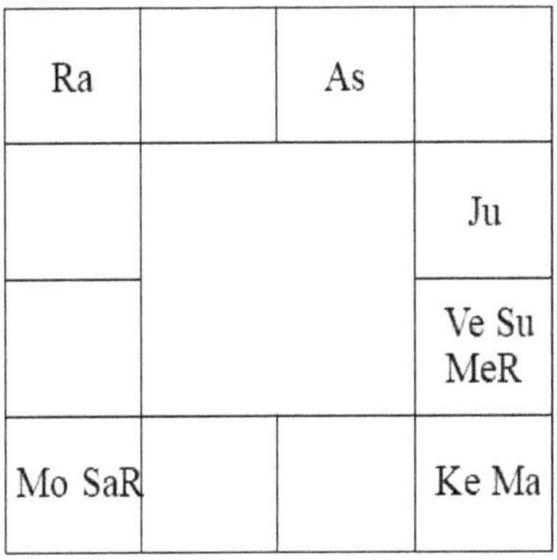

Venkatesha Trishamsha

D30

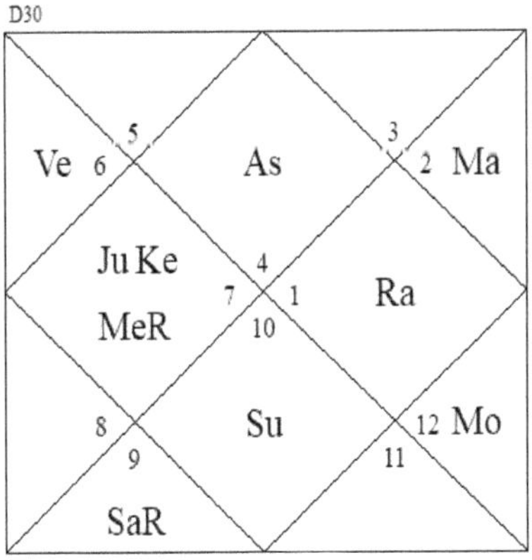

D30

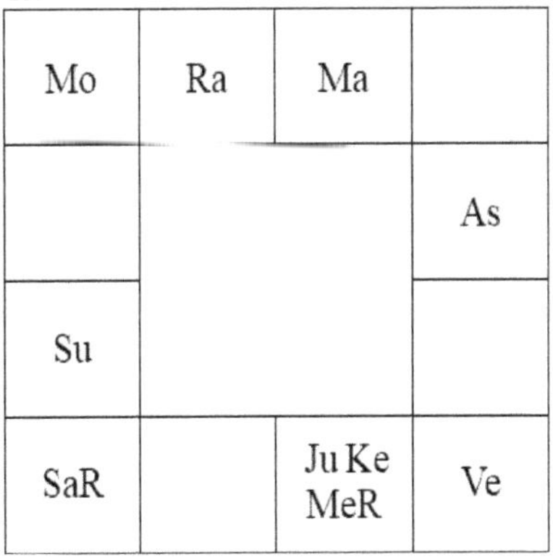

Parashar Trishamsha

D30

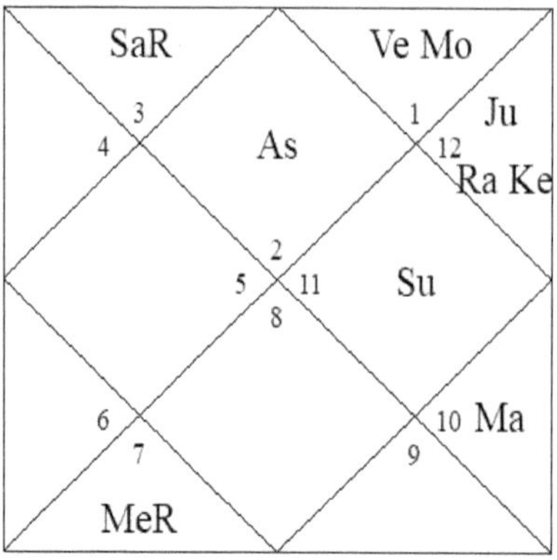

D30

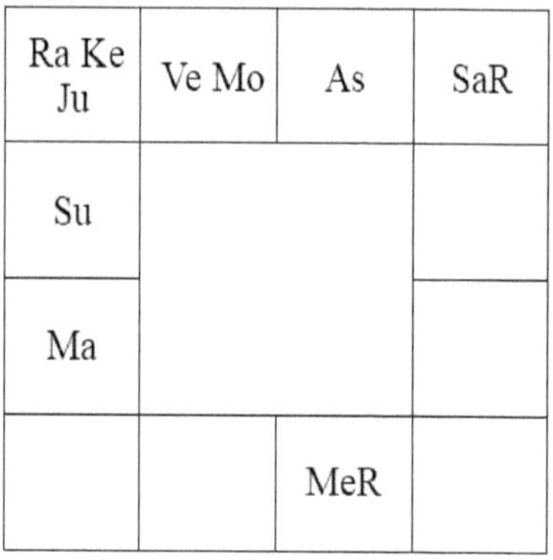

Iyer Trishamsha

D30 Iyer

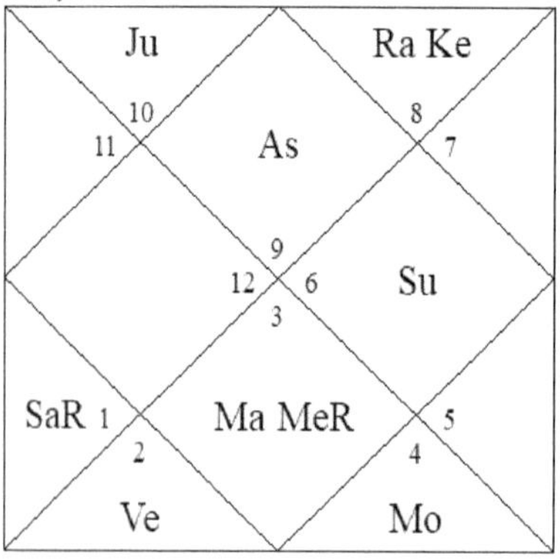

D30 Iyer

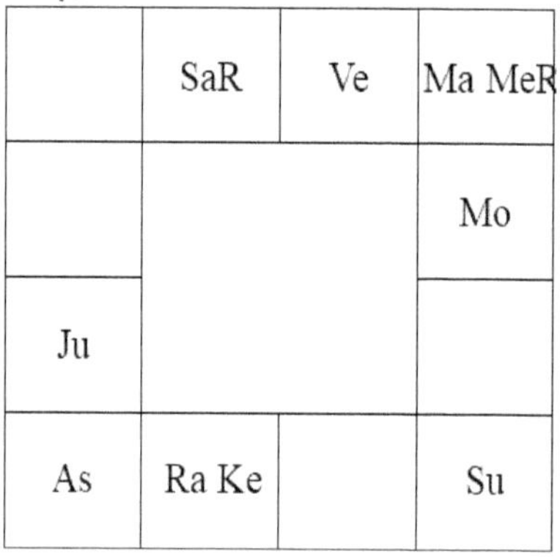

1. **Venkatesha Trishamsha** – lagan is aspected by Sun. lagan lord Moon is aspected by Venus.
2. **Parashar Trishamsha** – lagan is not related to any planet. Lagan lord Venus is with Moon and aspected by Mercury and Mars. This is a mixed indication.
3. **Iyer Trishamsha** – lagan is aspected by Mars and strong Mercury. The lagan lord Jupiter is in second house and the debilitation is cancelled by Saturn. Saturn is sign dispositor

of Jupiter. Mars is also aspecting Jupiter. This is a chart of mixed effects with good effects having an upper hand.

This chart belongs to a senior doctor who held high positions with government of India and was awarded Padam Vibhushan. He had to resign due to political interference. This is an example of mixed effects.

Example 3 – DOB 30 April 1945, TOB 10.27 (war time), POB Delhi

Birth Chart

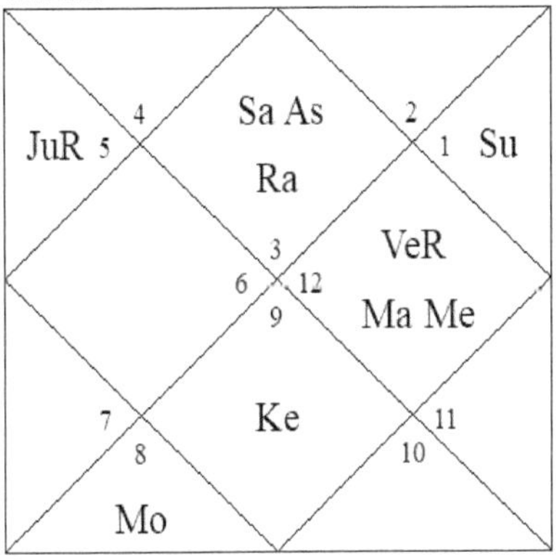

Birth Chart

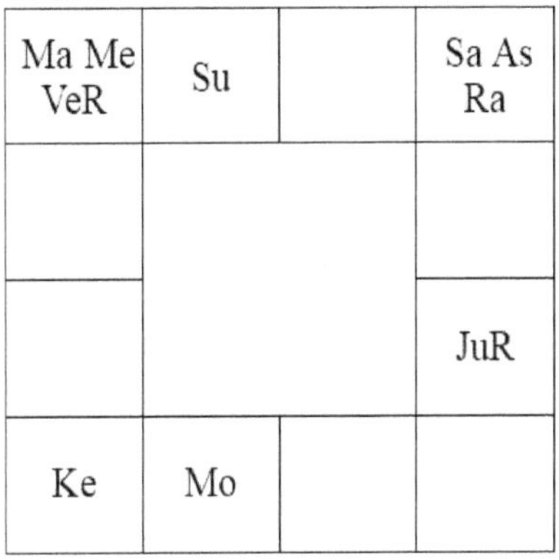

Venkatesha Trishamsha

D30

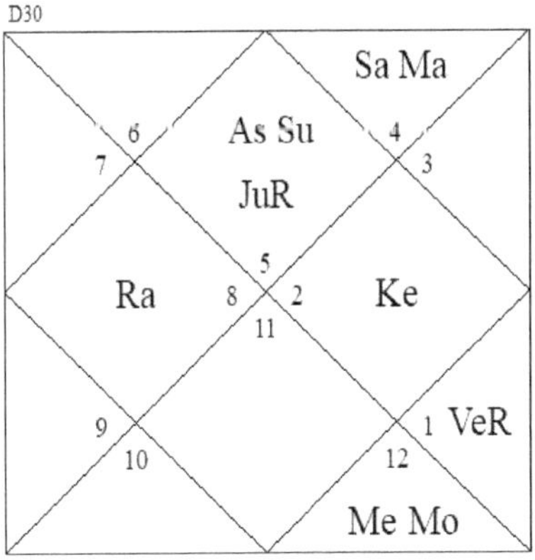

D30

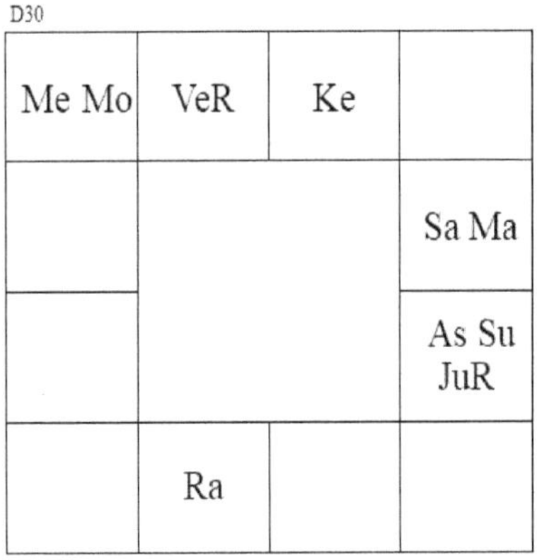

Parashar Trishamsha

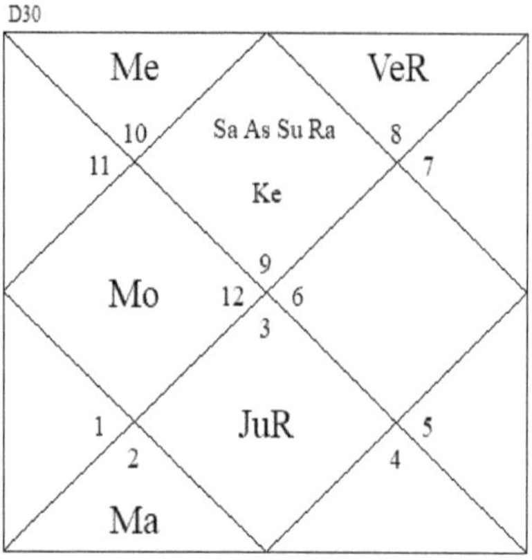

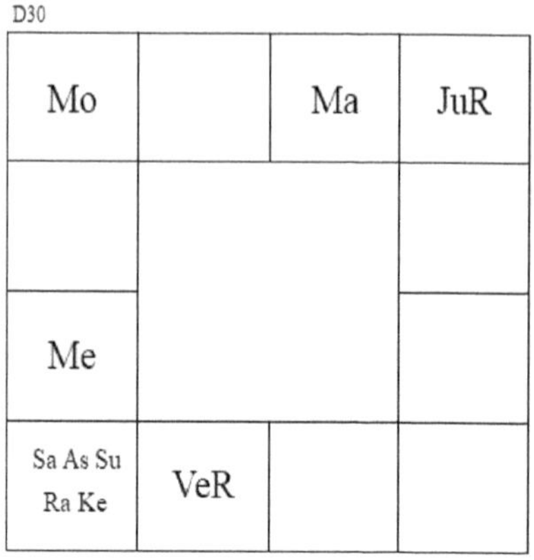

Iyer Trishamsha

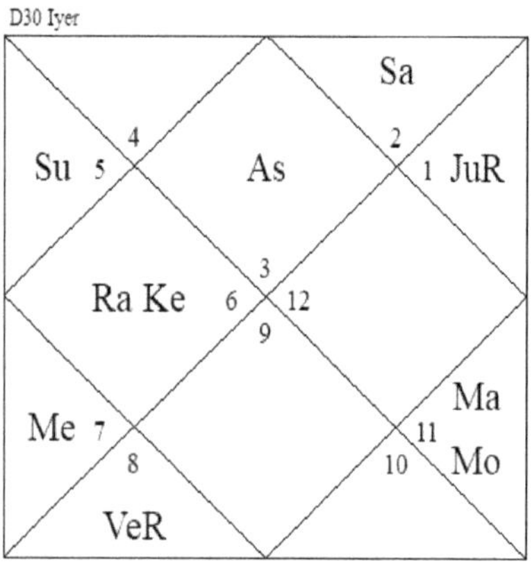

1. **Venkatesha Trishamsha** – lagan is having lagan lord and Jupiter. Lagan and lagan lord is not receiving any aspect. This shows it as a favorable chart and is not so in real life.
2. **Parashar Trishamsha** – lagan is occupied by Sun, Saturn and Rahu. It is aspected by lagan lord Jupiter and Mars. Without Jupiter aspect it is unfavorable chart. Lagan lord

Jupiter is also in RKA and aspected by Sun and Saturn. The actions can also invite evil effects.

3. **Iyer Trishamsha** – lagan is not related to any planet. Lagan lord is in trine and aspected by Jupiter. Inherent misfortunes are not present and the self-deeds do not invite misfortune.

This person is an engineer and had good service and successful business. He faced many problems in life but made a good standing by God's grace. We will term this Trishamsha as indicator of mixed fortunes.

Example 4 – DOB6 April 1990, TOB 5.23, POB Mathura

Birth Chart

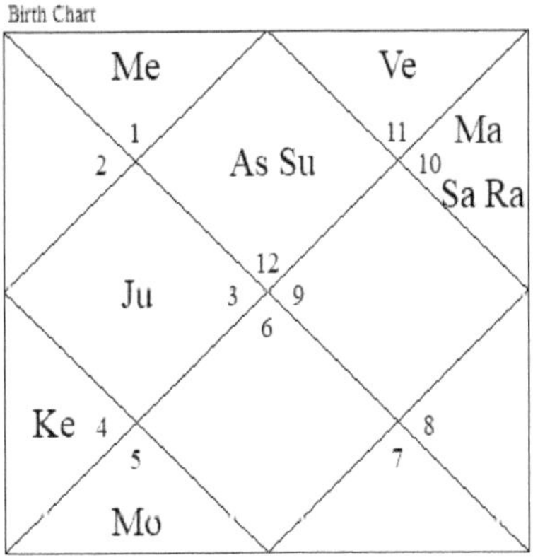

Birth Chart

As Su	Me		Ju
Ve			Ke
Sa Ra Ma			Mo

Venkatesha Trishamsha

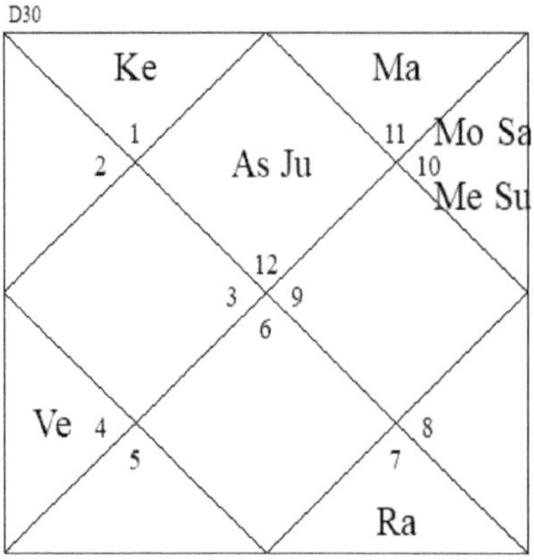

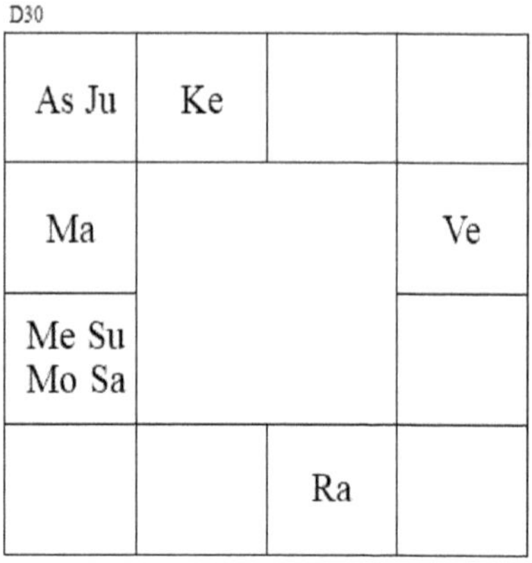

Parashar Trishamsha

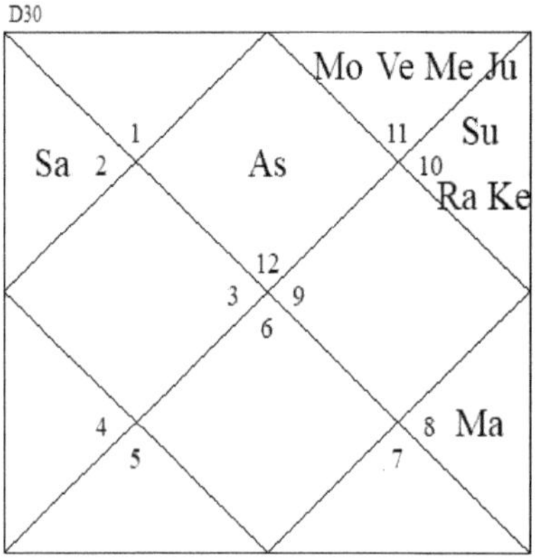

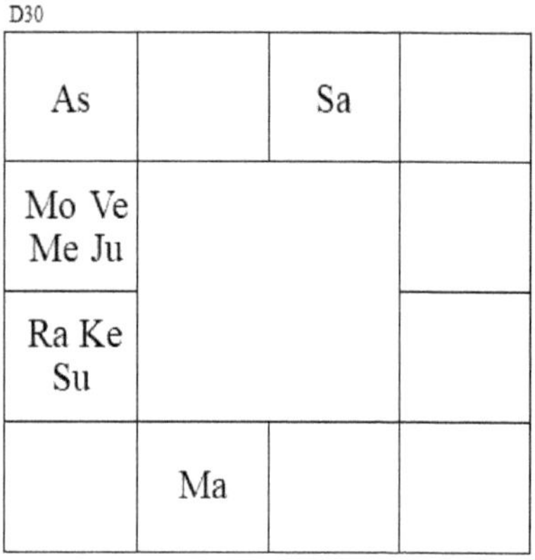

Iyer Trishamsha

D30 Iyer

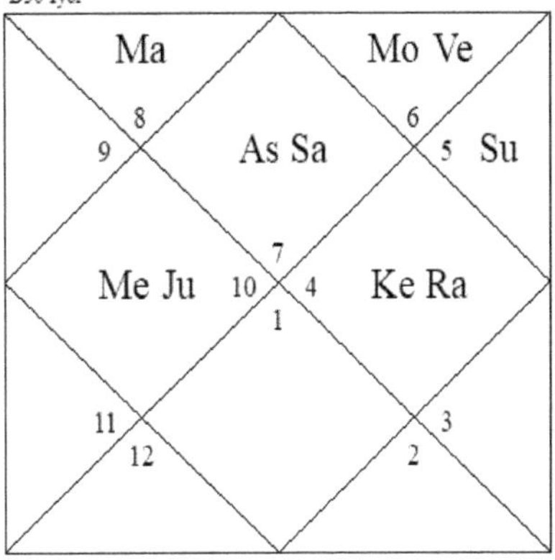

D30 Iyer

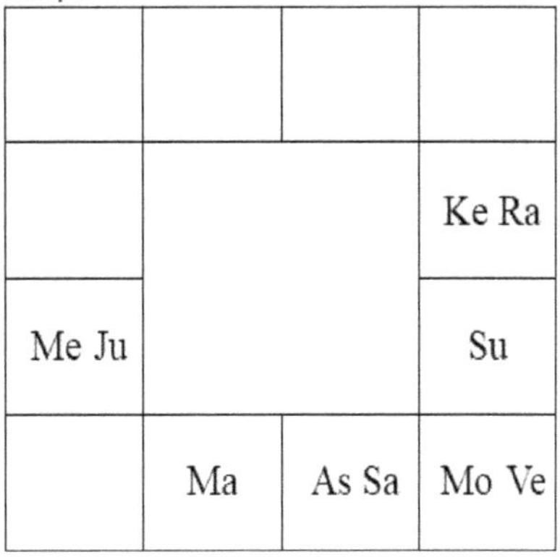

This boy is suffering from spinal cord atrophy and is in bed since 2006. He developed lungs problem in March 2019.

1. **Venkatesha Trishamsha** – lagan is occupied by its lord Jupiter. Lagan and lagan lord are in papa Kartari. Both are aspected by Saturn. It indicates unfavorable birth and also by self-actions.
2. **Parashar Trishamsha** – A benefic sign rises in lagan. Lagan is not aspected or occupied by any planet. Lagan lord is with three benefic and aspected by Mars. This Trishamsha is more towards favorable side.
3. **Iyer Trishamsha** – lagan is having exalted Saturn. He is not aspected by any planet. Lagan lord Venus is with Moon and is in papa Kartari. Both lagan and lagan lord are spoiled.

Example 5 – DOB 15 January 1952, TOB 20.09, POB Varanasi

Birth Chart

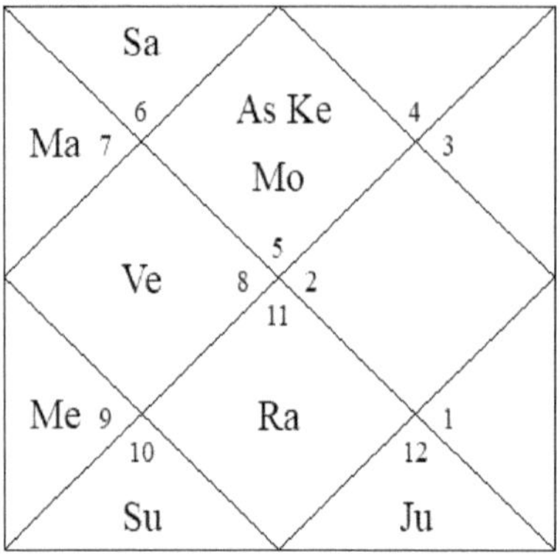

Birth Chart

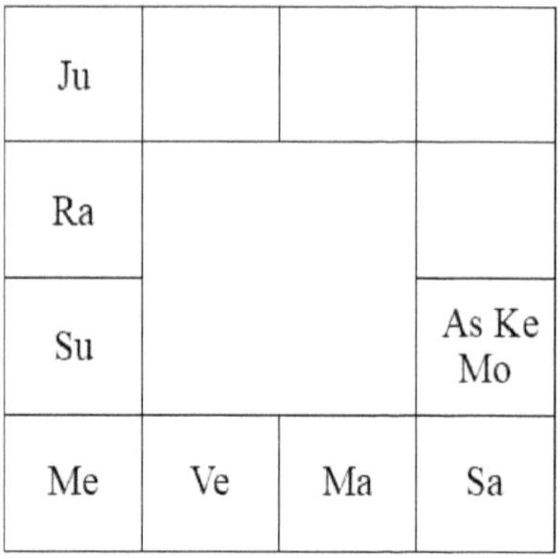

Venkatesha Trishamsha

D30

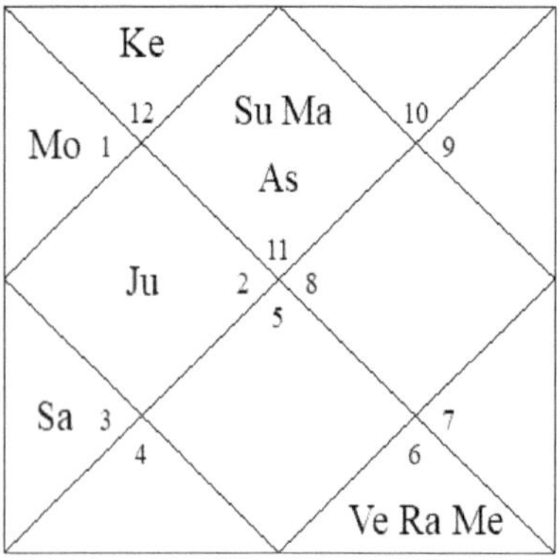

D30

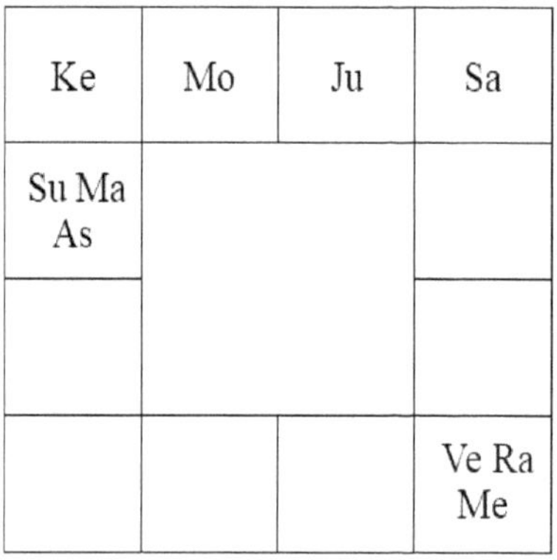

Parashar Trishamsha

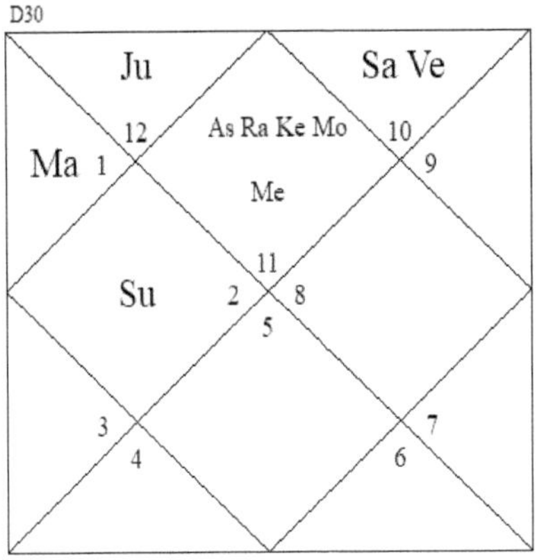

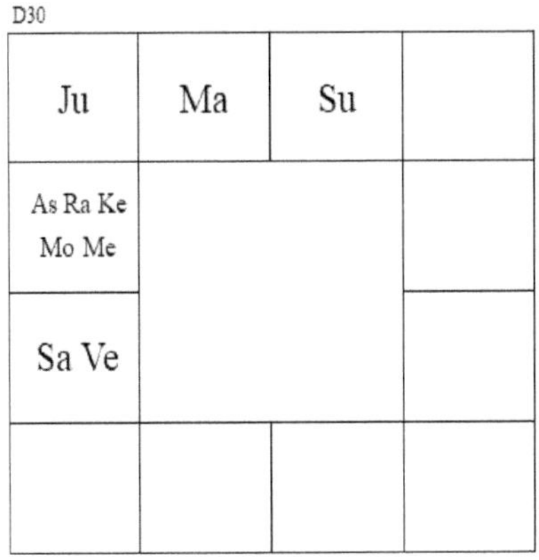

Iyer Trishamsha

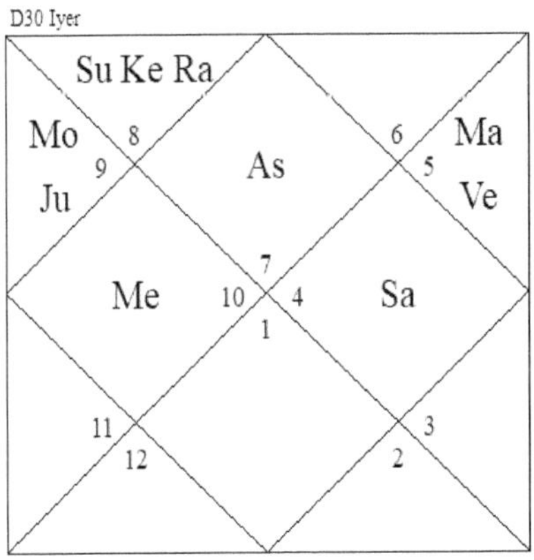

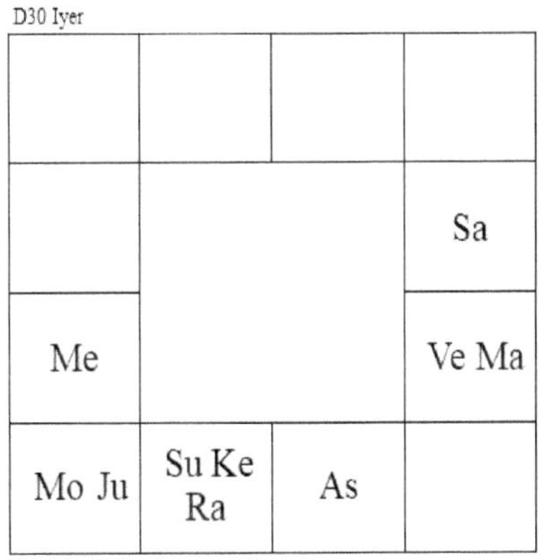

1. **Venkatesha Trishamsha** – Lagan is occupied by Sun and Mars. There is no benefic aspect. Lagan lord Saturn is well placed in trine and has no association or aspect. This shows an average birth.
2. **Parashar Trishamsha** – In this version lagan is having Rahu with two benefic. Lagan lord Saturn is in own sign and with Venus. Again, it is an average birth but no misfortune by own actions.

3. **Iyer Trishamsha** – Lagan is without any influence. Lagan lord is with Mars and is aspected by strong Jupiter. This is a favorable chart. Actions done under influence of Mars prove bad.

This chart is of highly successful businessmen of Indian origin and settled in USA. He holds a doctorate degree in engineering. He faced a setback in life due to hasty action but recovered.

Example 6 – DOB 24 June 1998, TOB 18.58, POB Delhi

Birth Chart

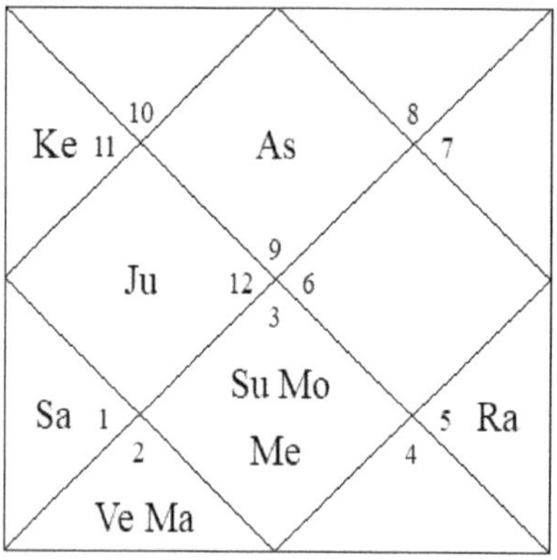

Birth Chart

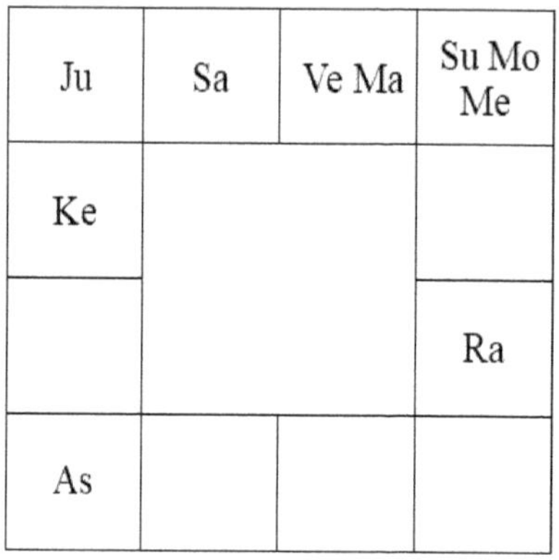

Venkatesha Trishamsha

D30

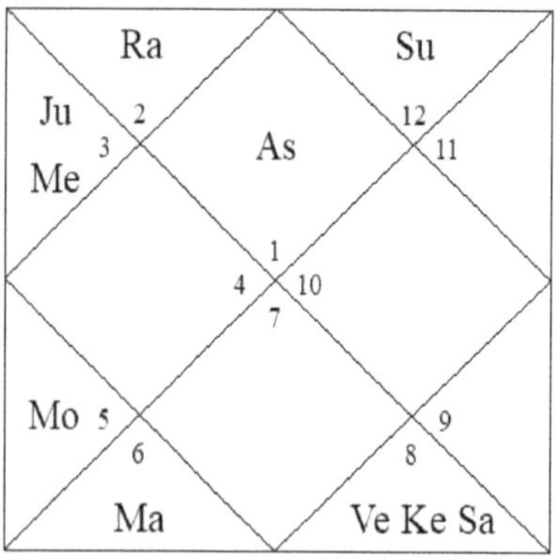

D30

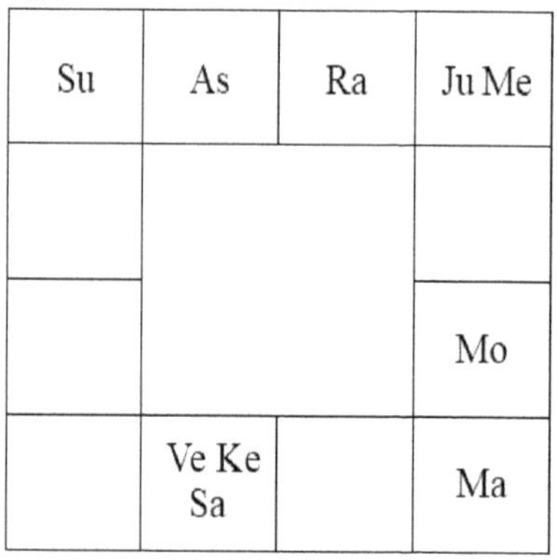

Parashar Trishamsha

D30

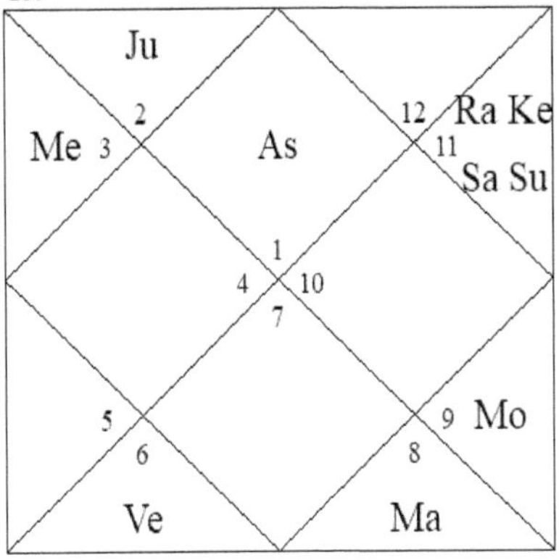

D30

	As	Ju	Me
Sa Su Ra Ke			
Mo	Ma		Ve

Iyer Trishamsha

D30 Iyer

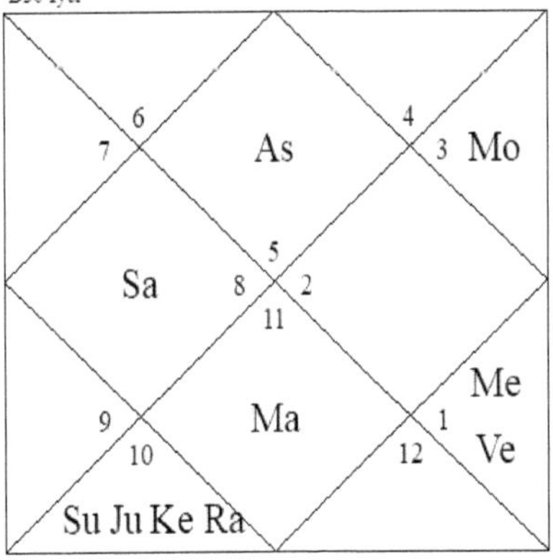

D30 Iyer

	Ve Me		Mo
Ma			
Su Ju Ke Ra			As
	Sa		

1. **Venkatesha Trishamsha** –_Lagan is in papa Kartari. It is aspected by its lord Mars and thus making it strong. Lagan lord is not having any aspect. This indicates a strong-willed person who can take quick decisions.
2. **Parashar Trishamsha** –_Lagan is aspected by Saturn. Lagan lord is also aspected by Saturn. Both are spoiled and make it an unfavorable chart by birth and by actions.

3. **Iyer Trishamsha** – This gives a better explanation. Lagan is aspected by Mars. Lagan lord is in RKA and aspected by Saturn. The problems are created by own actions.

This girl was born in a good family but ran away from her home and made her life miserable due to her actions.

Example 7 – DOB 5 September 1997, TOB 8.30, POB Delhi

Birth Chart

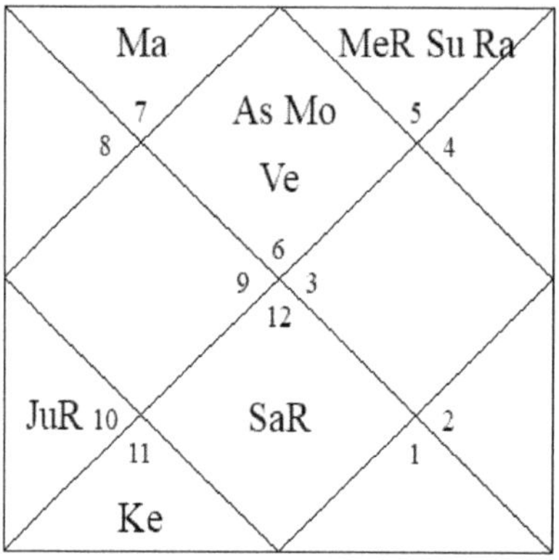

Birth Chart

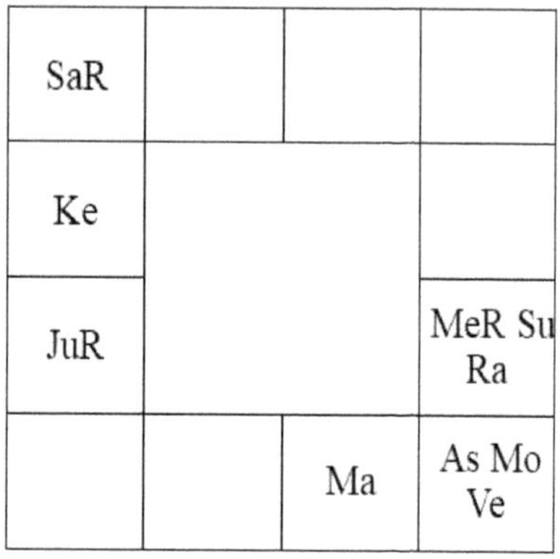

Venkatesh Trishamsha

D30

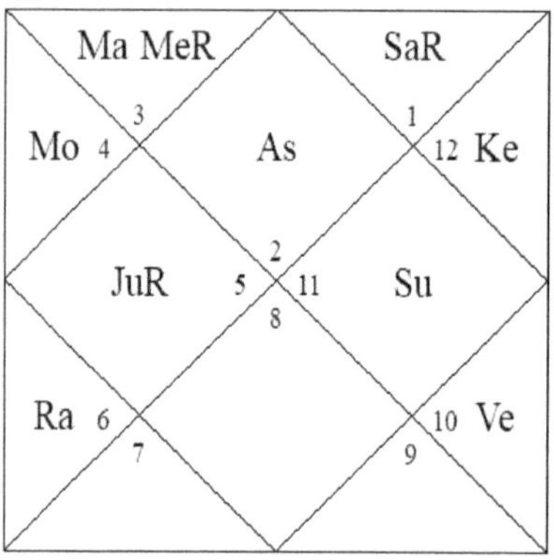

D30

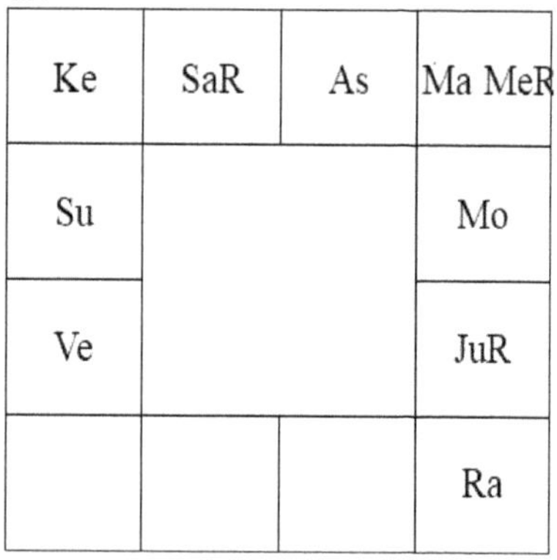

Parashar Trishamsha

D30

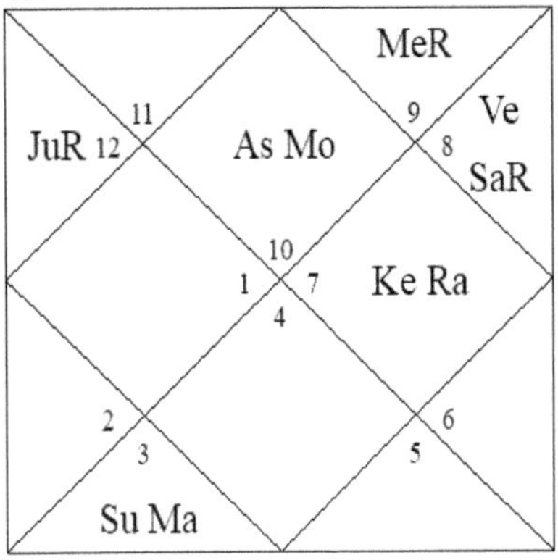

D30

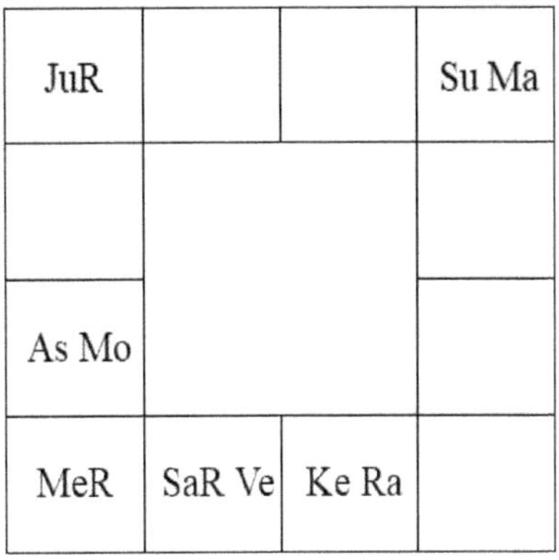

Iyer Trishamsha

D30 Iyer

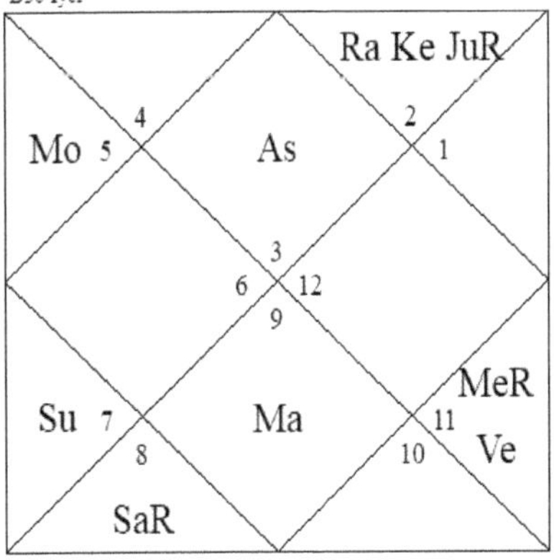

D30 Iyer

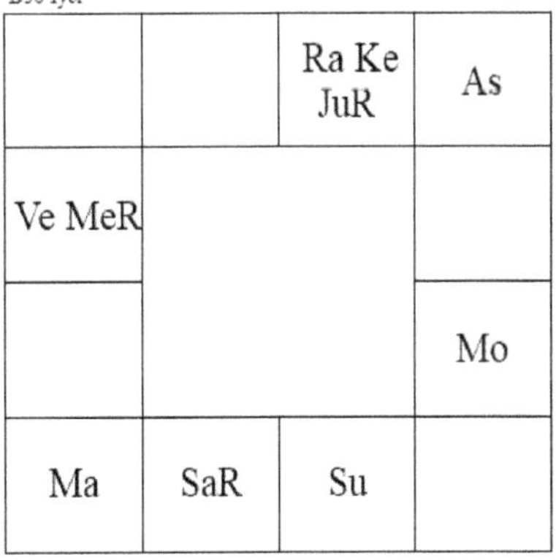

1. **Venkatesha Trishamsha** – Lagan is not associated with any planet. Not unfavorable by birth. Lagan lord is aspected by Moon, Mars and Saturn. Problems are self-generated.
2. **Parashar Trishamsha** – In this chart the lagan is occupied by Moon and aspected by Mars and Saturn. The birth is a mix of favorable and unfavorable effects. Lagan lord Saturn is well associated and gives no self-generated misfortunes.

3. **Iyer Trishamsha** – lagan is aspected by Mars and is not having any benefic relation. Lagan lord Mercury is with benefic and have no malefic relation. A good lagan lord assures no wrong doing by own actions. The main reason is debilitation of Sun.

This boy is mentally underdeveloped. He has not studied and behaves in a childish manner. As infant he consumed some worm with his food and has settled in his brain. The worm is not present now but has damaged his brain.

Example 8 – DOB 15 October 1973, TOB 22.58, POB Jaipur

Birth Chart

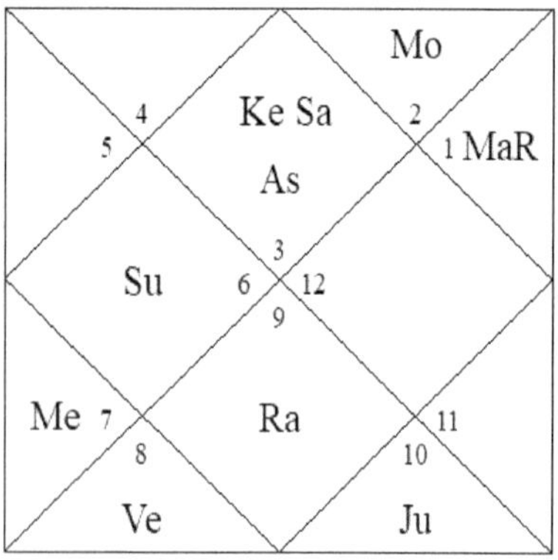

Birth Chart

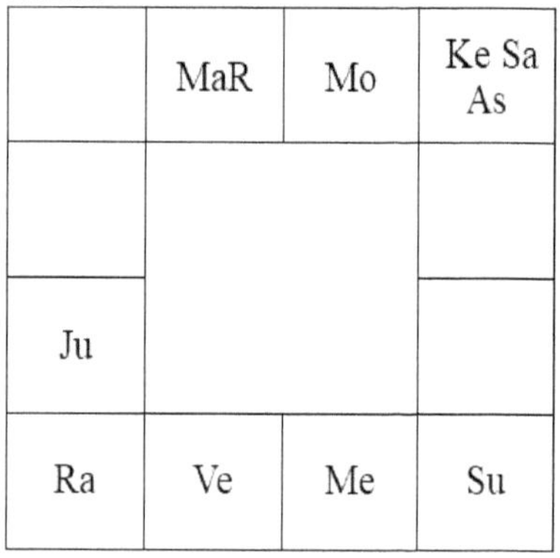

Venkatesha Trishamsha

D30

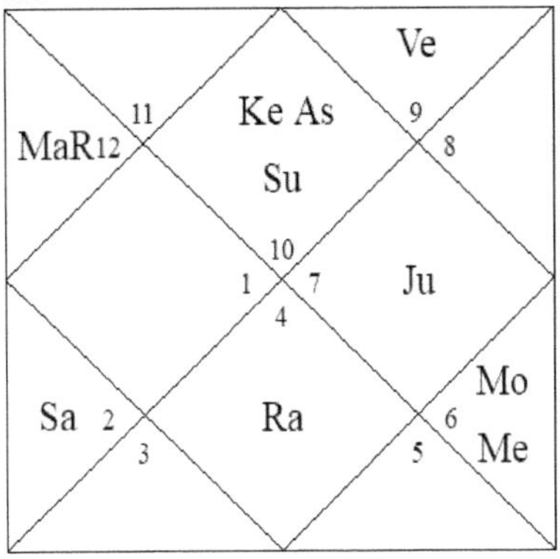

D30

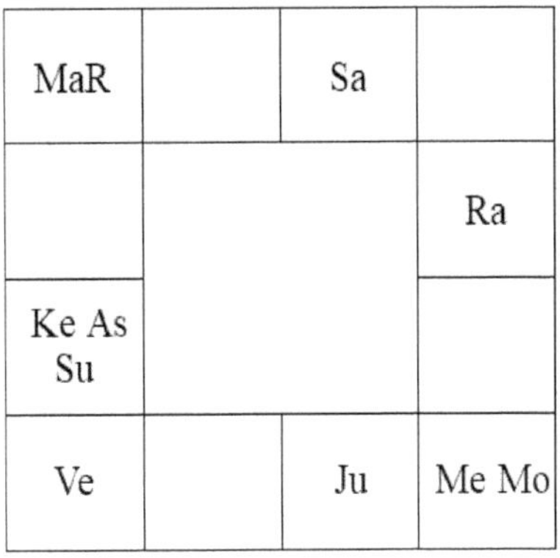

Parashar Trishamsha

D30

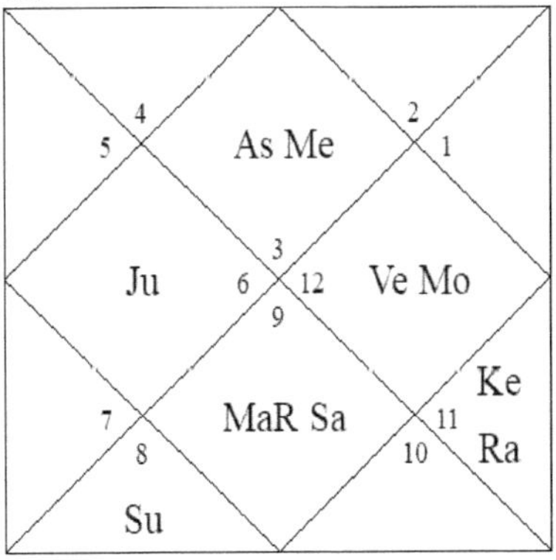

D30

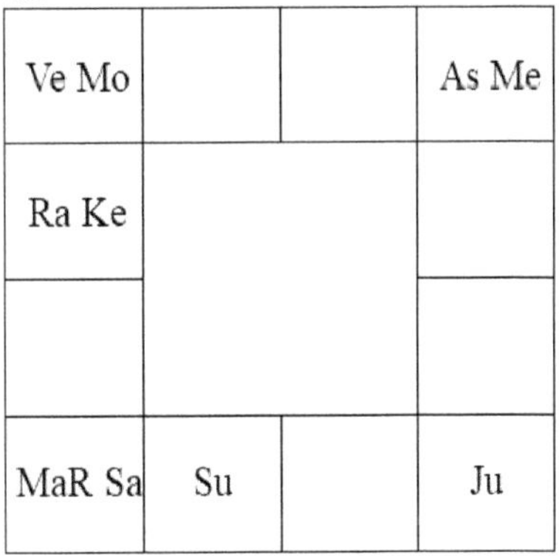

Iyer Trishamsha

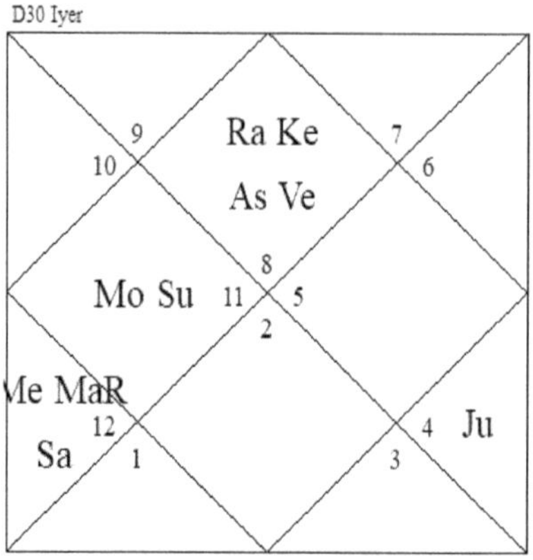

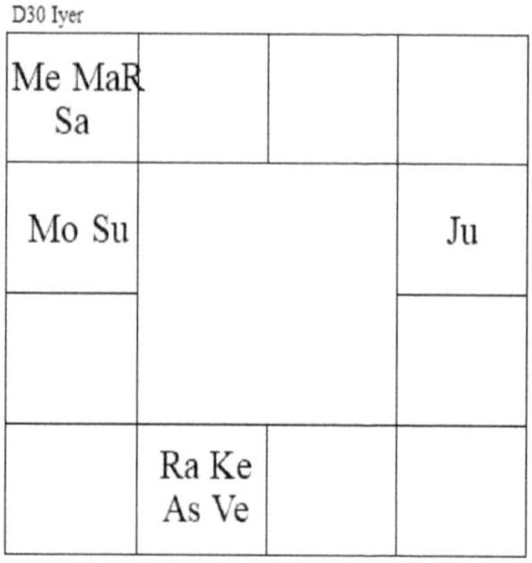

1. **Venkatesha Trishamsha** – Lagan is having Sun and Ketu. There is no benefic aspect. Lagan lord Saturn is also not having any benefic aspect. Lagan indicates a unfavorable birth. Misfortune is not created by self.
2. _**Parashar Trishamsha** – Lagan is occupied by its lord Mercury. Both lagan and lord are aspected by Mars and Saturn. The lagan and lagan lord are afflicted making it an unfavorable chart.
3. **Iyer Trishamsha** – Lagan is occupied by Rahu and Venus and is aspected by Jupiter. Lagan lord Mars is with Mercury and Saturn. He is again aspected by Jupiter. This chart promises mixed effects.

He was diagnosed with cancer and is fighting for recovery. Benefic relation with lagan and lagan lord can give cure.

Example 9 – DOB 13 May 1955, TOB 21.15, POB Rishikesh

Birth Chart

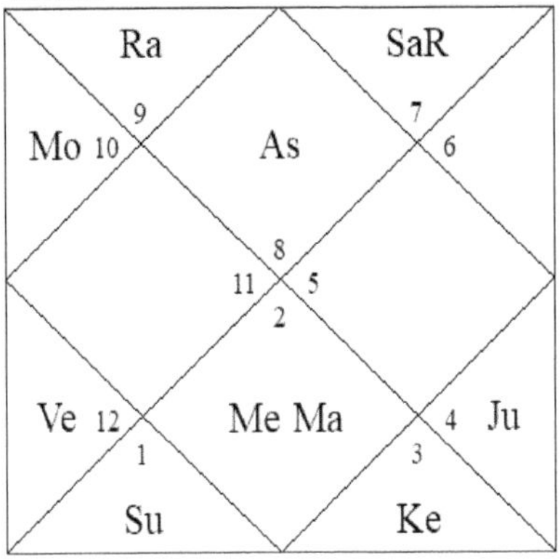

Birth Chart

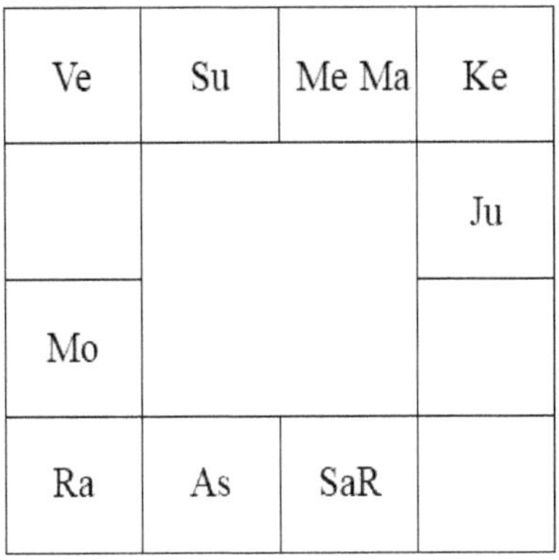

Venkatesha Trishamsha

D30

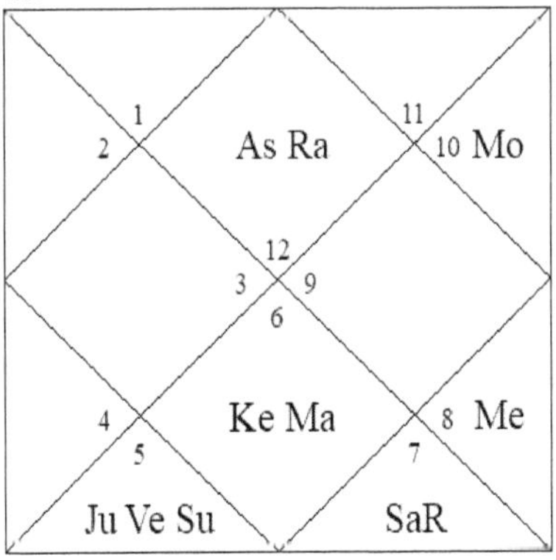

D30

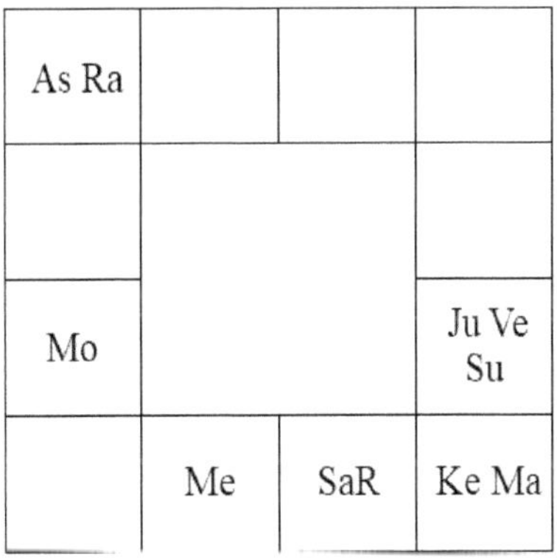

Parashar Trishamsha

D30

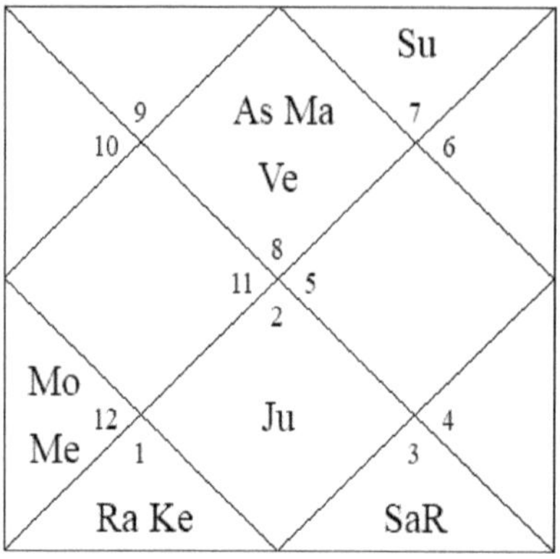

D30

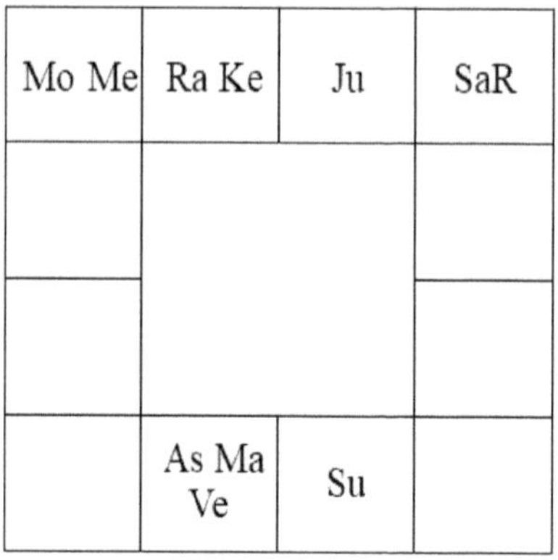

Iyer Trishamsha

D30 Iyer

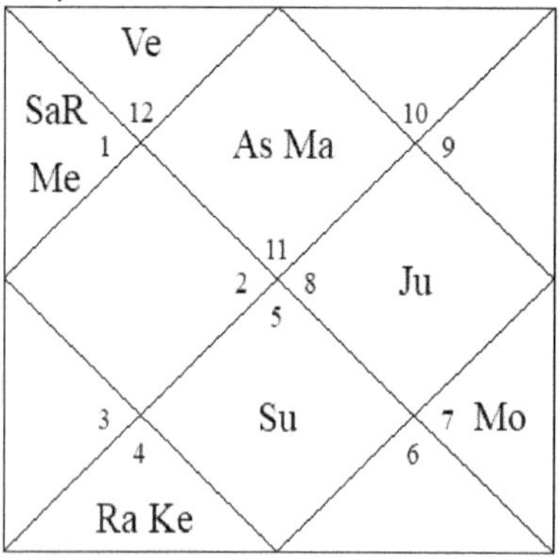

D30 Iyer

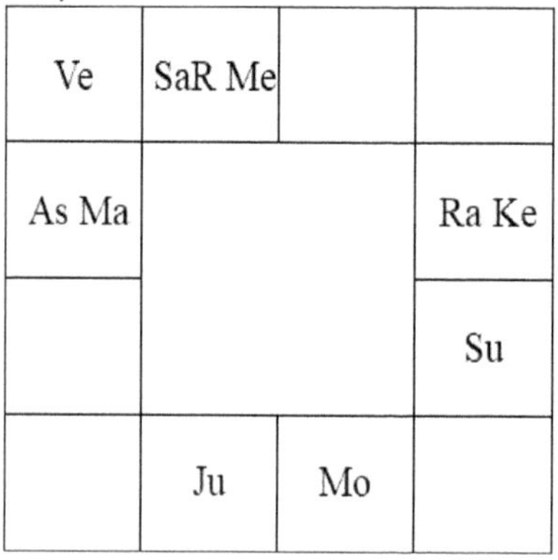

Venkatesha Trishamsha - Lagan is with Rahu and is aspected by Mars. This makes the chart as an unfavorable chart. Lagan lord Jupiter is with Venus and Sun. It has no other aspect. The misfortune is not by his actions.

Parashar Trishamsha_- Lagan is occupied by its lord Mars. Lagan is having Venus and is aspected by Jupiter. This shows a favorable birth and the lagan lord also provide good fortune by actions.

Iyer Trishamsha – Malefic sign rises in lagan. lagan contains Mars aspected by Sun. lagan has no benefic aspect. Lagan lord Saturn is with Mercury and is aspected by Moon. Actions are positive and support the results of lagan.

This person had a very difficult life. His transport business was grabbed by his partners. His family life was ruined due to his abusive wife. She took his property and his mother was on doles.

Example 10 – DOB 5 January 1928, TOB 17.26, POB Larkana, Pakistan

This chart is of Z. A. Bhutto. He was prime minister of Pakistan and was hanged to death. This happened on 4 April 1979. He has a fortunate birth but his actions took him towards misfortune.

Birth Chart

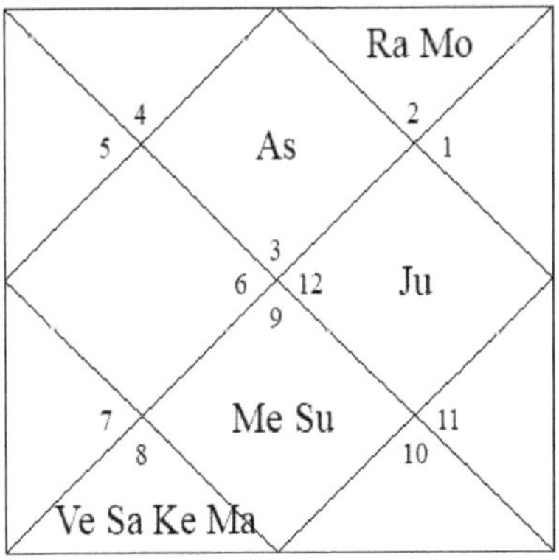

Birth Chart

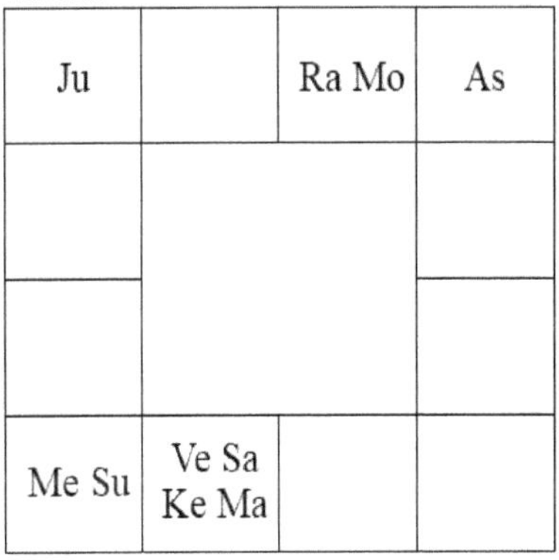

Venkatesha Trishamsha

D30

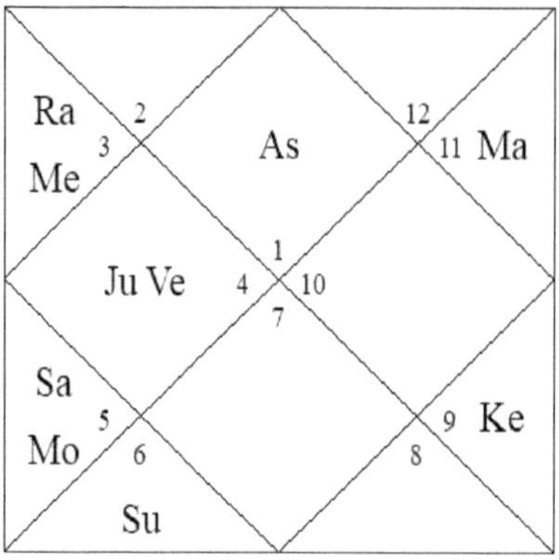

D30

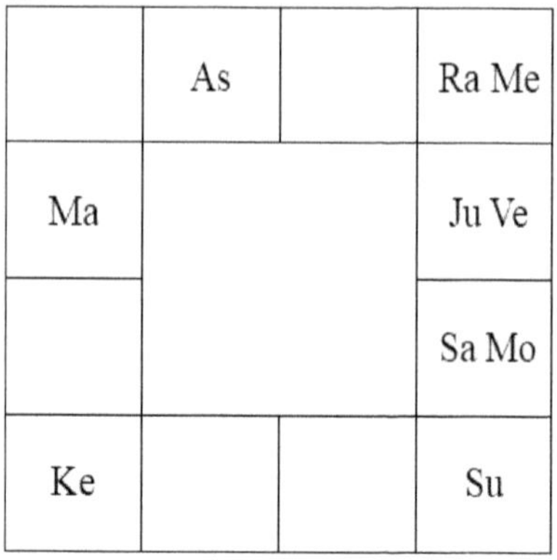

Parashar Trishamsha

D30

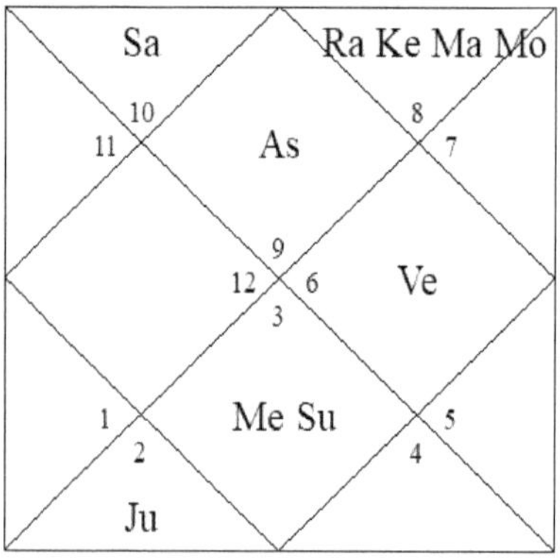

D30

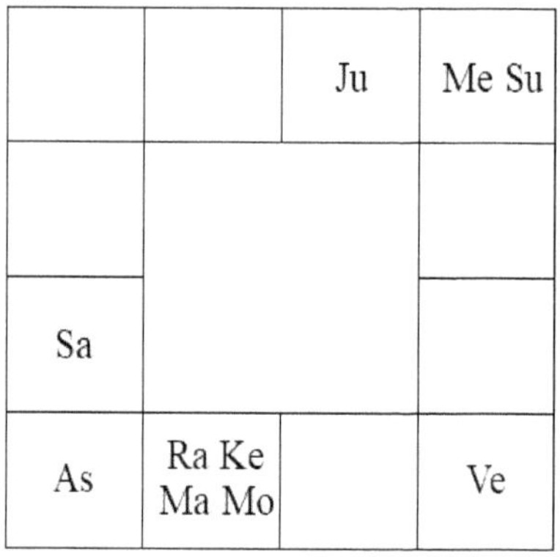

Iyer Trishamsha

D30 Iyer

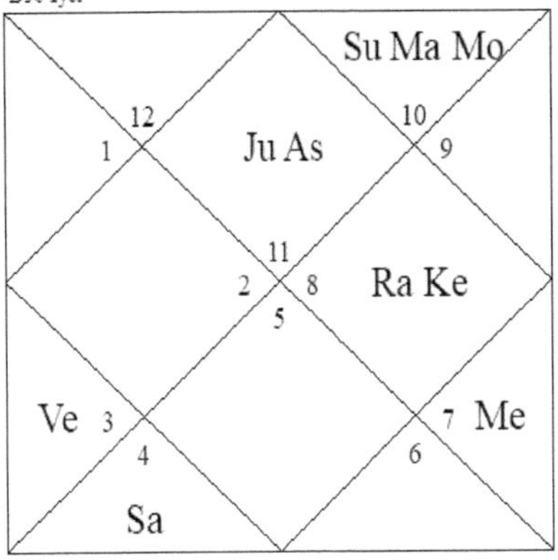

D30 Iyer

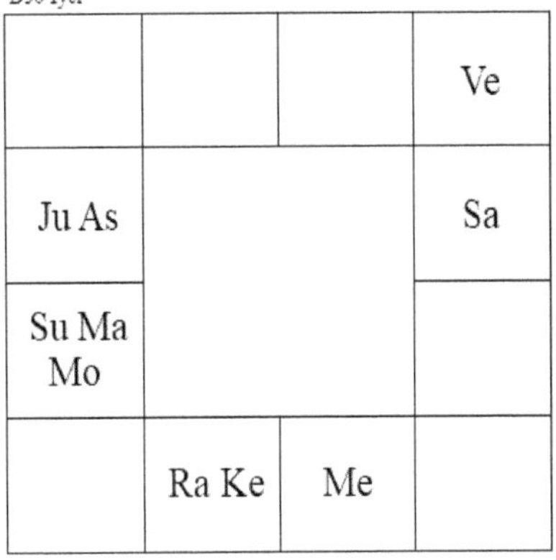

Venkatesha Trishamsha_- Lagan is under no influence by aspect or conjunction. Lagan lord Mars is aspected by Saturn and Moon. Saturn is sign dispositor of Mars. Lagan lord assumes strength.

Parashar Trishamsha_- Lagan is aspected by Mercury and Sun. lagan lord is highly afflicted by strong Mars and Moon. Affliction to Moon is seen.

Iyer Trishamsha_- Lagan is occupied by Jupiter alone. Jupiter has no aspect. This makes the birth a favorable birth. Lagan lord is aspected by Sun, Mars and Moon. Actions lead to misfortune. Moon is again involved.

Example 11 – DOB 4 March 1973, TOB 4.30, POB Dhamda

He was born in a well to do family. He inherited lot of land. His habit of taking drugs ruined him.

Birth Chart

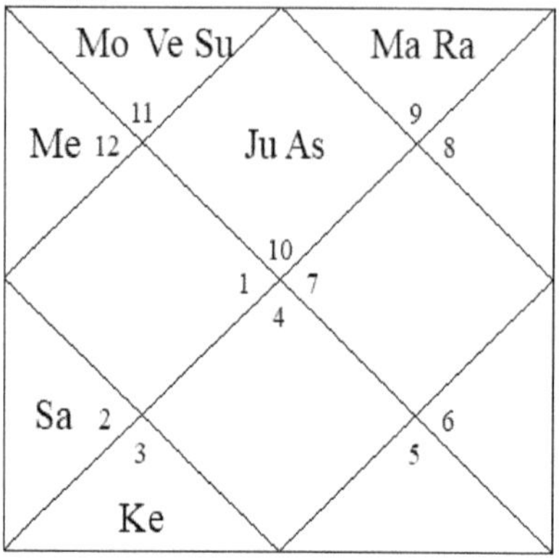

Birth Chart

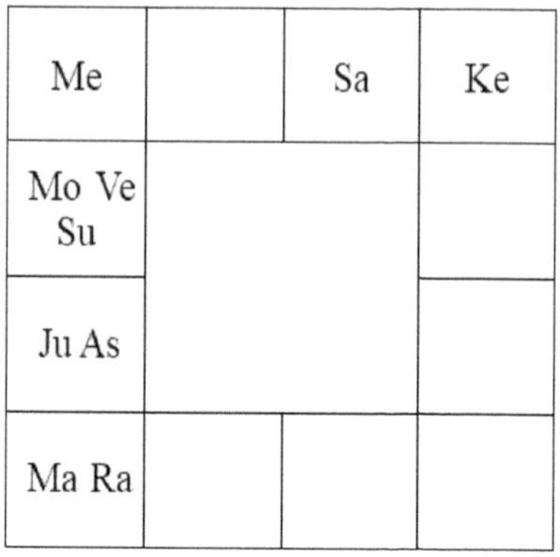

Venkatesha Trishamsha

D30

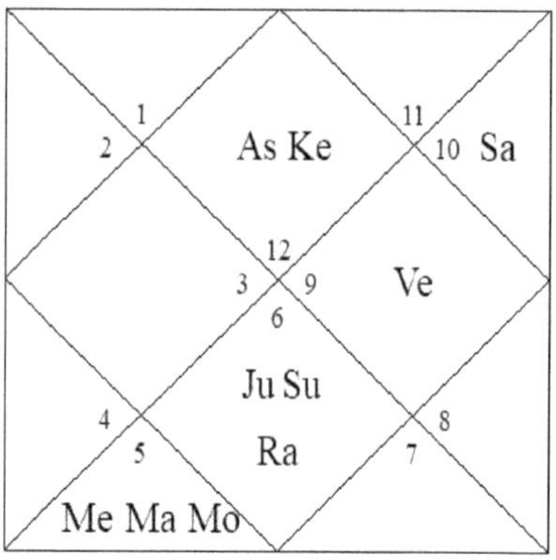

D30

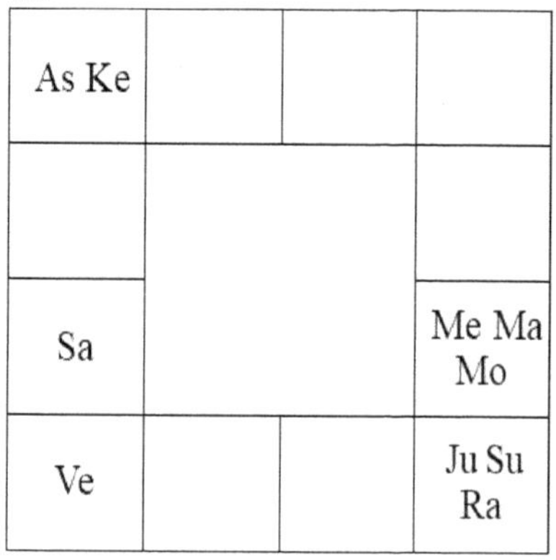

Parashar Trishamsha

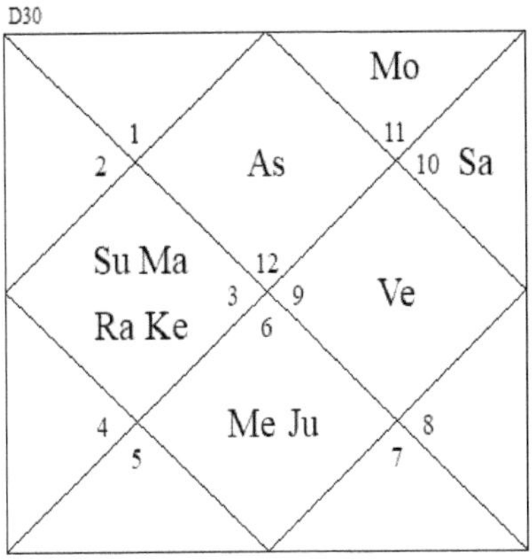

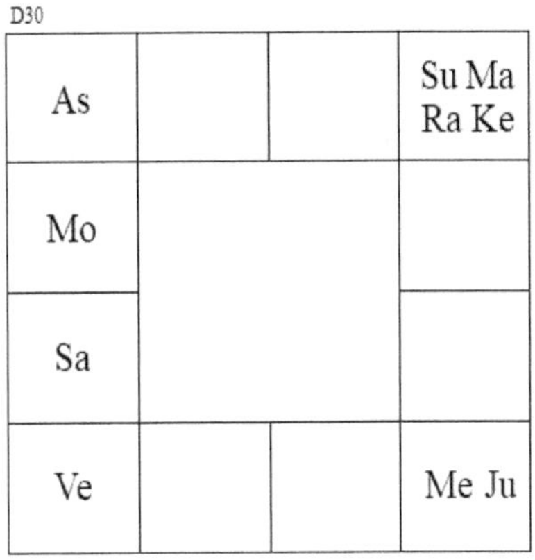

Iyer Trishamsha

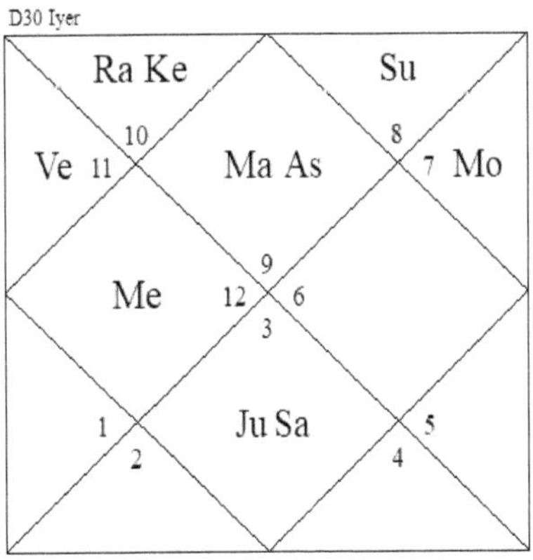

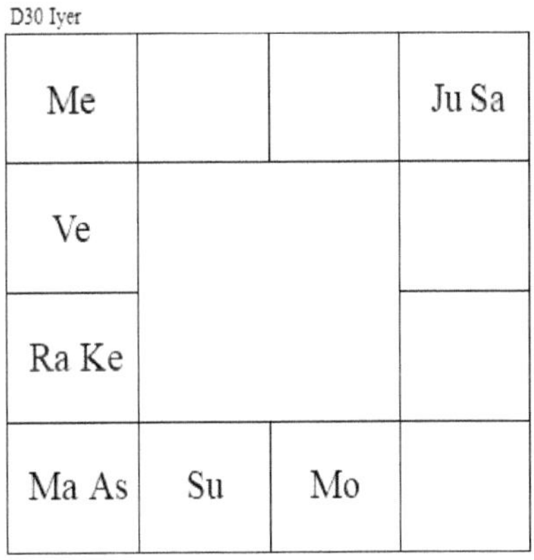

Venkatesha Trishamsha – lagan is in RKA. It is aspected by sun, Mars and Saturn. Aspect of Jupiter is the only saving grace. Birth is partly favorable. Lagan lord Jupiter is totally spoiled and has no benefic relation. He made his life miserable by own deeds.

Parashar Trishamsha – lagan is aspected by lord Jupiter. Saturn and Mercury are also aspect lagan. This is a favorable birth. Lagan lord is with Mercury and Mars is aspecting. It is a mix of good and bad action. This Trishamsha is not giving true story.

Iyer Trishamsha – lagan is in papa Kartari. Mars occupy lagan. It is aspected by Jupiter and Saturn. Aspect of lagan lord Jupiter gave a f favorable birth. The lagan lord is under malefic influence only. This explains the true story of this horoscope.

Example 12 – DOB 22 July 1972, TOB 18.00, POB Durg

In this horoscope both lagan and lagan lord are under malefic influence and there is no benefic relation. This is an unfortunate chart by birth and by deeds. He is charged with murder and leads a miserable life.

Birth Chart

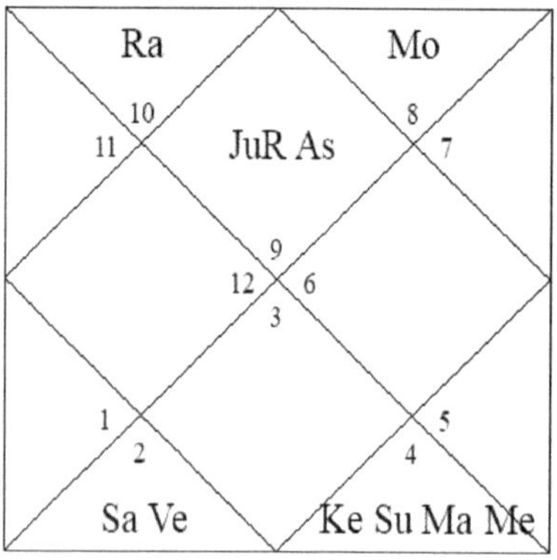

Birth Chart

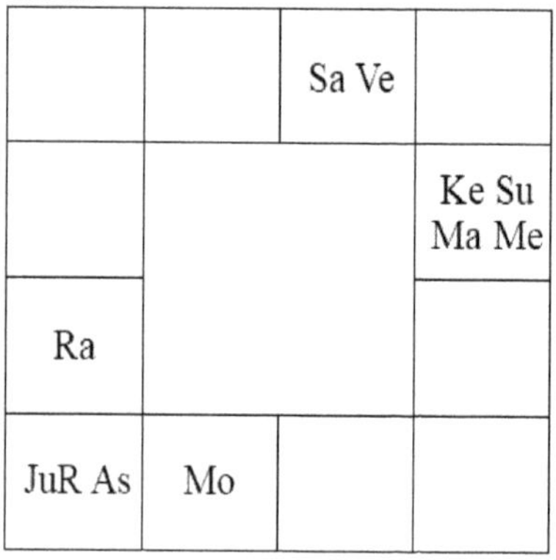

Venkatesha Trishamsha

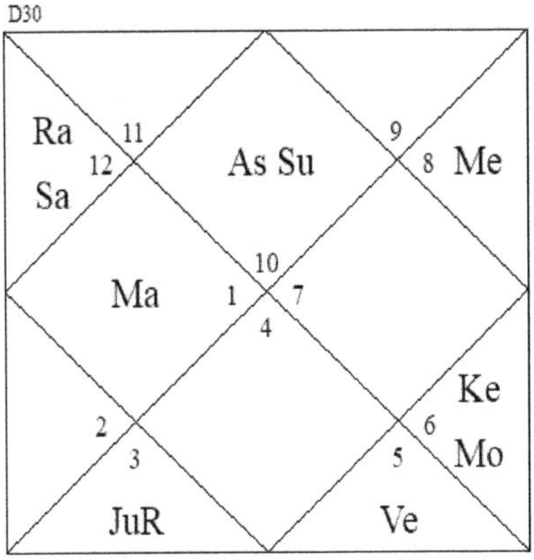

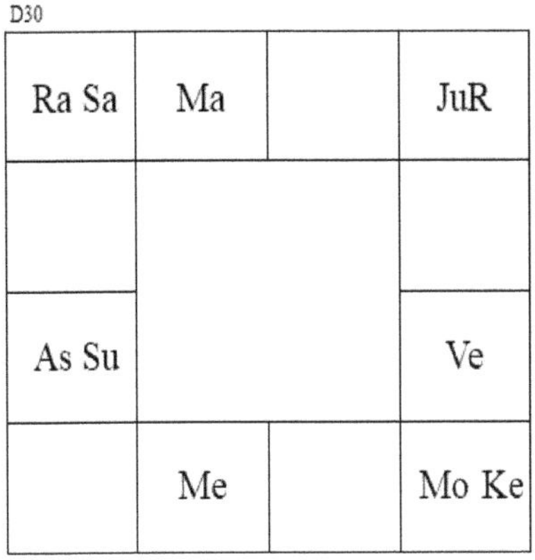

Parashar Trishamsha

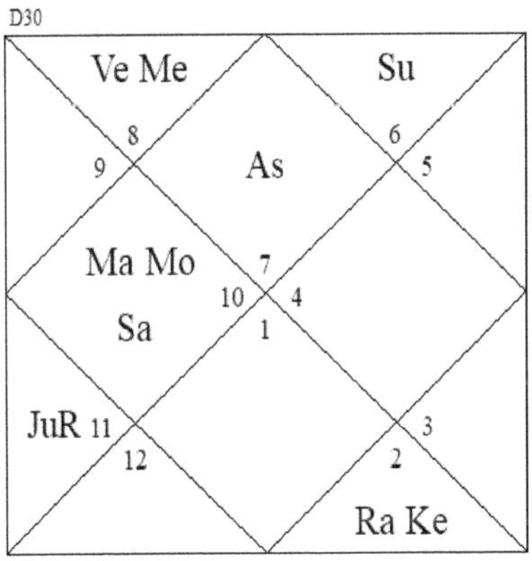

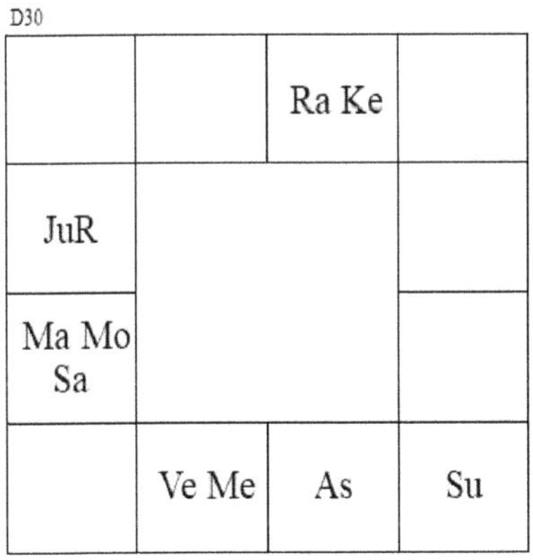

Iyer Trishamsha

D30 Iyer

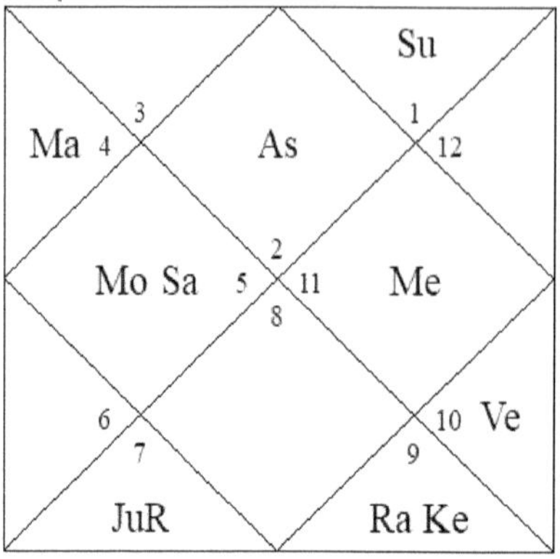

D30 Iyer

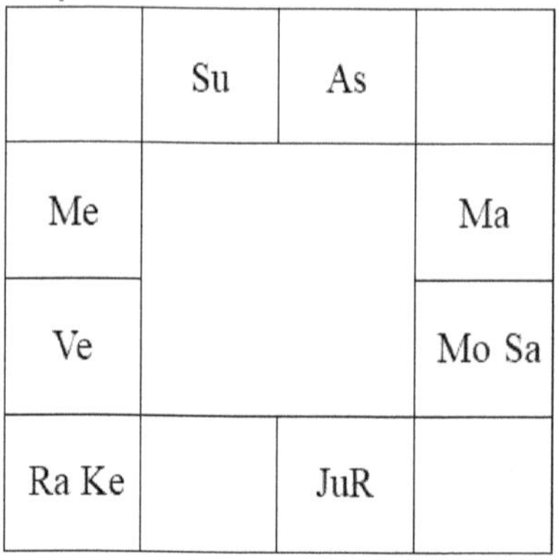

Venkatesha Trishamsha – lagan is occupied by Sun and have no other aspect. The sixth and eighth house has benefic and gives strength to lagan. Lagan lord Saturn is with Rahu and aspected by Moon. This chart is not giving true story.

Parashar Trishamsha – lagan is aspected by Jupiter and Saturn. Lagan lord Venus is with Mercury and is in RKA. This chart is also not giving true story.

Iyer Trishamsha – Lagan is aspected by Saturn and there is no benefic relation. Lagan lord Venus is aspected by Mars and is also not having any benefic relation. The birth and deeds are creating misfortune.

We now take an example of twins. The elder is leading a good life and younger is bankrupt and suffers from auto immune disease.

Elder

Example 13 – DOB 14 January 1966, TOB 2.47, POB Alwar

Birth Chart

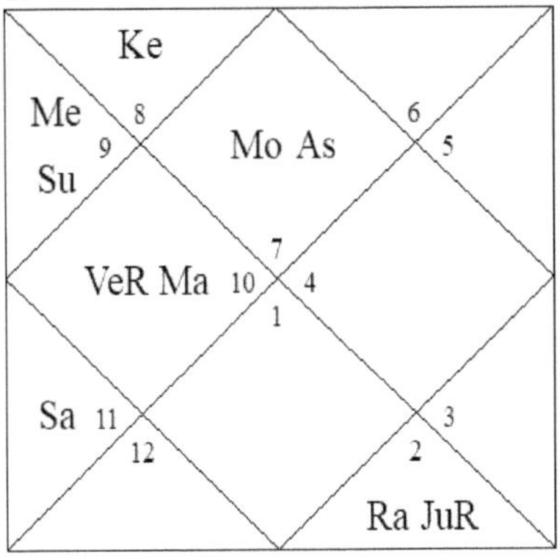

Birth Chart

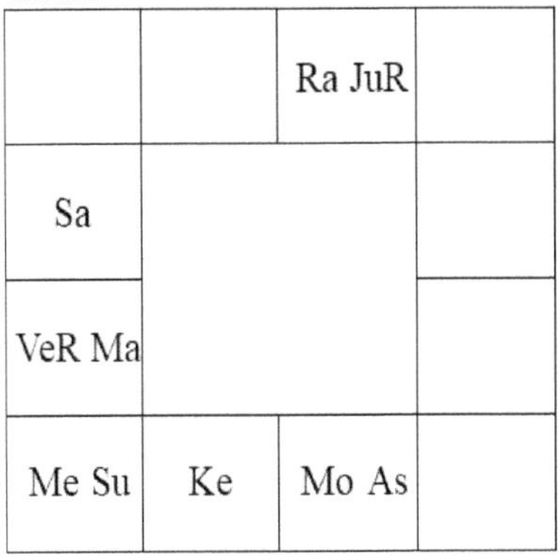

Venkatesha Trishamsha

D30

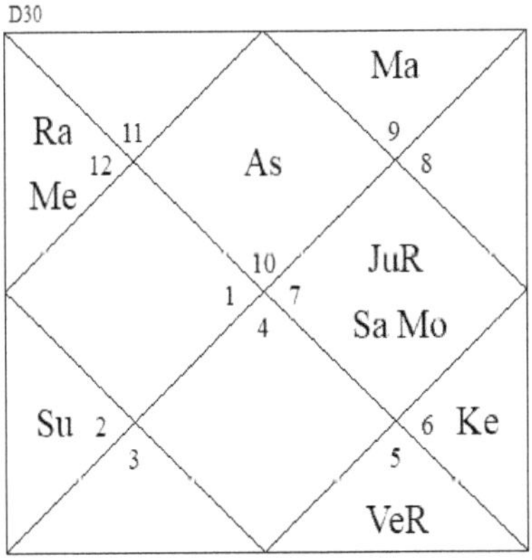

D30

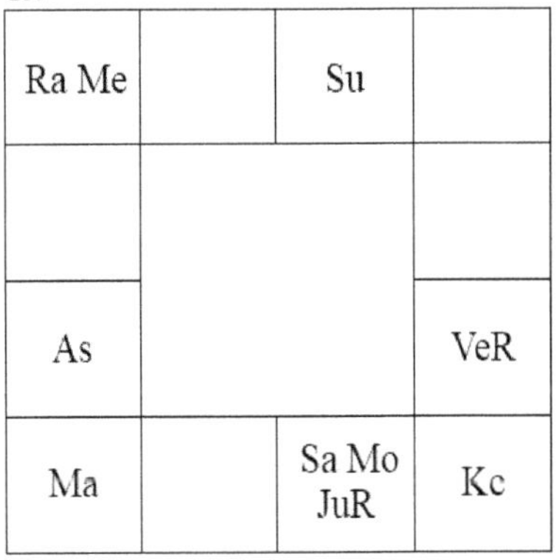

Parashar Trishamsha

D30

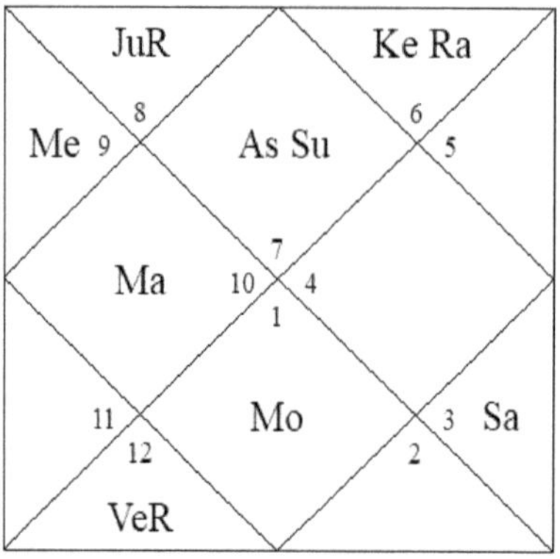

D30

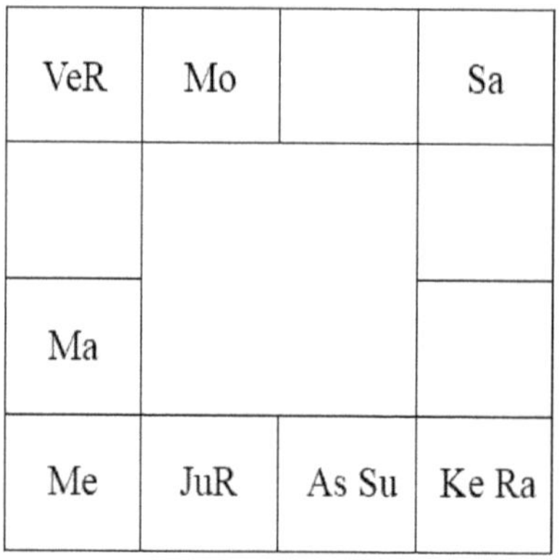

Iyer Trishamsha

D30 Iyer

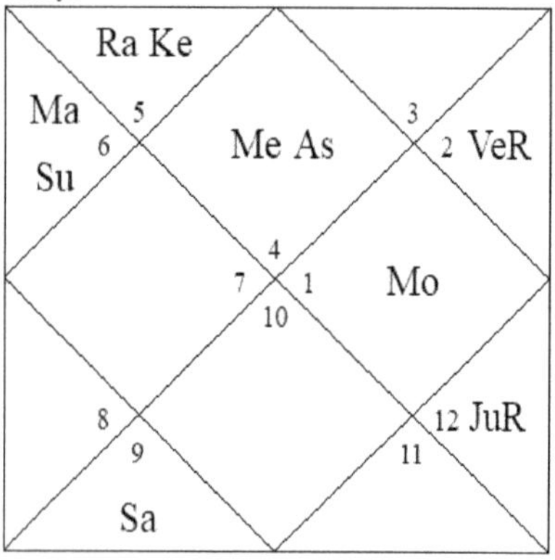

D30 Iyer

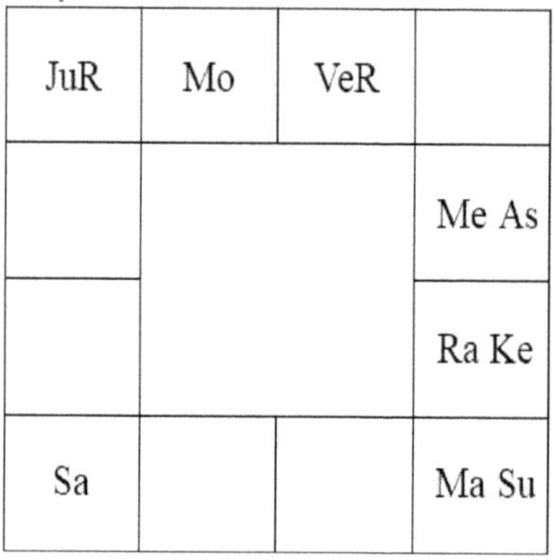

Venkatesha Trishamsha – Lagan is not occupied or aspected by any planet. The lagan lord Saturn is exalted and is with two benefic and involved with Gaja Keshari yoga. Both parameters are good.

Parashar Trishamsha – Lagan is occupied by Sun and is aspected by Moon. Lagan lord Venus is in RKA and aspected by Jupiter and Saturn. This shows a mixed life which is more towards favorable side.

Iyer Trishamsha – Lagan is having a benefic and aspected by a benefic Jupiter. Birth is favorable. Lagan lord Moon is in Subh Kartari and aspected by its sign lord Mars making it strong. This Trishamsha shows true story.

Younger

Example 14 – DOB 14 January 1966, TOB 3.24, POB Alwar

Birth Chart

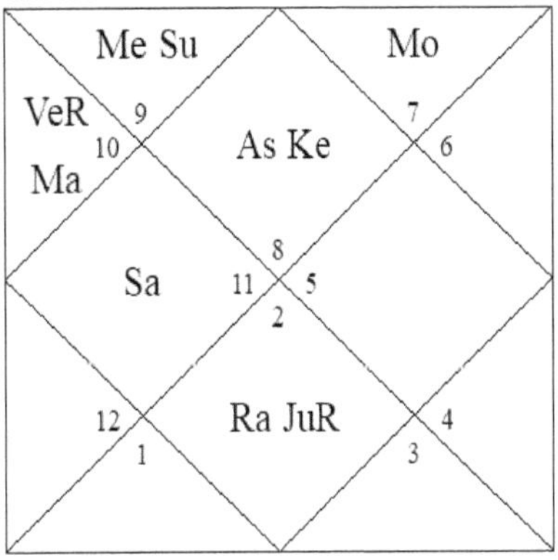

Birth Chart

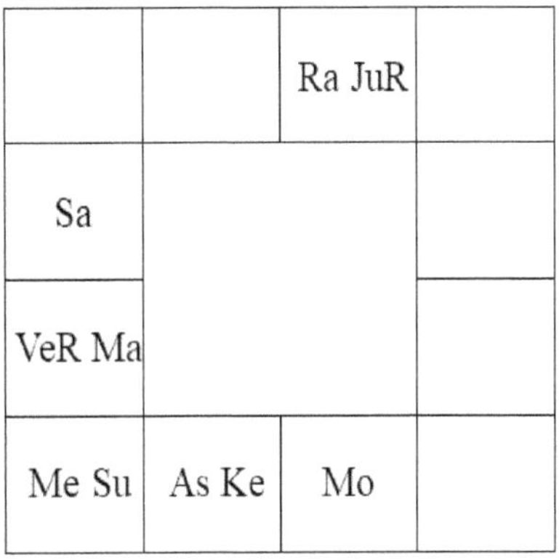

Venkatesha Trishamsha

D30

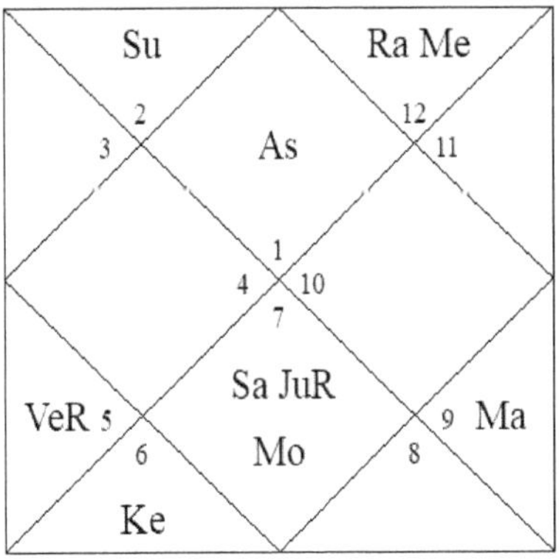

D30

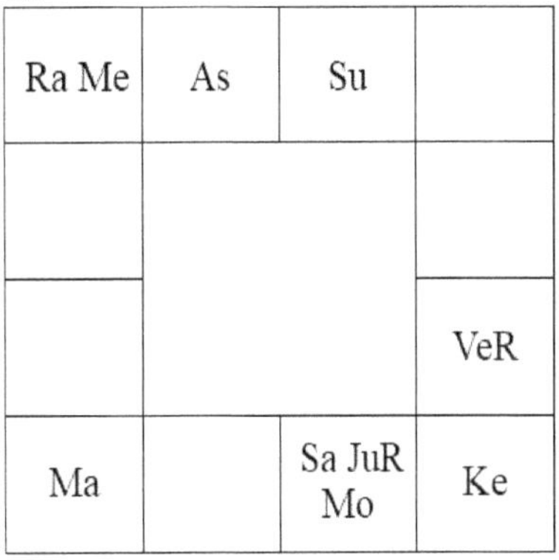

Parashar Trishamsha

D30

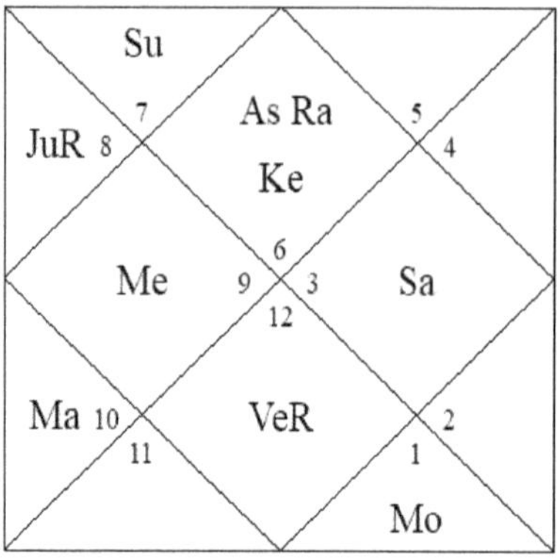

D30

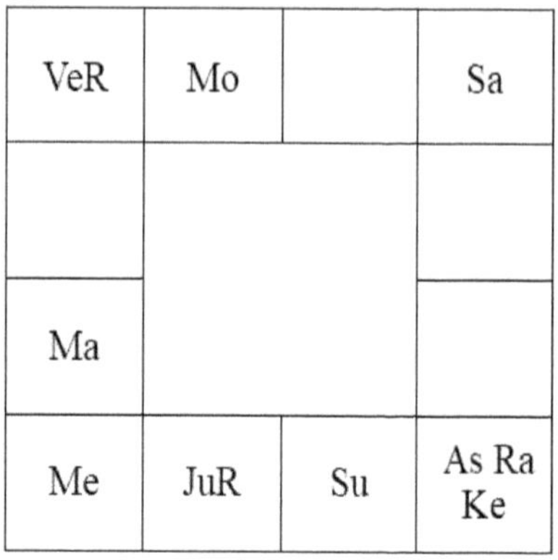

Iyer Trishamsha

D30 Iyer

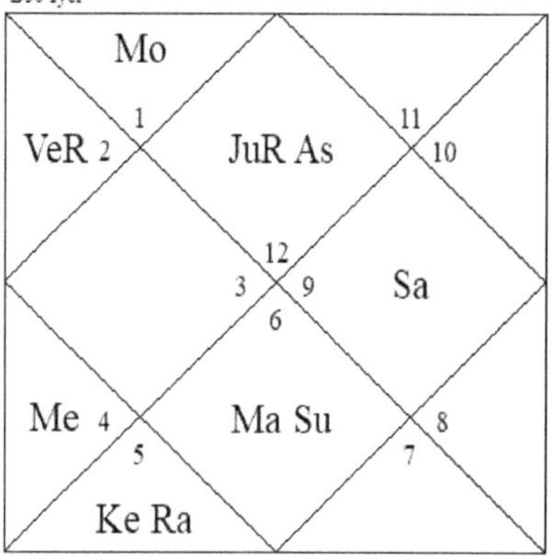

D30 Iyer

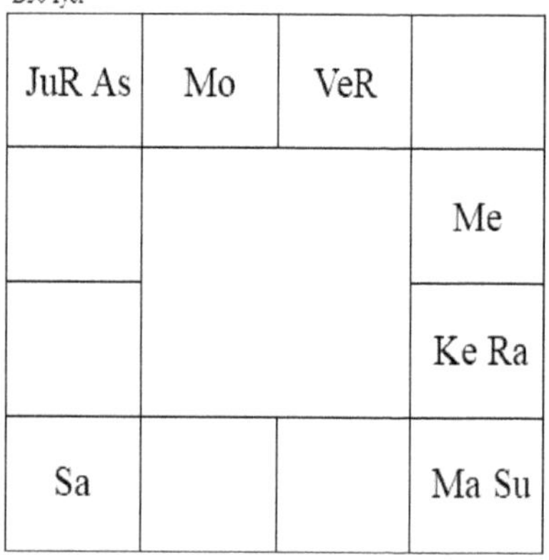

Venkatesha Trishamsha_– Lagan is having both malefic and benefic relation. Lagan lord Mars is aspected by Saturn only. This is a mixed chart and more towards misdeeds committed by him.

Parashar Trishamsha_– Lagan is in RKA and aspected by Venus. Lagan lord is aspected by Saturn. This is also not true.

Iyer Trishamsha_– Lagan and lagan lord both are under malefic influence and do not have any benefic relation. The birth and deeds are spoiled.

We can conclude that cyclical/ Iyer or Varanasi Trishamsha gives better results of physical and material life. The Parashar Trishamsha indicates Tatva.

Chapter 4
Examination

Examination of Trishamsha is an important step to analyze a horoscope. For examination of Trishamsha we will concentrate on four focal points. These are-

1. Lagan lord.
2. Eighth lord.
3. Moon.
4. Eighth house.

1. Lagan lord

For examination of lagan lord of Trishamsha, we must first decide that Trishamsha is a favorable chart or an unfavorable chart. For a favorable chart lagan lord gives benefic results and vice versa. We take the lagan lord of Trishamsha to birth chart. This will give good results to the significations of house occupied by it in birth chart if Trishamsha is a favorable chart. It will give bad results to the significations of house occupied by it in birth chart if Trishamsha chart is an unfavorable chart. It also imposes good or bad results on the planets aspected by it or associated with it.

2. Eighth lord

Now the eighth lord of Trishamsha chart is taken to birth chart. The eighth lord of Trishamsha is always malefic. It spoils the significations of the house in which he is placed in birth chart. The significations of the planets are also destroyed. The aspect or association of eighth lord is also harmful.

3. Moon

Moon is seen for endurance of a person to face the misfortunes. A strong Moon is when it is related to Mars and Saturn by sign and by conjunction or aspect. Moon in sign of Mars and associated with Saturn or in the sign of Saturn and associated with Mars is praised as giver of Sanyas. Such a Moon gives mental strength to face adversities of life. Benefic sign and relation of benefic makes a person mentally soft.

4. Eighth house

Eighth house is the longevity of Trishamsha. A benefic eighth house will increase the longevity and a malefic eighth house will decrease the longevity. It is applied to both favorable and unfavorable charts. In an unfavorable Trishamsha a benefic eighth house will end the unfortunate life and can give a fortunate life. The best situation is having a favorable Trishamsha and a strong and benefic eighth house which will give a long fortunate life. Mixed effect on eighth house will give mixed results.

The following additional rules can be considered.

1. We can apply the first two points in other divisional charts.
2. PAC of benefic or malefic will modify the results.
   We will now see the application on example charts. These are applied on Parashar and cyclical (Iyer) Trishamsha only.

Example 1 – DOB 23 May 1948, TOB 20.01.45, POB Bareilly

Birth Chart

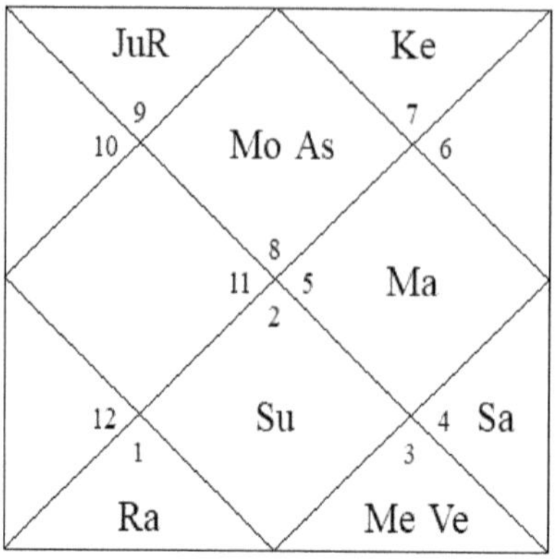

Birth Chart

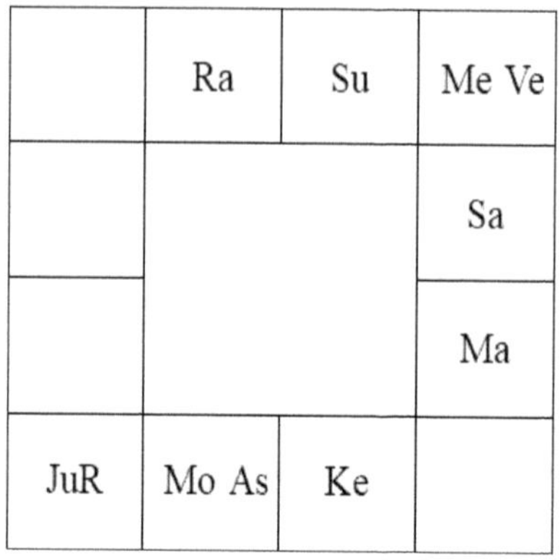

Parashar Trishamsha

D30

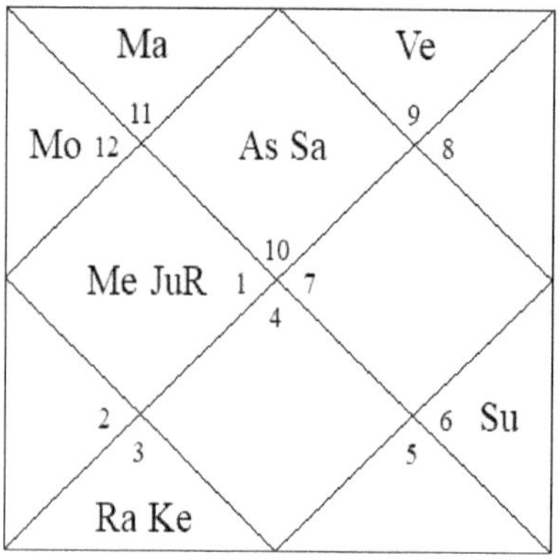

D30

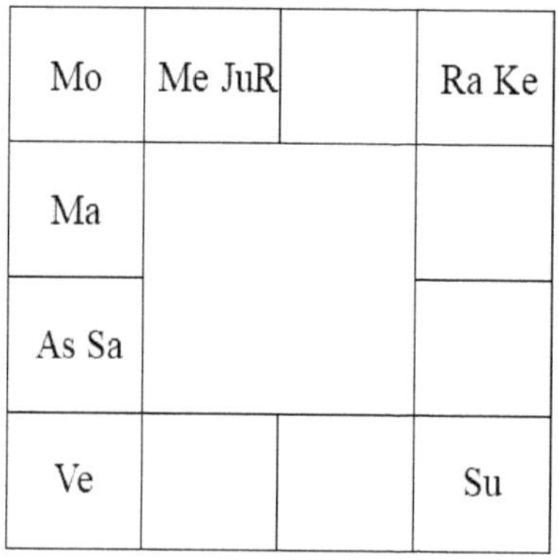

Iyer Trishamsha

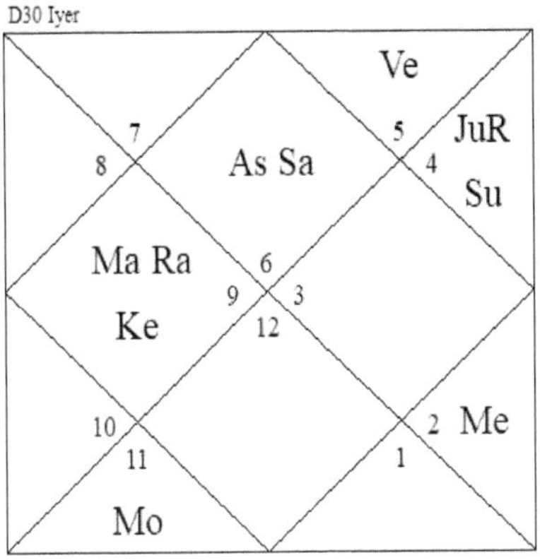

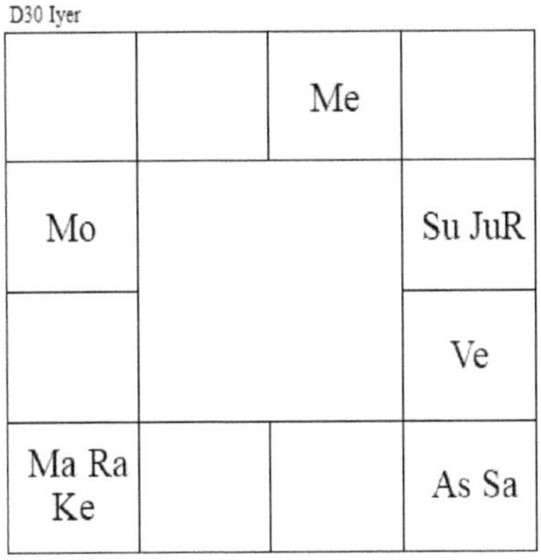

This example given is a favorable birth. We will analyze Trishamsha charts to examine it.

1. Parashar Trishamsha

a. **Lagan lord** - Lagan lord is Saturn. He is placed in ninth house in birth chart. He has given good results of ninth house.

b. **Eighth lord** - Eighth lord is Sun. Sun is placed in seventh house in birth chart. He is not related to any planet. His wife expired at an early age.

c. **Moon** – Moon is in the sign of Saturn and aspected by Saturn and Mars. This has given mental capacity to face bad times with wisdom.

d. **Eighth house** – Eighth house is in RKA and is aspected by Saturn and Sun. Saturn is lagan lord. This is a favorable chart thus fortune is for long duration. It is confirmed.

2. Iyer Trishamsha

a. **Lagan lord** – Lagan lord is Mercury and is placed in eighth house with Venus and is aspected by second and fifth lord making it strong. This makes him dedicated.

b. **Eighth lord** – Eighth lord is Mars. Mars is in tenth house in birth horoscope. Mars is Digbali and aspected by Jupiter. He faced many challenges in profession but the Jupiter provided protection. This Trishamsha shows this event clearly.

c. **Moon** – Moon is in Aquarius which is sign of Saturn and is aspected by Venus. It is a perfect combination which enables him to face misfortune.

d. **Eighth house** – Eighth house is Aries. This gives long life of fortune. This gives better explanation. He is still enjoying high position.

Example 2 – DOB 22 August 1931, TOB 23.08.56, POB Bulandshahr

Birth Chart

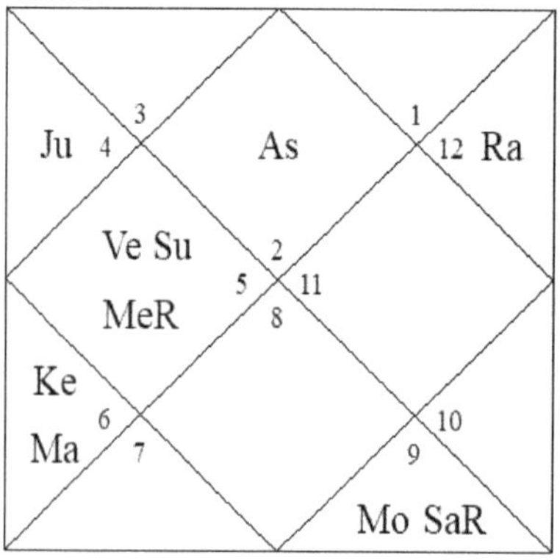

Birth Chart

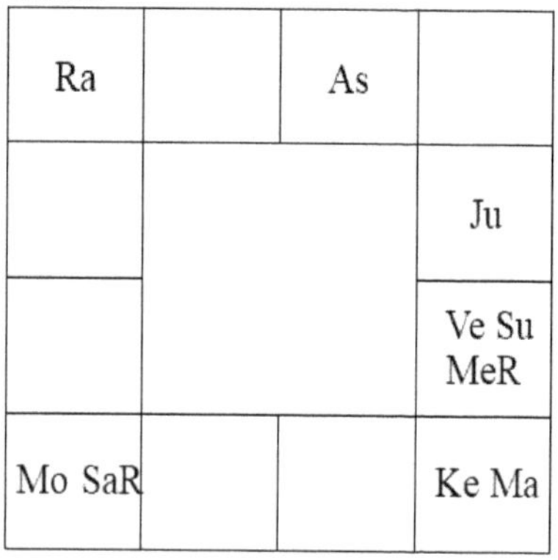

Parashar Trishamsha

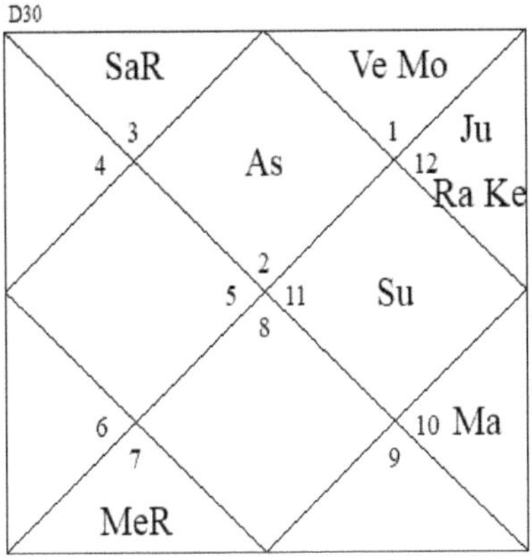

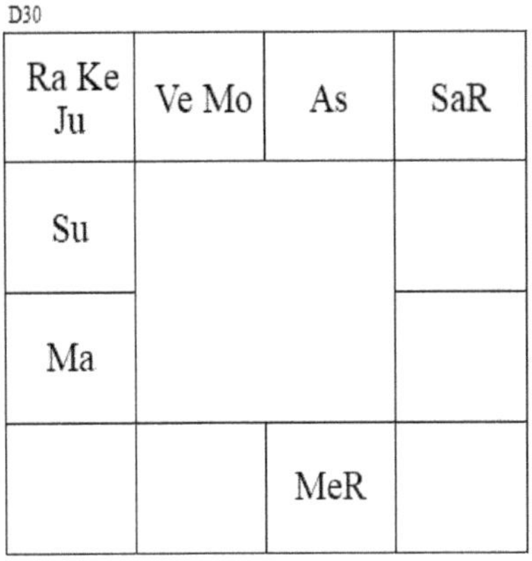

Iyer Trishamsha

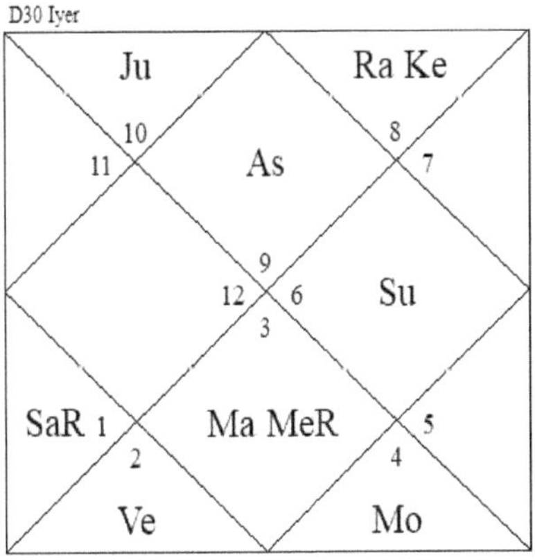

1. Parashar Trishamsha

a. **Lagan lord** – Lagan lord is Venus. In birth chart Venus is in fourth house in Leo. It is in conjunction with Sun and Mercury. So, it is related with fourth house and fourth lord. This provides happiness of family.

b. **Eighth lord -** Eighth lord is Jupiter. Jupiter is exalted in third house and indicates loss of courage and younger siblings.

c. **Moon** – Moon is in the sign of Mars. It is with Venus and is aspected by exalted Mars and Mercury. Moon is strong to face misfortunes.

d. **Eighth house** – Eighth house is aspected by Saturn and has no benefic relation. The fortunes should have ended but it is not so. He was having name fame and good practice as a doctor even after retirement.

2. Iyer Trishamsha

a. **Lagan lord** – Lagan lord is Jupiter. Jupiter is exalted in third house and is not aspected by any planet. It gives respect from siblings.

b. **Eighth lord** – Eighth lord is Moon. Moon is in Sagittarius in eighth house of birth chart. It is with Saturn and aspected by Mars. Moon gives problems to eighth, ninth and tenth house. Saturn is lord of ninth and tenth house. He had to quit his job suddenly.

c. **Moon** – Moon is in Cancer and is aspected by Jupiter. There is no association of Mars or Saturn. He likes to avoid problems and wisely steers away from them.

d. **Eighth house** – Eighth house has Moon in own sign and aspected by Jupiter. He still has fortune after retirement.

Example 3 – DOB 30 April 1945, TOB 10.27 (war time), POB Delhi

Birth Chart

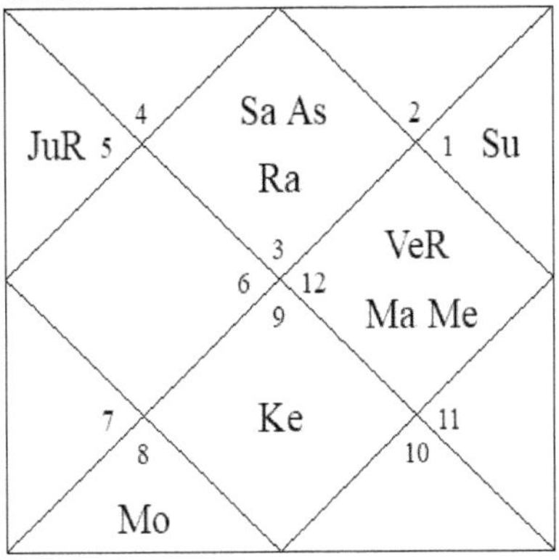

Birth Chart

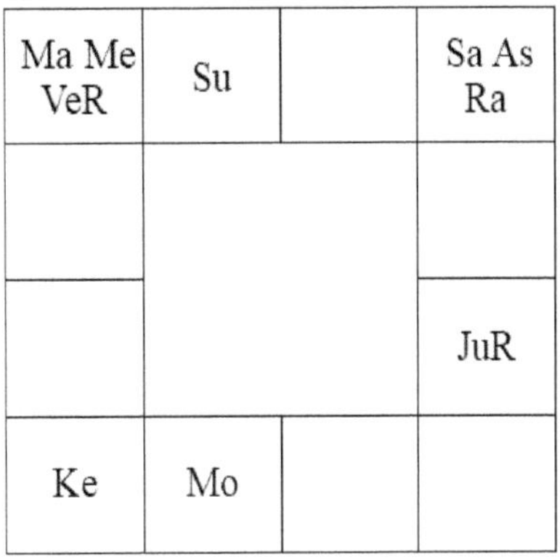

Parashar Trishamsha

D30

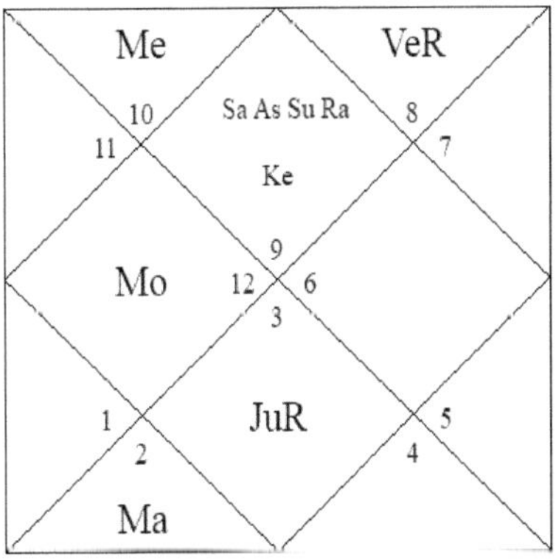

D30

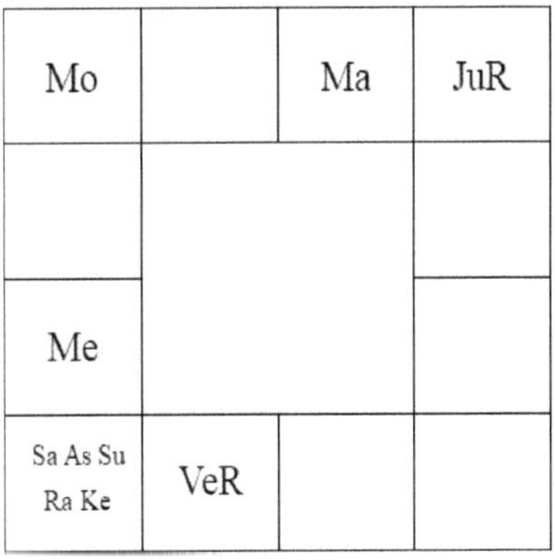

Iyer Trishamsha

D30 Iyer

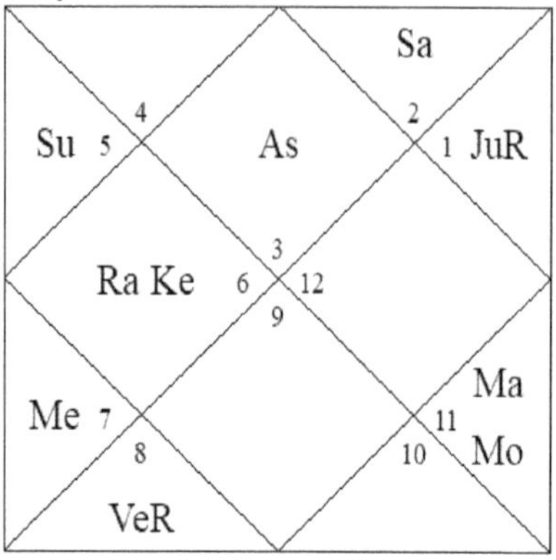

D30 Iyer

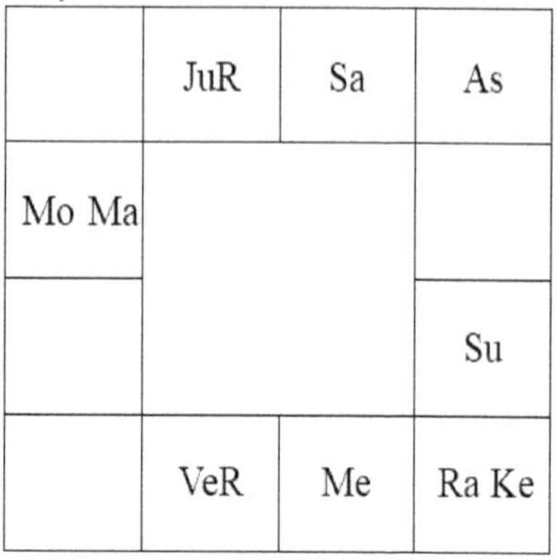

1. Parashar Trishamsha

a. **Lagan lord** – Lagan lord is Jupiter. In birth chart Jupiter is in third house aspected by Saturn. It gives mixed courage and average relations with coborn.

b. **Eighth lord** - Eighth lord is Moon. Moon is placed in sixth house in birth and has no aspect. Moon gives illness and enemies.

c. **Moon** – Moon is in the sign of Jupiter and is not associated with any planet. He avoids misfortunes by wise action and does not like to face problems.

d. **Eighth house** – Eighth house is aspected by Mercury. There is no other relation. The life of fortune is long.

2. Iyer Trishamsha

a. **Lagan lord** – Lagan lord is Mercury. Mercury is placed in tenth house in birth horoscope. He is with Mars and Venus and is aspected by Saturn. This gives good position in profession.

b. **Eighth lord** – Eighth lord is Saturn. Saturn is in lagan with Rahu. As eighth lord it gives physical problems. Saturn is aspecting tenth house and three planets placed in tenth house. Saturn is aspecting tenth lord Jupiter. This made him to quit his good job. Jupiter is seventh lord also and gives problems in married life also.

c. **Moon** – Moon is in Aquarius with Mars and is aspected by Sun and Saturn. He is mentally capable of facing challenges of life.

d. **Eighth house** – Eighth house has no aspect or conjunction. It is neutral and the fortune life is not dependent on external influence.

Example 4 – DOB 6 April 1990, TOB 5.23, POB Mathura

Birth Chart

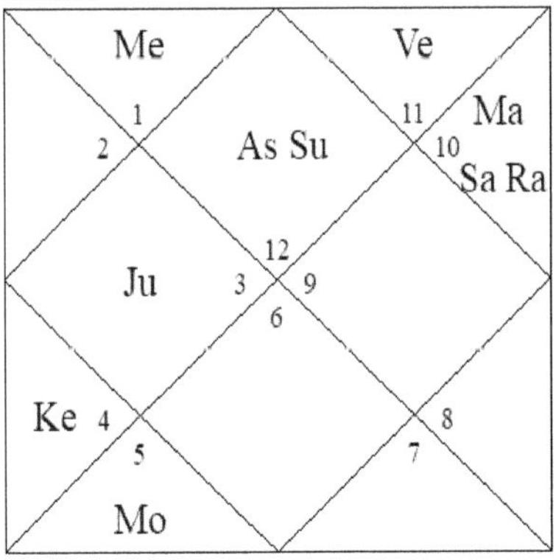

Birth Chart

As Su	Me		Ju
Ve			Ke
Sa Ra Ma			Mo

Parashar Trishamsha

D30

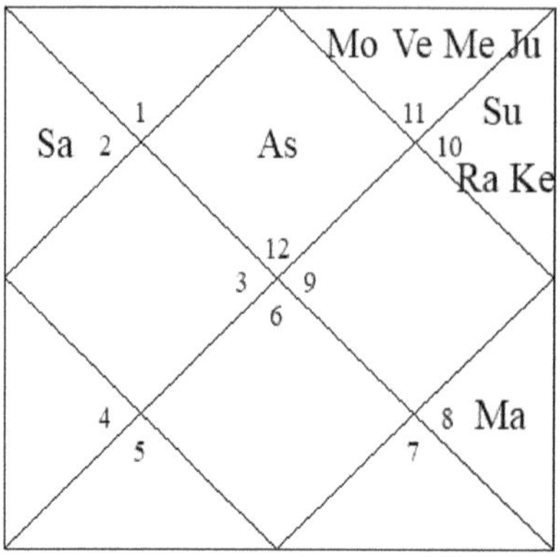

D30

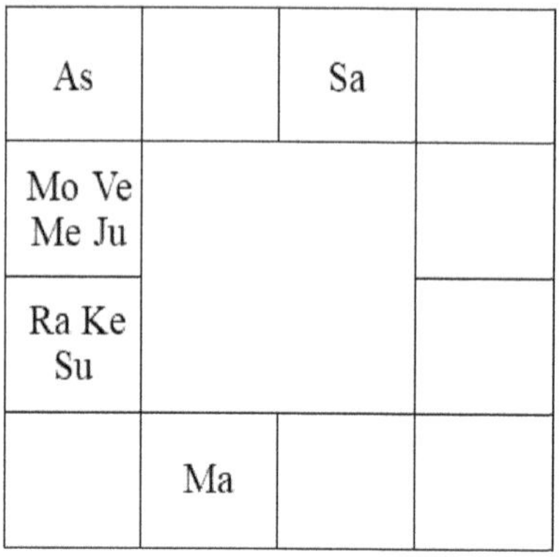

Iyer Trishamsha

D30 Iyer

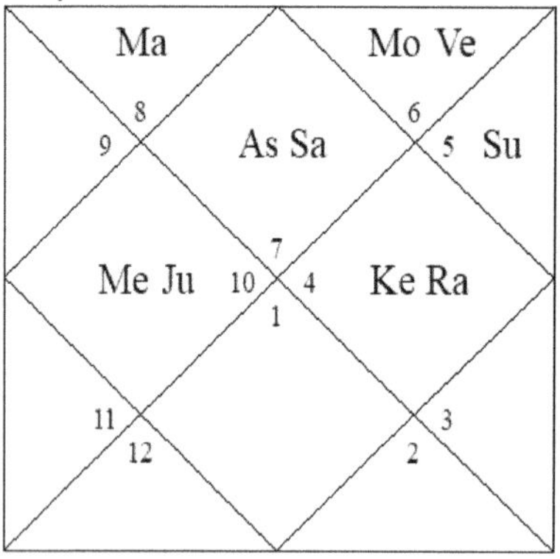

D30 Iyer

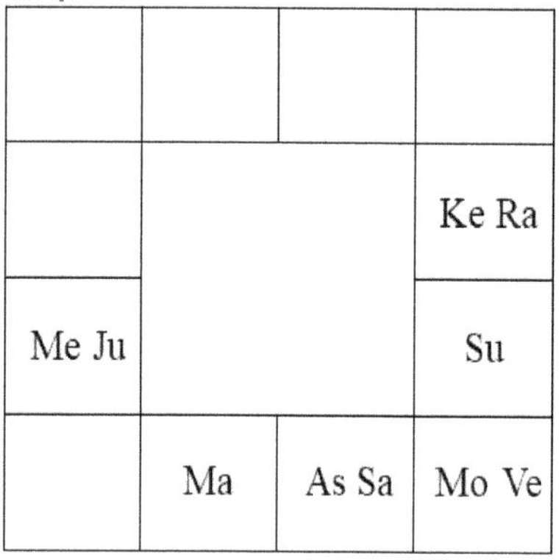

1. Parashar Trishamsha

a. **Lagan lord** – Lagan lord is Jupiter. In birth chart Jupiter is in fourth house and has no aspect. This is a chart of misfortune. The placement of lagan lord gives loss of happiness and problems to family.

b. **Eighth lord** - Eighth lord is Venus. Venus is in Aquarius in papa Kartari and in twelfth house. He is in bed for last sixteen years due to papa Kartari. Venus is aspecting Moon giving mental agony.

c. **Moon** – Moon is in the sign of Saturn. Moon is with three benefic and aspected by Mars and Saturn. He is facing all problems with courage.

d. **Eighth house** – Eighth house is aspected by Jupiter. This Trishamsha is an unfortunate chart. This gives problems for long duration.

2. Iyer Trishamsha

a. **Lagan lord and eighth lord** – Lagan lord and eighth lord is Venus. In birth horoscope Venus is highly afflicted and is giving lot of problems.

b. **Eighth lord** – Same a lagan lord.

c. **Moon** – Moon is in Virgo with debilitated Venus. It is aspected by Jupiter. It is on papa Kartari and this Moon is not free to bear the pains.

d. **Eighth house** – Mars and Jupiter are aspecting eighth house. This is both benefic and malefic relation. The misfortunes and fortunes are both present.

Example 5 – DOB 15 January 1952, TOB 20.09, POB Varanasi

Birth Chart

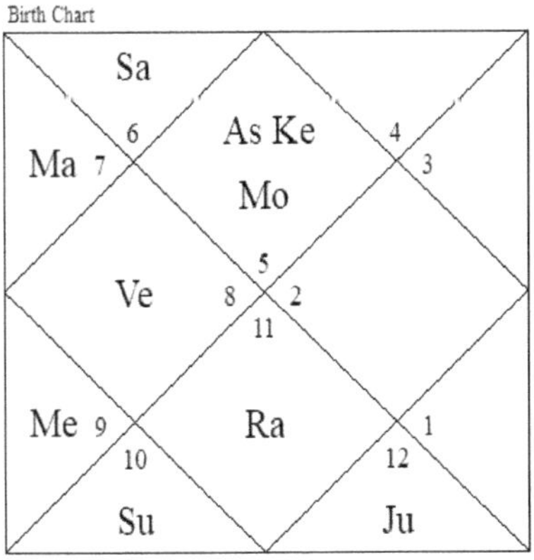

Birth Chart

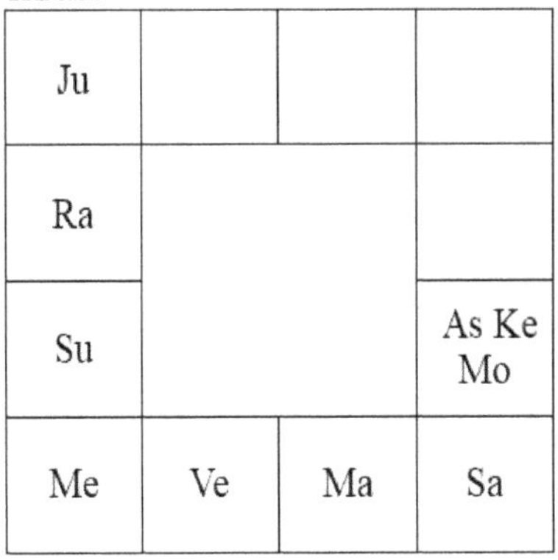

Parashar Trishamsha

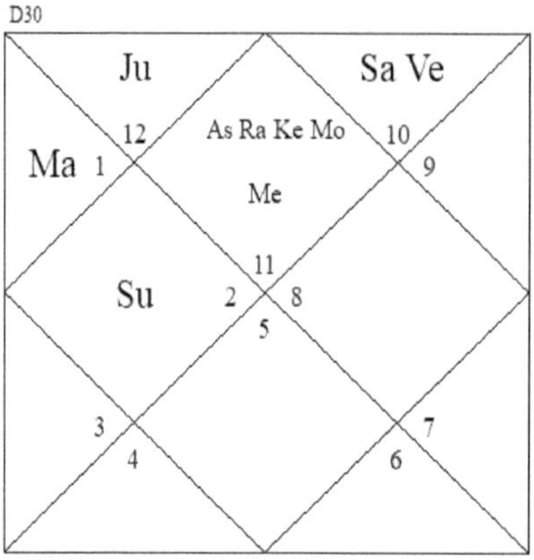

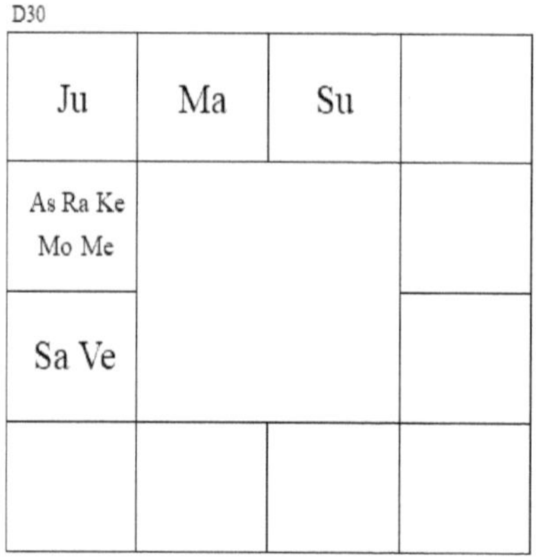

Iyer Trishamsha

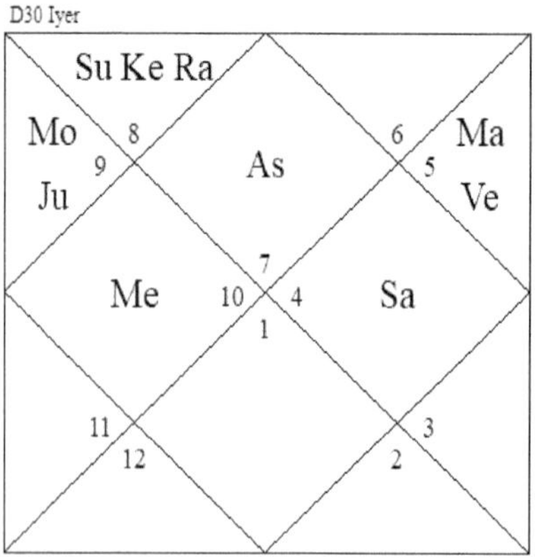

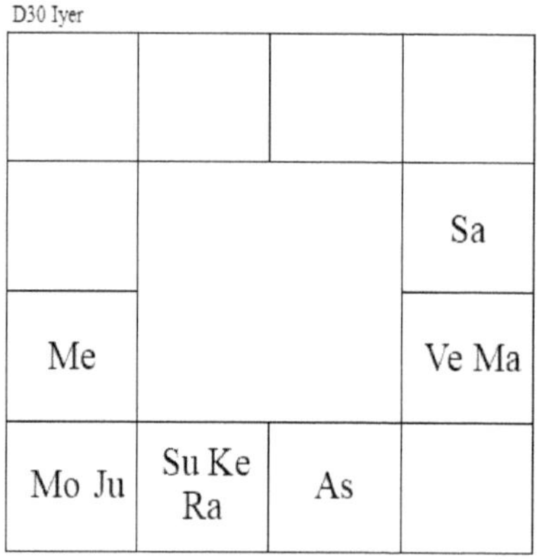

1. Parashar Trishamsha

a. **Lagan lord** – Lagan lord is Saturn. In birth chart Saturn is in second house. Saturn is aspecting Venus and Jupiter. Being in second house it has given wealth and birth in good family. Saturn aspect is also promoting the significations of houses owned by Venus and Jupiter.

b. **Eighth lord** - Eighth lord is Mercury. Mercury is in fifth house and indicates problems to children. The lagan lord is also aspecting the fifth lord and gives protection to children.

c. **Moon** – Moon is in the sign of Saturn, Aquarius. Moon is with Rahu and Mercury. He gets upset by problems because of Rahu but his Mercury intelligence gives support to his mind.

d. **Eighth house** – Eighth house is aspected by Jupiter. It gives durable fortune.

2. Iyer Trishamsha

a. **Lagan lord and eighth lord** – Lagan lord and eighth lord is Venus. In birth horoscope Venus is in fourth house and is playing dual role. He migrated to USA leaving his home in India and made another home abroad.

b. **Eighth lord** – Same a lagan lord.

c. **Moon** – Moon is in Sagittarius and is with Jupiter. Moon is related to benefic only and as such he will not face any major problems to face them.

d. **Eighth house** – It is in RKA and aspected by Sun. the fortunate life can be terminated. He had faced problems in life also.

Example 6 – DOB 24 June 1998, TOB 18.58, POB Delhi

Birth Chart

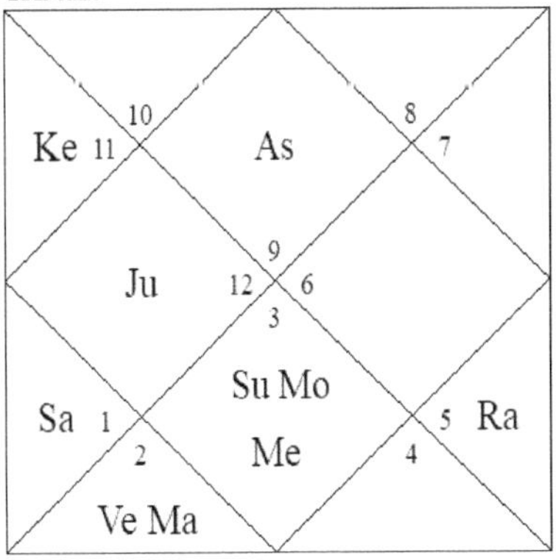

Birth Chart

Ju	Sa	Ve Ma	Su Mo Me
Ke			
			Ra
As			

Parashar Trishamsha

D30

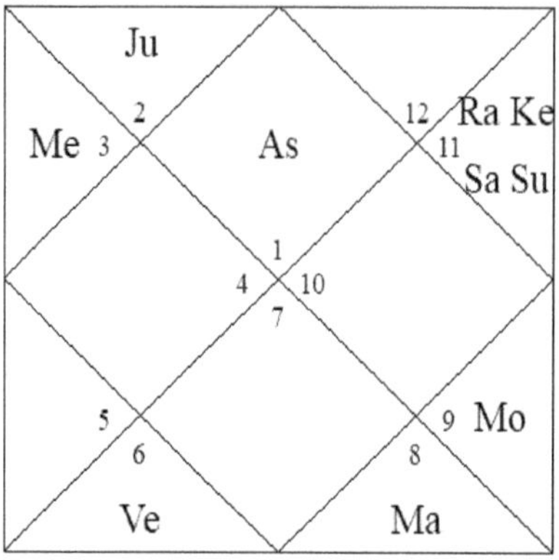

D30

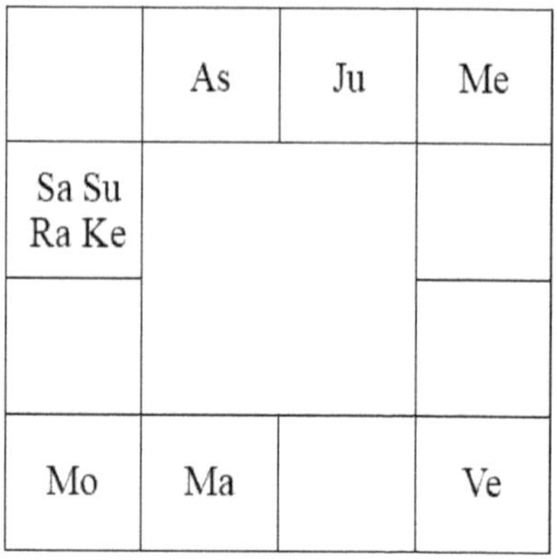

Iyer Trishamsha

D30 Iyer

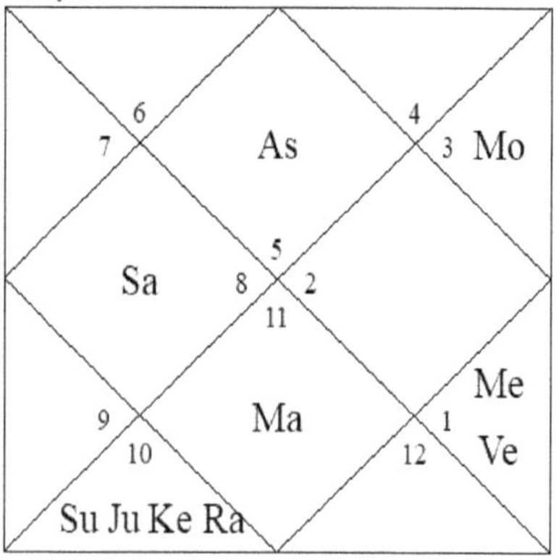

D30 Iyer

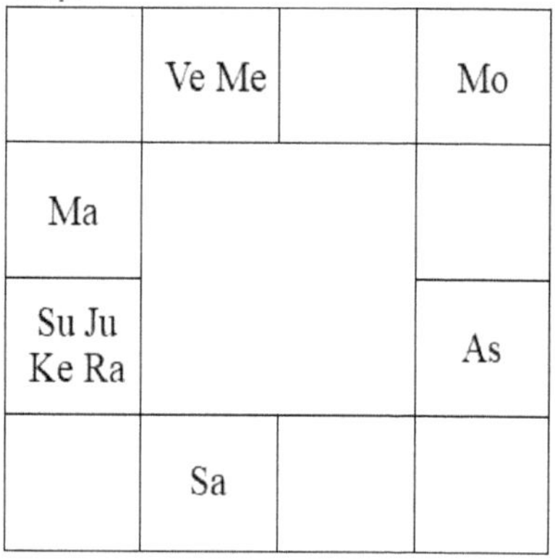

1. Parashar Trishamsha

a. **Lagan lord and eighth lord** – Lagan lord and eighth lord is Mars. Mars is in sixth house of birth chart and is with sixth lord. This is not a fortunate chart and this placement gives enemies and illness. Mars is aspecting ninth house and lagan. It spoils the dharma and self. Aspect of Mars on lagan gives her determination. She ran away from her home and ruined her life.

b. **Eighth lord** – Same as lagan lord.
c. **Moon** – Moon is in Sagittarius, a sign of Jupiter. It is aspected by Mercury. She cannot face adversities of life.
d. **Eighth house** – Mars is in eighth house in Scorpio. It is aspected by Jupiter and Saturn. The unfortunate life is long.

2. Iyer Trishamsha

a. **Lagan lord** – Lagan lord is Sun. In birth horoscope Sun is in seventh house with seventh lord Mercury. It is with Moon. The seventh house, seventh lord are under affliction. It is with eighth lord Moon and spoils the manglya house.
b. **Eighth lord** – Eighth lord of Trishamsha is Jupiter. Jupiter is in fourth house in birth chart. Jupiter is in papa Kartari. This gives better explanation of the event.
c. **Moon** – Moon is in Gemini and not has any other relation. This is an immature mind.
d. **Eighth house** – In this Trishamsha the eighth house is average. The unfortunate trends can be corrected.

Example 7 – DOB 5 September 1997, TOB 8.30, POB Delhi

Birth Chart

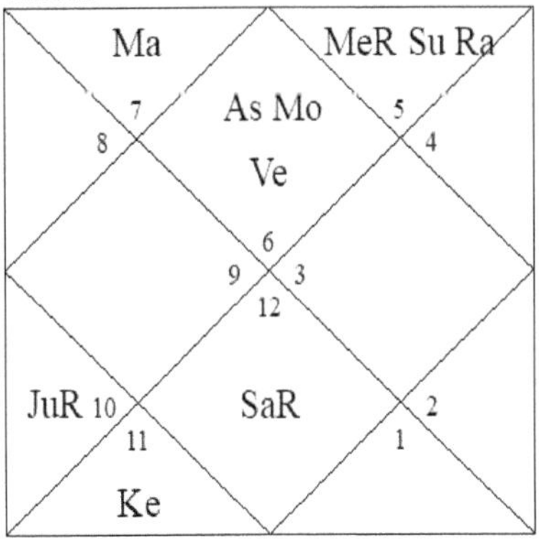

Birth Chart

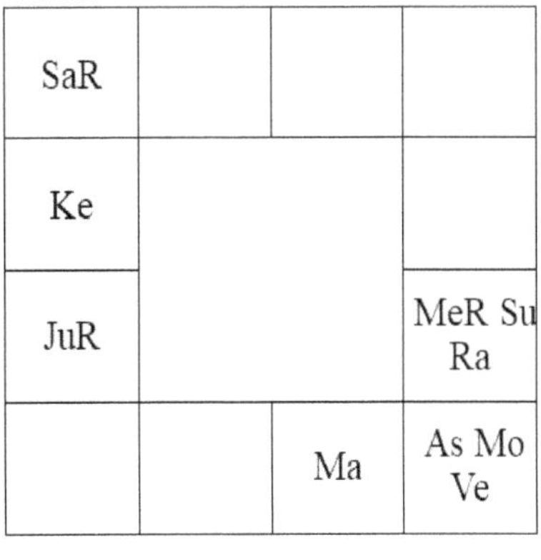

Parashar Trishamsha

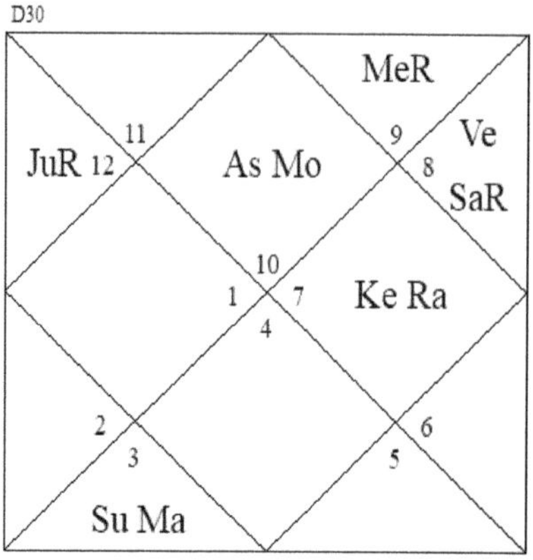

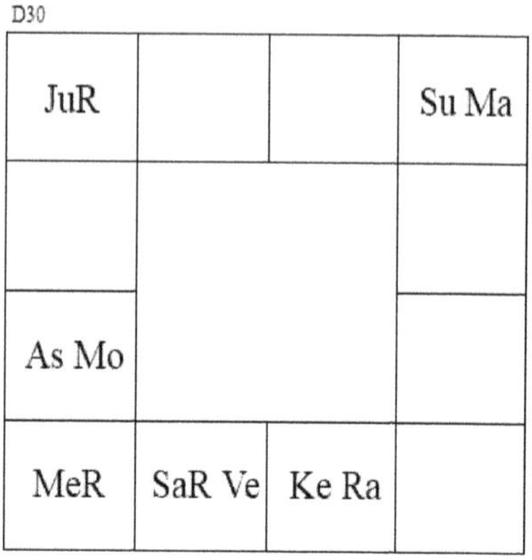

Iyer Trishamsha

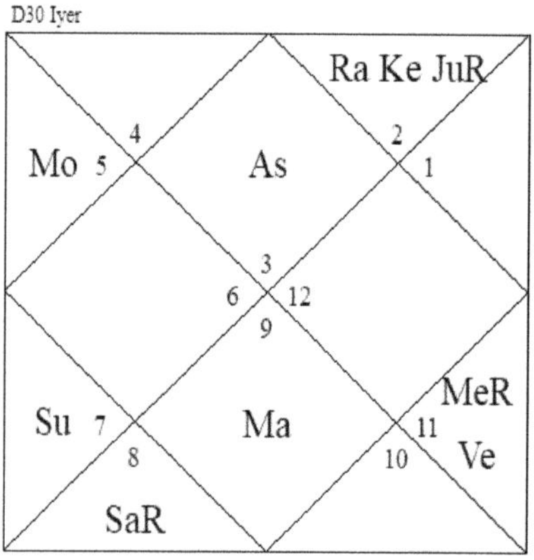

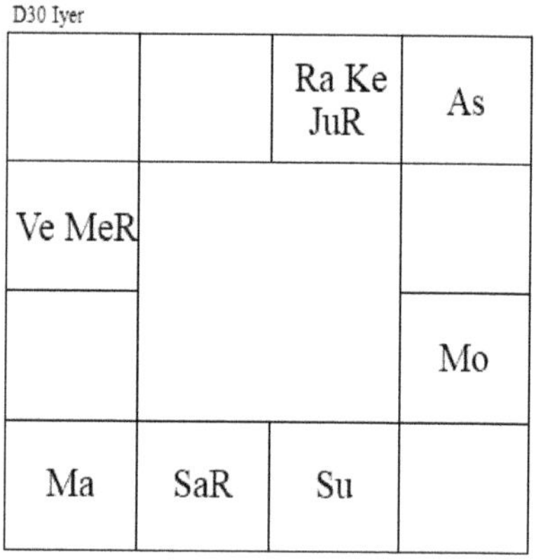

1. Parashar Trishamsha

a. **Lagan lord** – Lagan lord Saturn is in seventh house in Trishamsha. It is aspecting Moon and Venus. Venus is ninth lord. Ninth house is also aspected by Saturn. This way the ninth house and lord are under bad influence. This is spoiling the fate and father.

b. **Eighth lord** – Eighth lord is Sun. In birth chart Sun is in twelfth house with Rahu and Mercury. He is not able to enjoy his bed. He is mentally ill and is confined to bed.

c. **Moon** – Moon is in Capricorn and is aspected by Saturn and Mars which is making him strong to face the adversities.

d. **Eighth house** – Leo is the sign in eighth house. It is aspected by Saturn only. The misfortune is of long duration.

2. Iyer Trishamsha

a. **Lagan lord** – Lagan lord is Mercury. Mercury is in twelfth house of birth chart. It is with Rahu and Sun. This situation is already discussed above.

b. **Eighth lord** – Eighth lord is Saturn. In Parashar Trishamsha Saturn is lagan lord. This is spoiling seventh house. Due to illness, he cannot get married.

c. **Moon** – Moon is in third house in Leo and is aspected by Mercury, Venus and Saturn. Mental attitude is soft and cannot face problems.

d. **Eighth house** – Capricorn is aspected by Saturn and Jupiter. The misfortunes are to be faced for a long time.

Example 8 – DOB 15 October 1973, TOB 22.58, POB Jaipur

Birth Chart

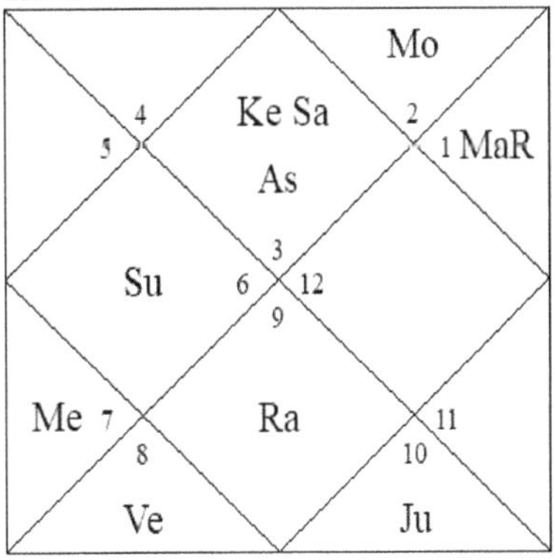

Birth Chart

	MaR	Mo	Ke Sa As
Ju			
Ra	Ve	Me	Su

Parashar Trishamsha

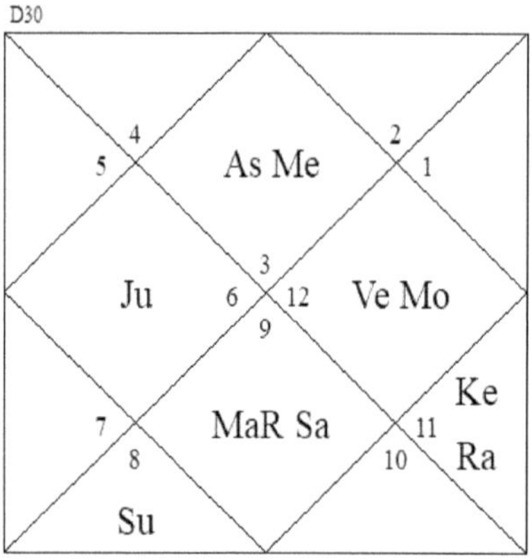

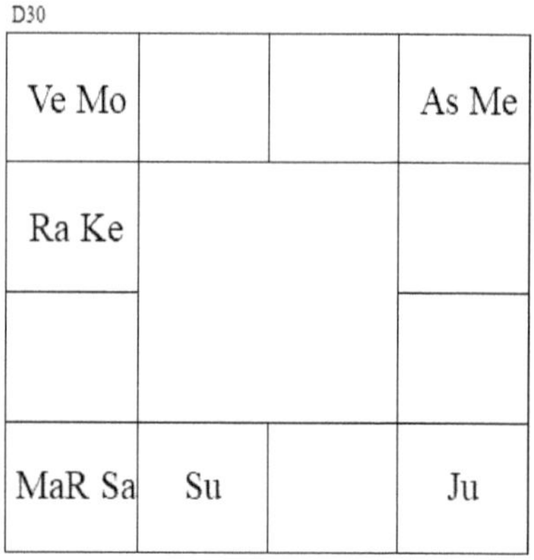

Iyer Trishamsha

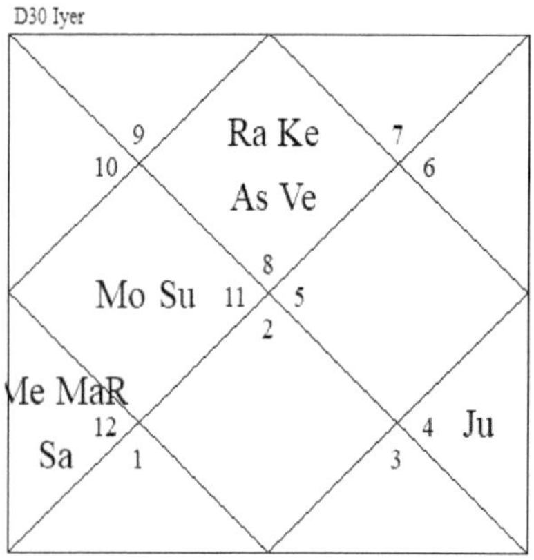

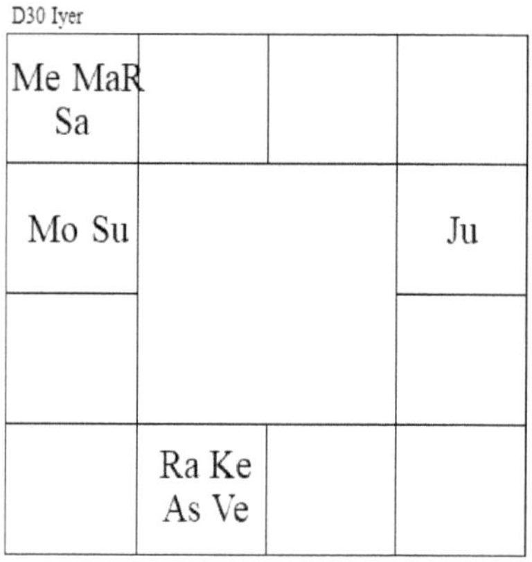

1. Parashar Trishamsha

a. **Lagan lord** – Lagan lord Mercury is in fifth house in birth chart. It is aspecting Mars. Mars is sixth lord. Mercury is thus afflicting fifth house and sixth house. This gives illness with sufferings.

b. **Eighth lord** – Eighth lord is Saturn. Saturn is in lagan with Ketu. Lagan is body and he is suffering with cancer.

c. **Moon** – Moon is in tenth house with exalted Venus. It is aspected by Jupiter and Saturn. This Moon is providing wisdom to face illness.

d. **Eighth house** – Eighth house is in papa Kartari and is aspected by Jupiter. Jupiter is prolonging the life of misfortune.

2. Iyer Trishamsha

a. **Lagan lord** – Lagan lord of Trishamsha is Mars. Mars is sixth lord of birth and aspects lagan lord Mercury. The body is suffering with illness.

b. **Eighth lord** – Eighth lord is Mercury. We have discussed Mercury already.

c. **Moon** – Moon is in Aquarius with Sun He has no aspect on him. Moon being in Aquarius gives some mental strength to face the illness.

d. **Eighth house** – It is aspected by Mars only which gives hope of ending misfortunes early.

Example 9 – DOB 13 May 1955, TOB 21.15, POB Rishikesh

Birth Chart

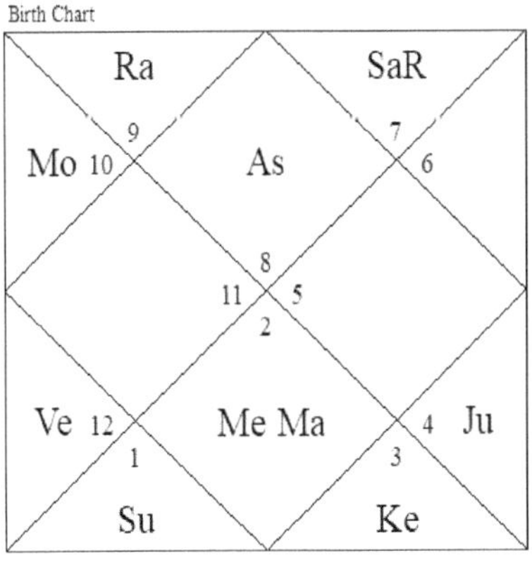

Birth Chart

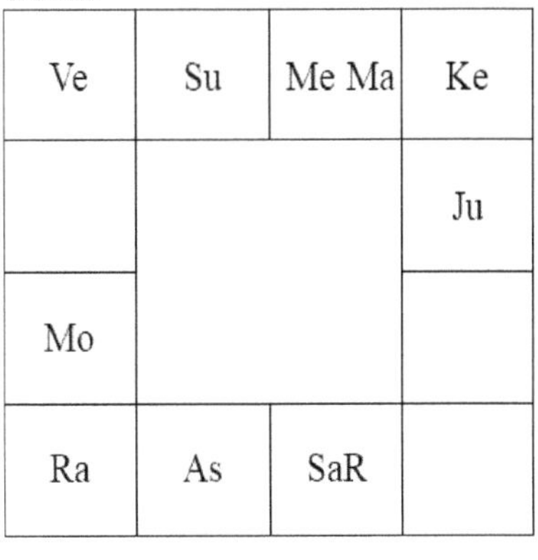

Parashar Trishamsha

D30

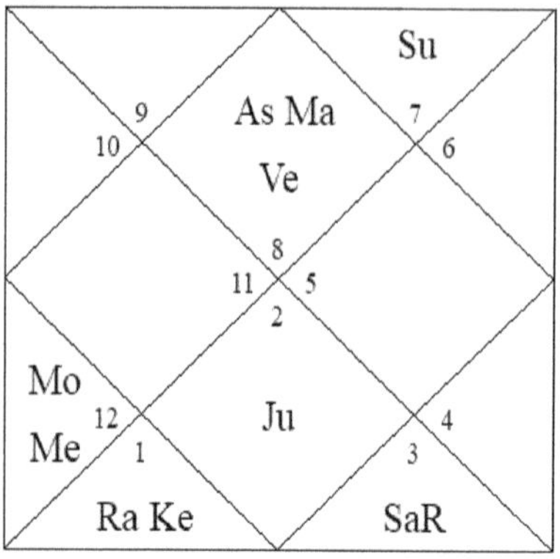

D30

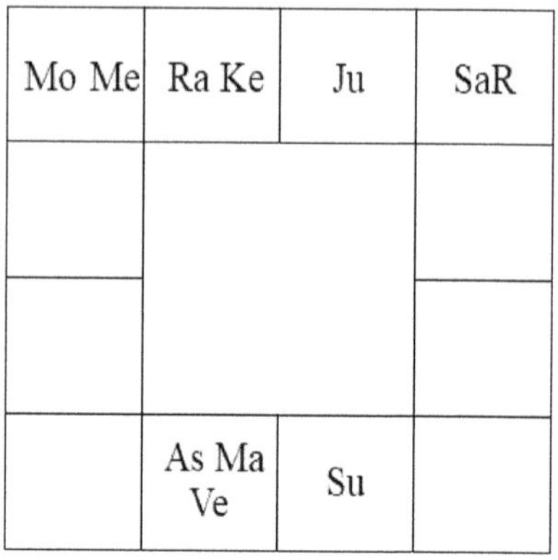

Iyer Trishamsha

D30 Iyer

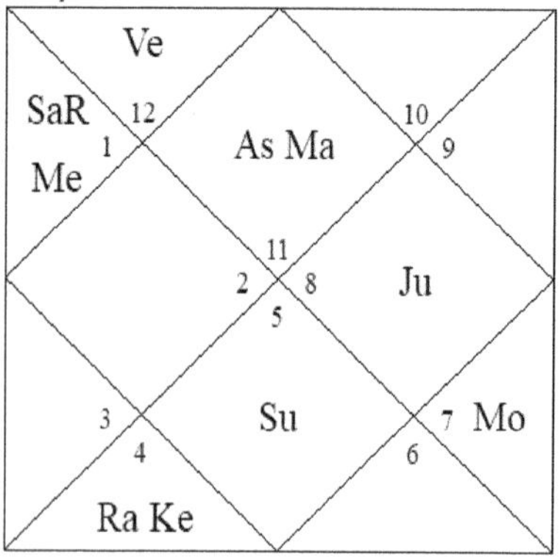

D30 Iyer

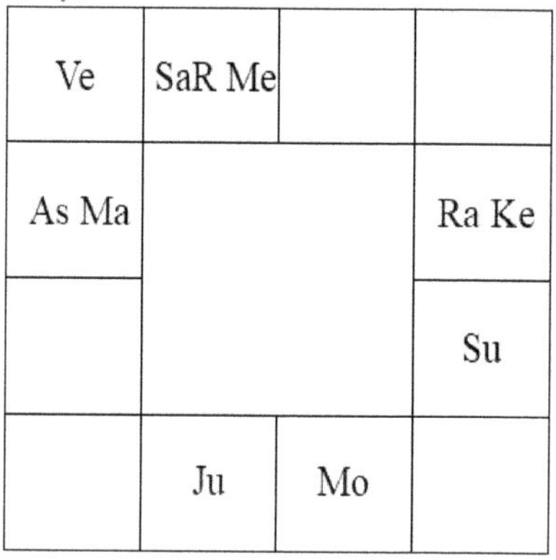

1. Parashar Trishamsha –

a. **Lagan lord** – Lagan lord of Trishamsha is Mars. Mars is in seventh house in birth horoscope. It is aspecting lagan which is in papa Kartari. The physical problems are present.

b. **Eighth Lord** – Eighth lord is Mercury. In birth chart Mercury is in seventh house with lagan lord Mars and aspects lagan. The physical problems are many folds. The seventh house is also spoiled.

c. **Moon** – Moon is with Mercury in Pisces. It is aspected by Saturn. It is an average situation.
d. **Eighth house** – Eighth house is occupied by Saturn and aspected by Mars. The life of Trishamsha is short.

2. Iyer Trishamsha –

a. **Lagan lord** – Lagan lord is Saturn and is placed in twelfth house in birth. It is aspected by Sun. Saturn is spoiling wealth and fate. Its aspect on sixth house is making the enemies strong. His business was grabbed by partners.
b. **Eighth lord** – Eighth lord is Mercury. In birth chart Mercury is in seventh house with lagan lord Mars and aspects lagan. The physical problems are many fold. The seventh house is spoiled.
c. **Moon** – Moon is in Libra and is aspected by Saturn and Mercury. He is mentally soft and is not able to fight back.
d. **Eighth house** – Eighth house is in Kartari. It is aspected by Venus thus giving long life to miseries. His miseries ended with his death only.

This person had a very difficult life. His transport business was grabbed by his partners. His family life was ruined due to his abusive wife. She took his property and his mother was on doles.

Example 10 – DOB 5 January 1928, TOB 17.26, POB Larkana, Pakistan

Birth Chart

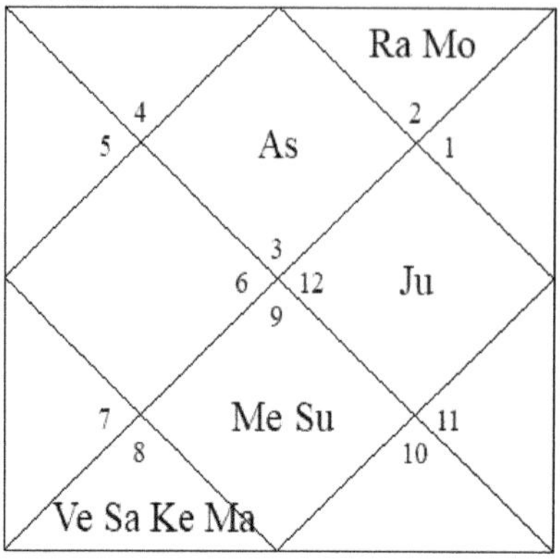

Birth Chart

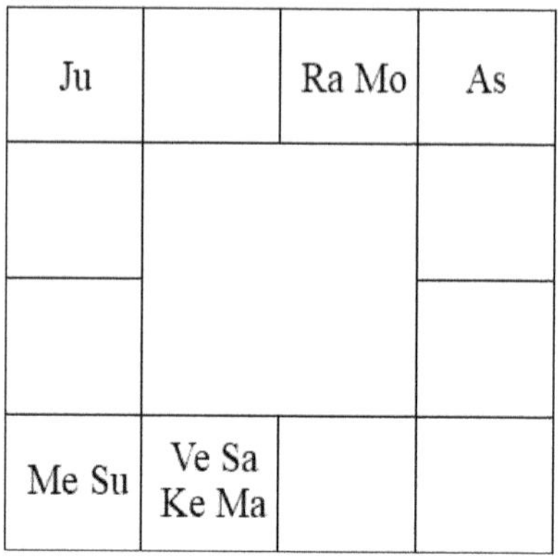

Parashar Trishamsha

D30

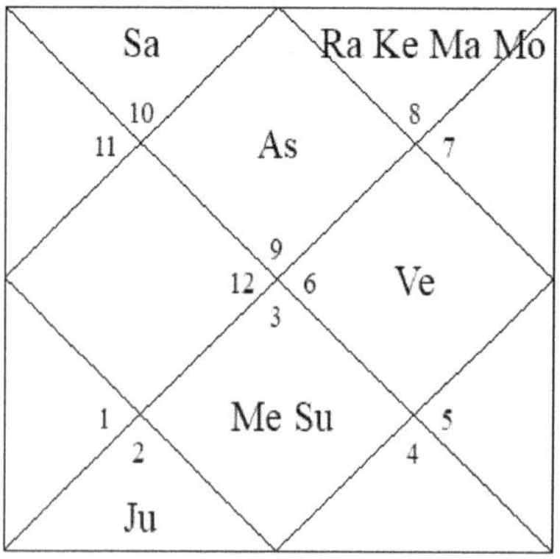

D30

Iyer Trishamsha

D30 Iyer

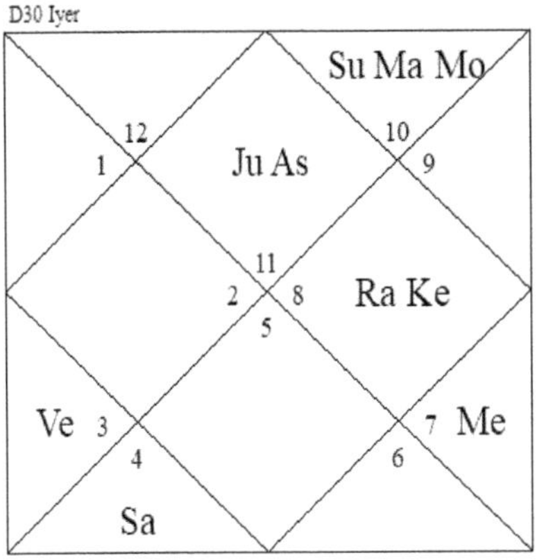

D30 Iyer

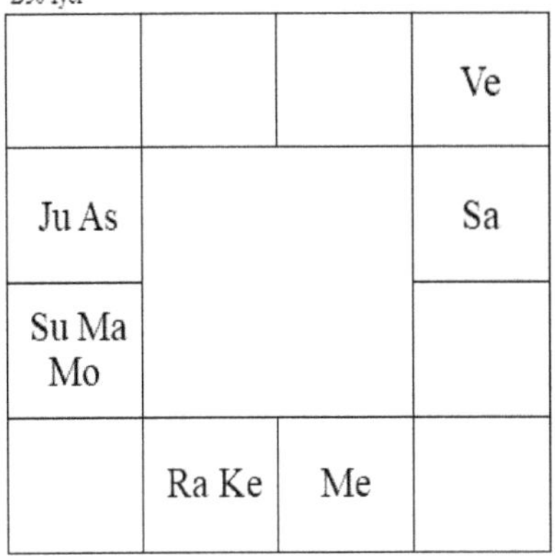

This chart is of Z. A. Bhutto. He was prime minister of Pakistan and was hanged to death. This happened on 4th April 1979. He has a fortunate birth but his actions took him towards misfortune.

1. Parashar Trishamsha –

a. **Lagan lord** – Lagan lord is Jupiter. In birth chart Jupiter is in tenth house. It is a fortunate birth and Jupiter promotes tenth house. Jupiter is aspecting second, sixth and seventh house. Wealth, family and enemies are blessed.

b. **Eighth lord** – Eighth lord is Moon. Moon is in twelfth house with Rahu. It is aspecting three planets in sixth house and spoiled the significations of them.

c. **Moon** – Moon is in Scorpio with Mars. It also conjoined with Rahu and is aspected by Jupiter. He was capable to face challenges of life.

d. **Eighth house** – Saturn is aspecting eighth house and cutting short the life of fortunes.

2. Iyer Trishamsha –

a. **Lagan lord -** Lagan lord is Saturn. Saturn is in sixth house with Venus, Mars and Ketu. It is aspecting Moon. Since it a fortunate birth Saturn is promoting the significations of these planets.

b. **Eighth lord** – Eighth lord is Mercury. Mercury is in seventh house aspecting lagan of Gemini sign. It is with Sun who is lord of ninth house. Thus, lagan and ninth are spoiled. He was hanged as his luck ran out.

c. **Moon** – Moon is in Capricorn with Sun and Mars. It is aspected by Saturn. Mental capacity to endure problems is present.

d. **Eighth house** – Saturn is aspecting eighth house and cutting short the life of fortunes.

Example 11 – DOB 4 March 1973, TOB 4.30, POB Dhamda

Birth Chart

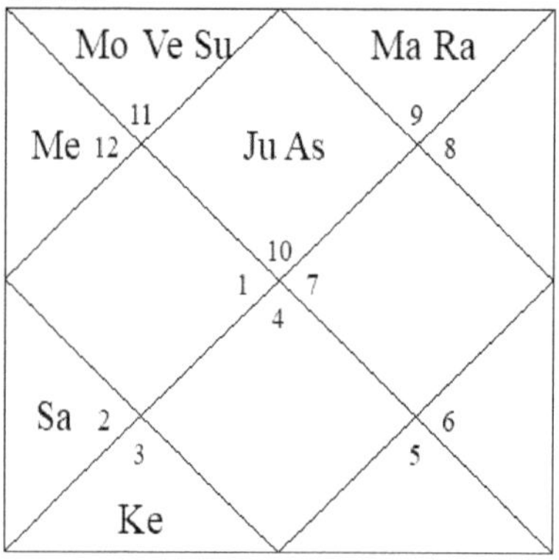

Birth Chart

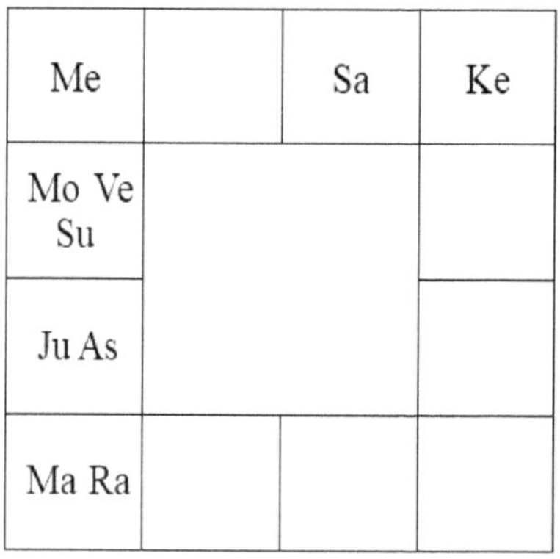

Parashar Trishamsha

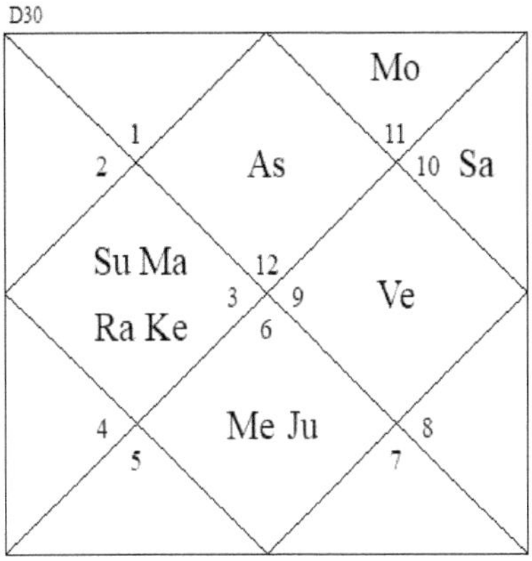

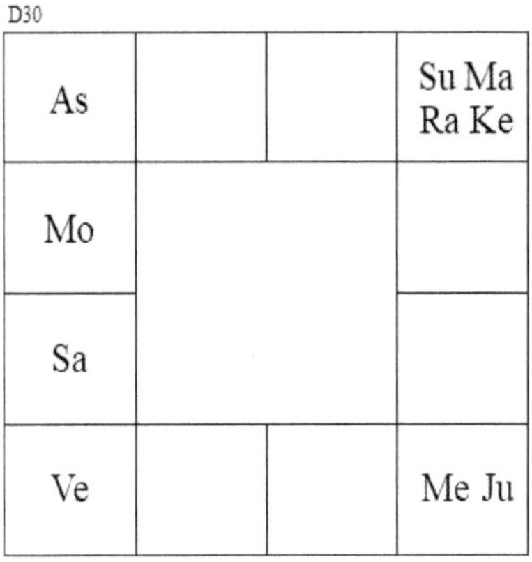

Iyer Trishamsha

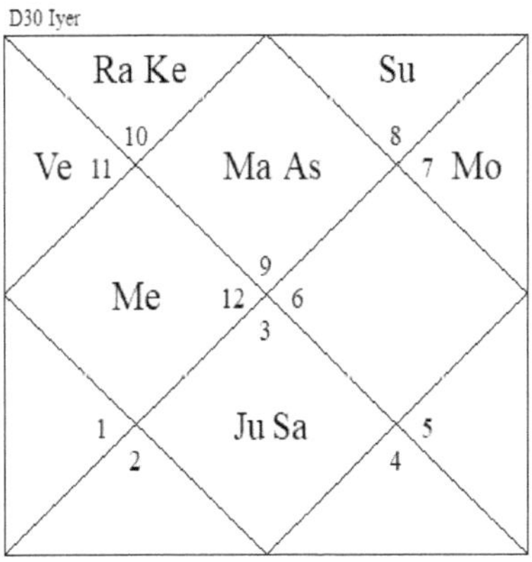

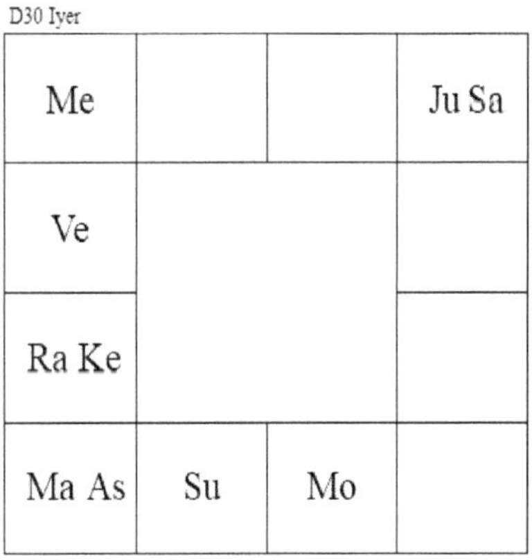

He was born in a well to do family. He inherited lot of land. His habit of taking drugs ruined him.

1. Parashar Trishamsha –

a. **Lagan lord** – Lagan lord Jupiter is in lagan in birth chart. Jupiter is aspecting lagan lord Saturn and has given good physical strength.
b. **Eighth lord** – Venus is eighth lord. Venus is in second house in birth. This spoils his wealth and eating habits.

Venus is with Sun and Moon. They are seventh and eighth lord and afflict these significations.

c. **Moon** – Moon is in Aquarius and has no relation with any other planet. No support to bear the misfortune is present.
d. **Eighth house** – Eighth house has a malefic aspect of Saturn. The life of misfortune is short.

2. Iyer Trishamsha

a. **Lagan lord** – Lagan lord is Jupiter which has been discussed in Parashar Trishamsha.
b. **Eighth lord** – Moon is eighth lord of Trishamsha. Moon is in second house of birth. It has spoiled the second house as discussed above.
c. **Moon-** Moon is in Libra and is aspected by Jupiter. Moon is soft and he cannot fight the bad cravings.
d. **Eighth house** – Eighth house is in RKA and aspected by Mars. The unfortunate life will end suddenly.

Example 12 – DOB 22 July 1972, TOB 18.00, POB Durg

In this horoscope both lagan and lagan lord are under malefic influence and there is no benefic relation. This is an unfortunate chart by birth and by deeds. He is charged with murder and leads a miserable life.

Birth Chart

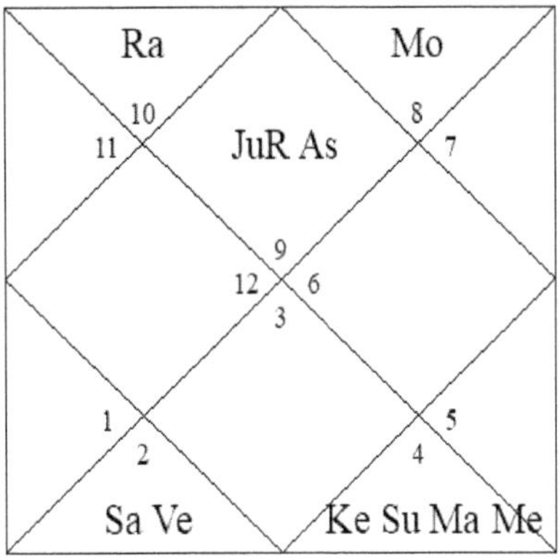

Birth Chart

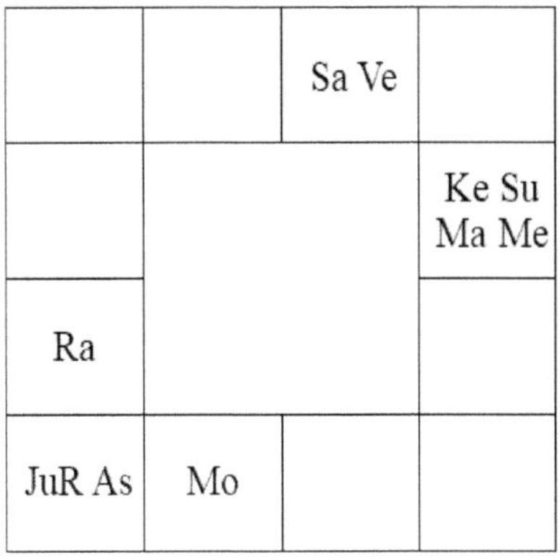

Parashar Trishamsha

D30

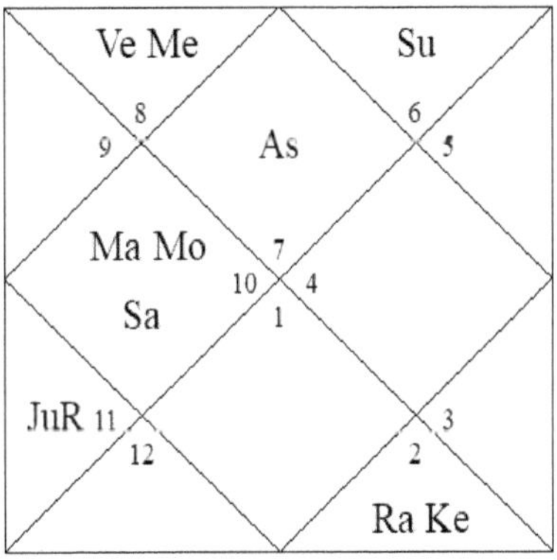

D30

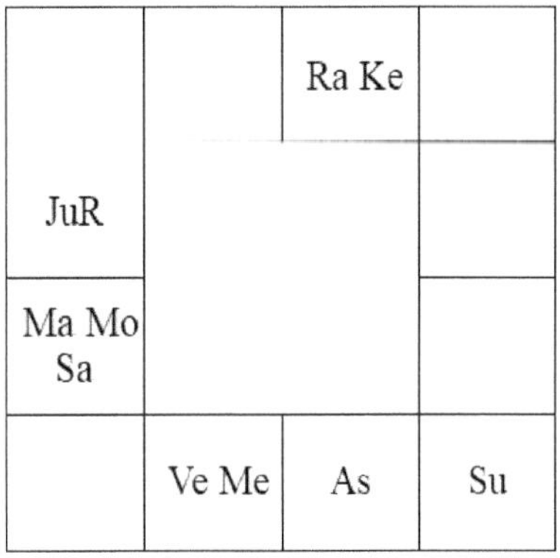

Iyer Trishamsha

D30 Iyer

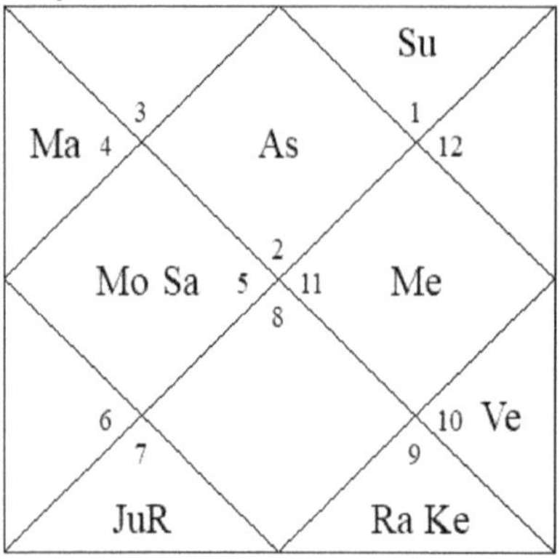

D30 Iyer

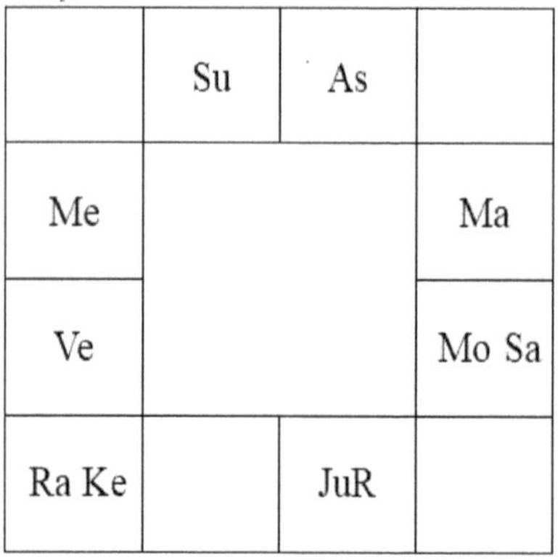

In this horoscope both lagan and lagan lord are under malefic influence and there is no benefic relation. This is an unfortunate chart by birth and by deeds. He is charged with murder and leads a miserable life.

1. Parashar Trishamsha

a. **Lagan lord and eighth lord** – Venus is both lagan and eighth lord of Trishamsha. Venus is placed in sixth house with Saturn. It is aspecting Moon.

b. **Moon** – Moon is in Capricorn and is with Mars and Saturn. He can endure all misfortunes with courage.

c. **Eighth house** – Eighth house has Rahu and is aspected by its lord Venus and Mercury. The life of misery is long.

2. Iyer Trishamsha –

a. **Lagan lord** – Here also the lagan lord is Venus.

b. **Eighth lord** – Jupiter is eighth lord and is placed in lagan. It aspects the trines and seventh house. His family life is ruined.

c. **Moon** – Moon is in Leo with Saturn. He can face the adverse situations.

d. **Eighth house** – Rahu is placed there giving short life to misfortunes.

We now take an example of twins. The elder is leading a good life and younger is bankrupt and suffers from auto immune disease.

Elder

Example 13 – DOB 14 January 1966, TOB 2.47, POB Alwar

Birth Chart

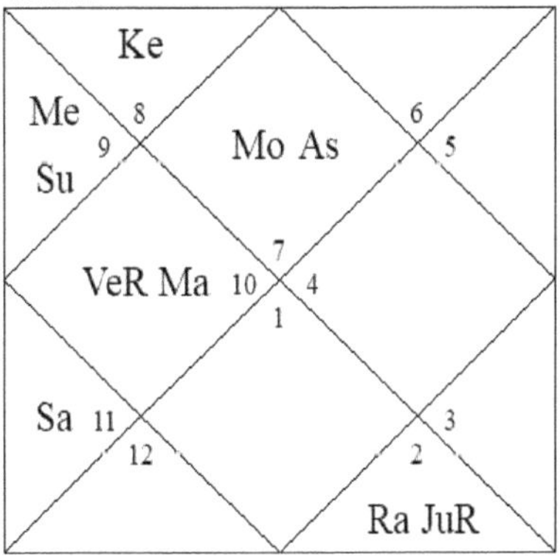

Birth Chart

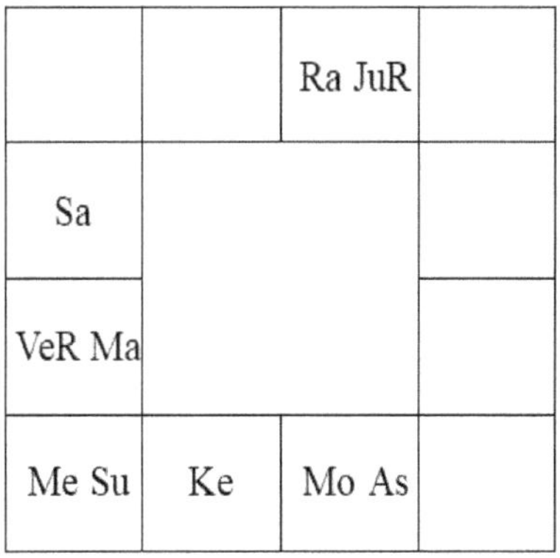

Parashar Trishamsha

D30

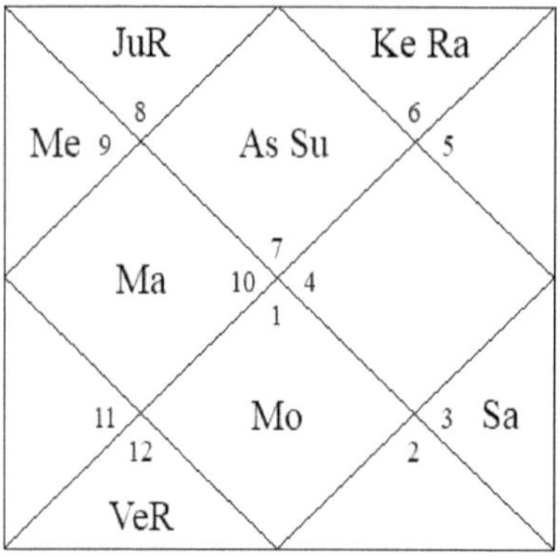

D30

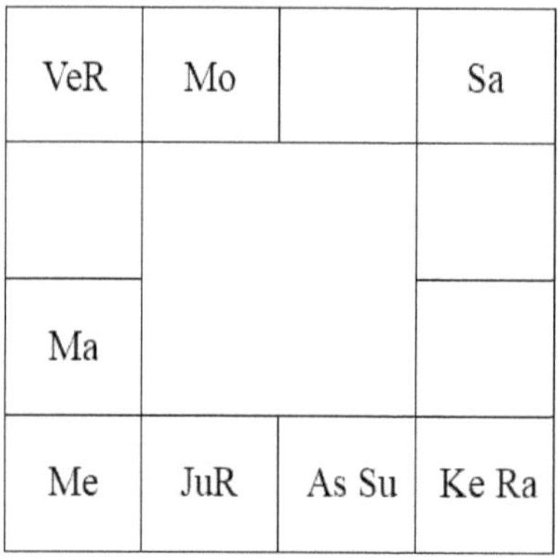

Iyer Trishamsha

D30 Iyer

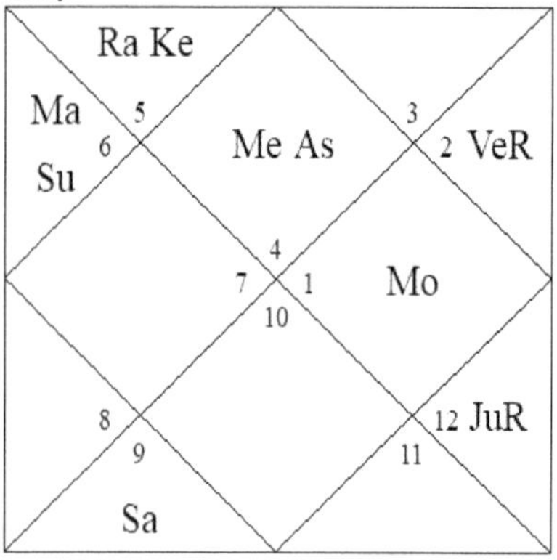

D30 Iyer

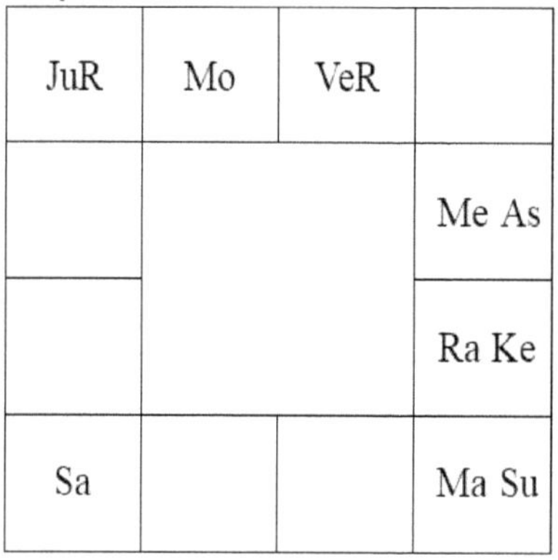

1. Parashar Trishamsha

a. **Lagan lord and Eighth lord** – Lagan lord and eighth lord is Venus. This Venus plays a dual role here because it is a fortunate chart. Venus is in fourth house in birth. It is with Mars and is not aspecting any planet. Mixed results will be experienced for fourth, second, seventh, lagan, and eighth house.

b. **Moon-** Moon is in Aries and is aspected by Mars. He has capacity to face adversities with courage and aggression.

c. **Eighth house** – Eighth house has no planet but aspected by Jupiter. The fortunes will have long life.

Younger

Example 14 – DOB 14 January 1966, TOB 3.24, POB Alwar

Birth Chart

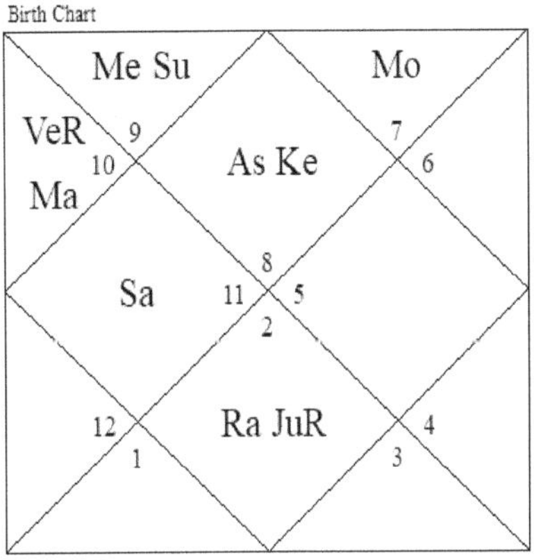

Birth Chart

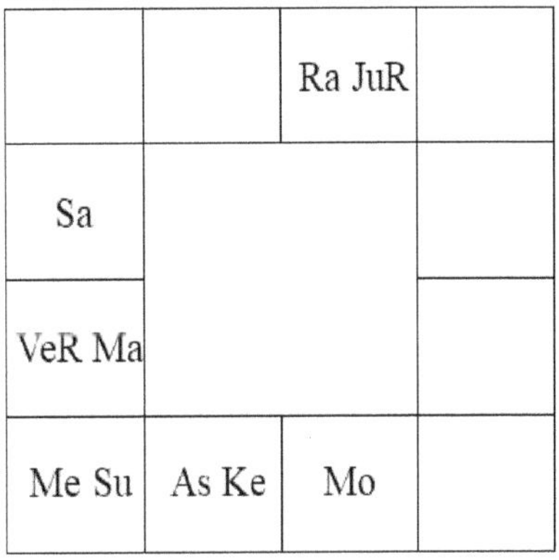

Parashar Trishamsha

D30

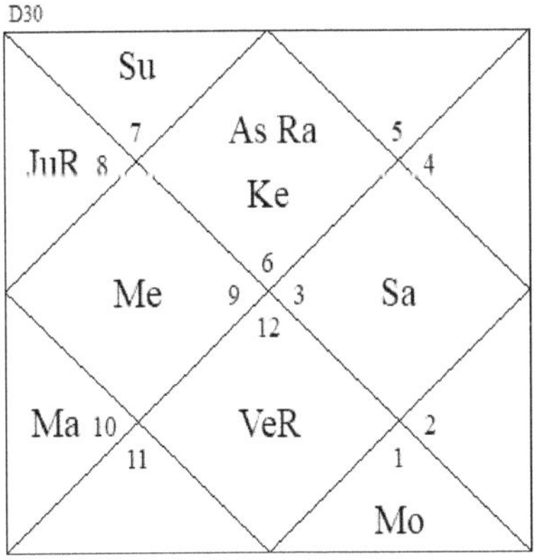

D30

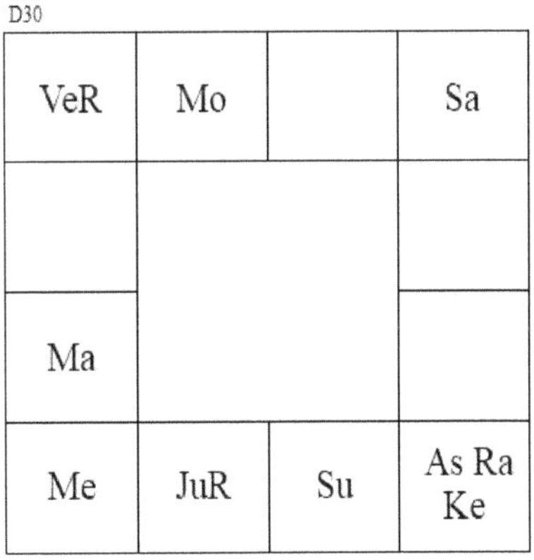

Iyer Trishamsha

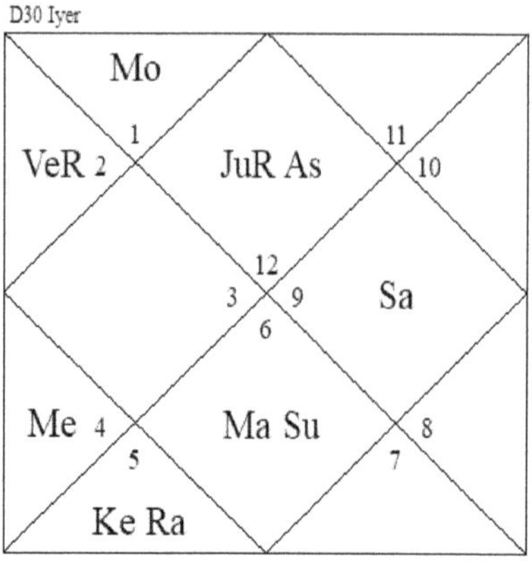

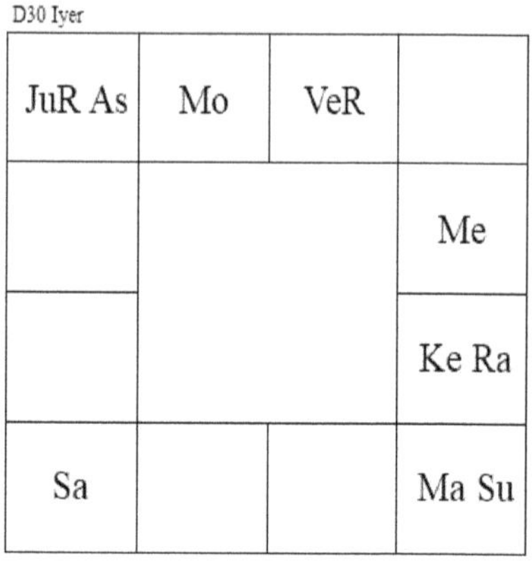

1. Parashar Trishamsha

a. **Lagan lord** – Lagan lord is Mercury. Mercury is in second house in birth horoscope. It is with Sun and has no aspect. Since it is a misfortune chart as such second house is spoiled. Sun is lord of tenth giving set back to profession.

b. **Eighth lord** – Lord of eighth house is Mars. Mars is in third house with Venus. Mars is lagan lord giving physical problems. Venus is twelfth and seventh lord. It gives wasteful expenditure and problems in married life.

c. **Moon** – Moon is in Aries and aspected by Mars. He faces problems with courage.

d. **Eighth house** – Moon is in eighth house and is aspected by twelfth lord Sun. The longevity of misfortune is short.

2. Iyer Trishamsha

a. **Lagan lord** – Jupiter is the lagan lord of Trishamsha. Jupiter is with Rahu in seventh house in birth. It gets no aspect. The seventh house is afflicted.

b. **Eighth lord** – Venus is eighth lord and is with Mars. Mars is lagan lord giving problems to self.
c. **Moon** – Moon is in Aries in Subh Kartari and aspected by Mars. Moon is strong to face adversities.
d. **Eighth house** – Eighth house is aspected by Moon giving long life to miseries.

We can conclude that cyclical/ Iyer or Varanasi Trishamsha gives better results of physical and material life.

Chapter 5
Marriage Matters

Trishamsha plays a very important role in marriage of a person. This is used as a confirmation of Navamsha in the marriage matters. We will apply the Trishamsha in the following matters.

1. Early marriage.
2. Happy or unhappy marriage.
3. Death or separation in marriage.
4. Denial of marriage.

1. Early marriage

Every society has an average age for marriage of boys and girls. When marriage or **affair** happens earlier than this age then it is termed as early marriage. We will use Navamsha and Trishamsha to confirm it. First, we check Navamsha for promise or desire of marriage. The Trishamsha is then examined. The rule of early marriage for Trishamsha is given.

Rule

Note a planet which is connected to lagan/ lagan lord of birth chart by conjunction or aspects. This planet when connected with lagan of Trishamsha will indicate early marriage or affair.

We will examine this in Parashar and Iyer Trishamsha with Navamsha.

Example 1 – DOB 4 March 1973, TOB 4.30, POB Dhamda

This person is unmarried as of now. At the age of 16 years, he married a girl without the knowledge of parents and brought her home. After persuasion by family, he sent her back and never married again.

Birth Chart

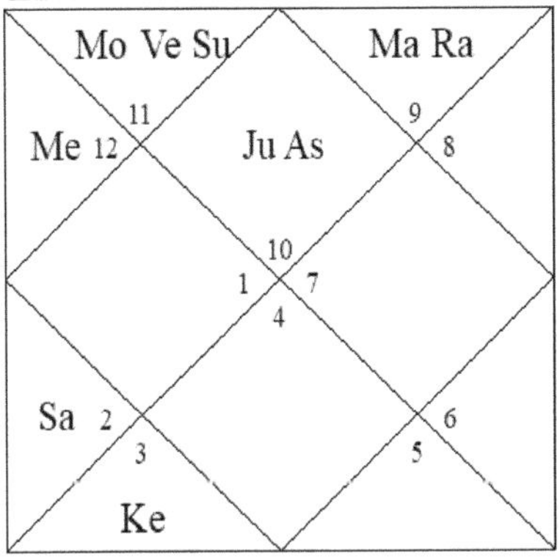

Birth Chart

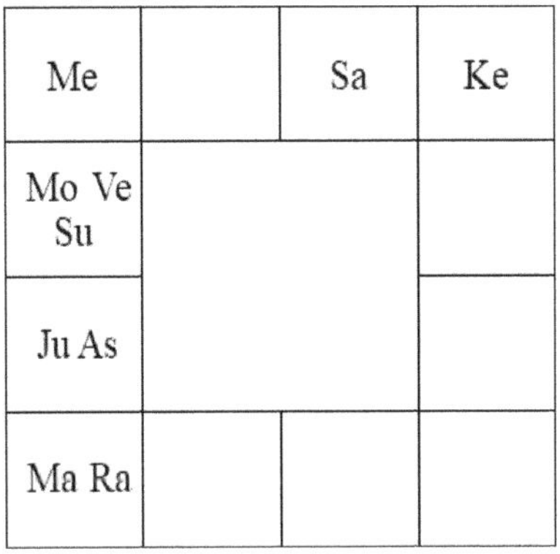

D30

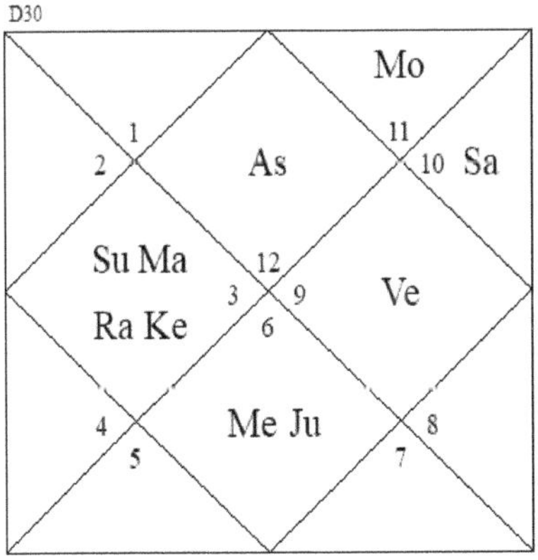

D30

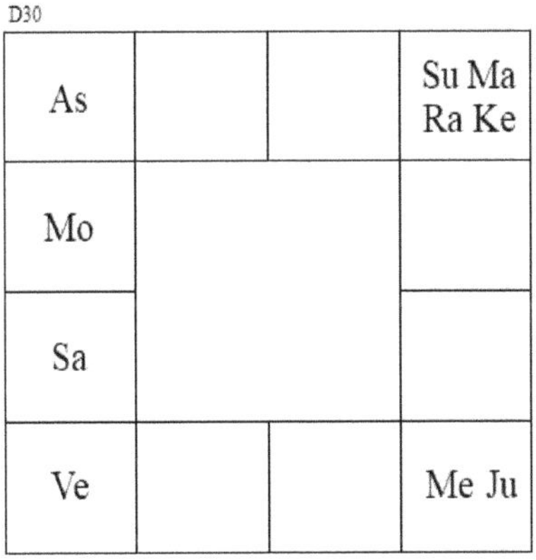

D30 Iyer

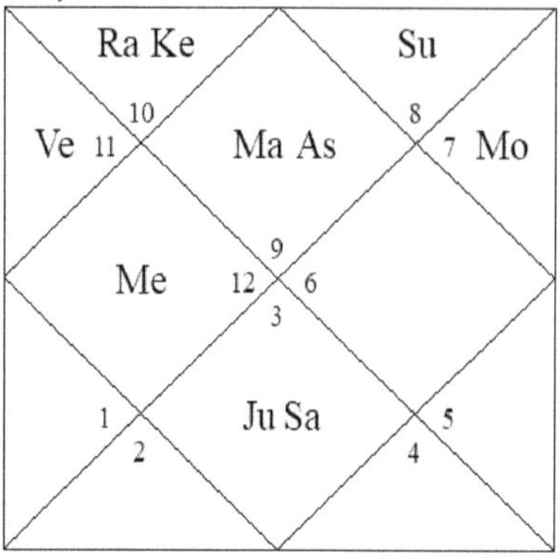

D30 Iyer

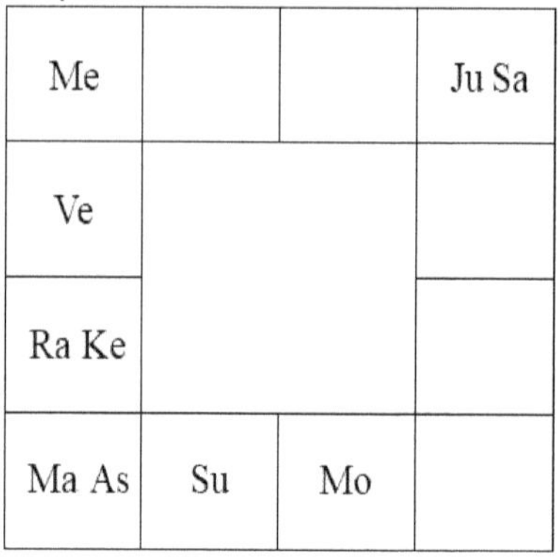

Birth horoscope – Lagan is occupied by Jupiter.

Parashar Trishamsha – Jupiter is aspecting lagan in this chart also.

Iyer Trishamsha – Jupiter is aspecting lagan of this Trishamsha also. Sixth house is aspected by Sun. seventh house has Saturn and eighth house has Ketu and are aspected by Mars. This way Jupiter is connected to lagan of birth horoscope and in Trishamsha charts. This gives an early affair.

Example 2 – DOB 29 January 1954, TOB 4.30, POB KOSCIUSKO USA

Birth Chart

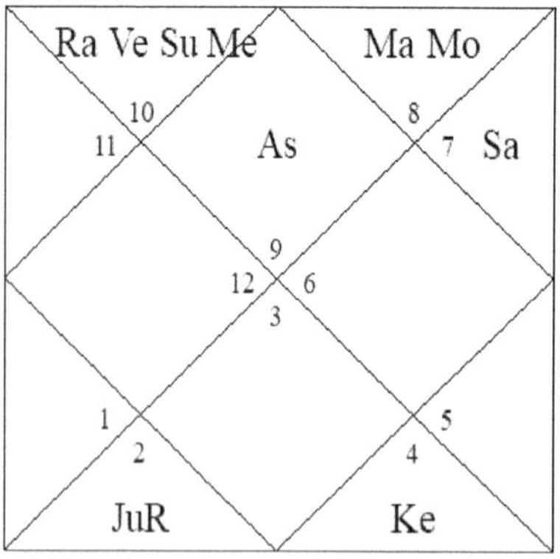

Birth Chart

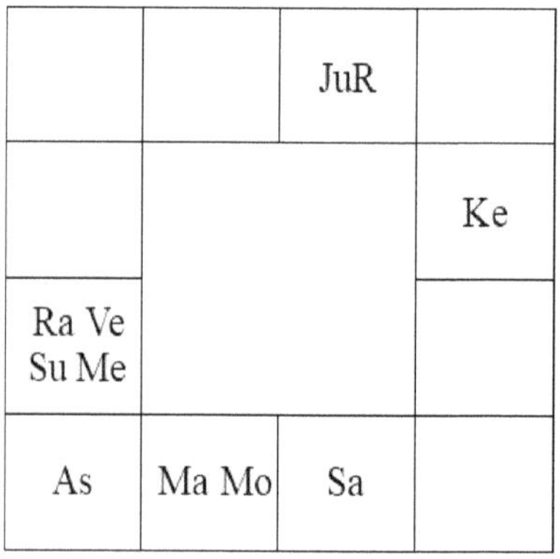

D30

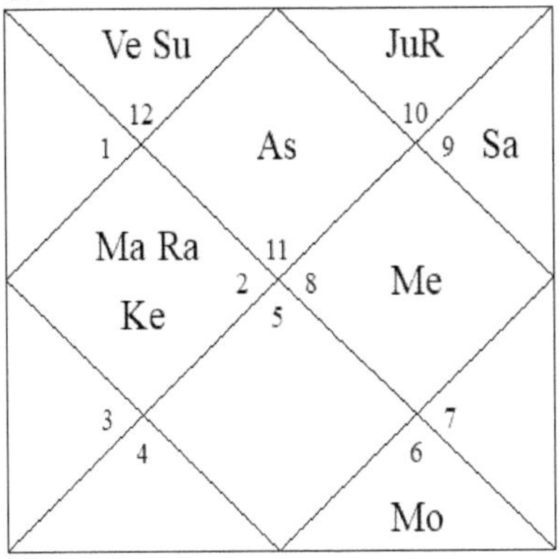

D30

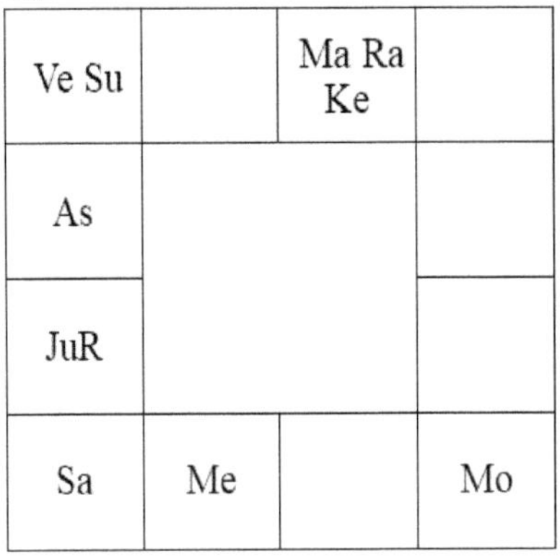

D30 Iyer

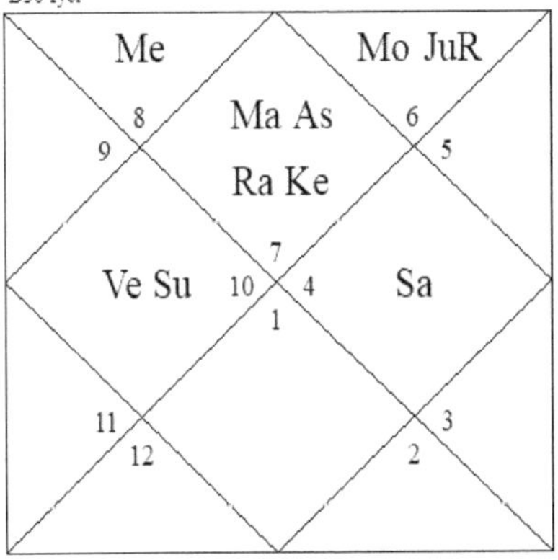

D30 Iyer

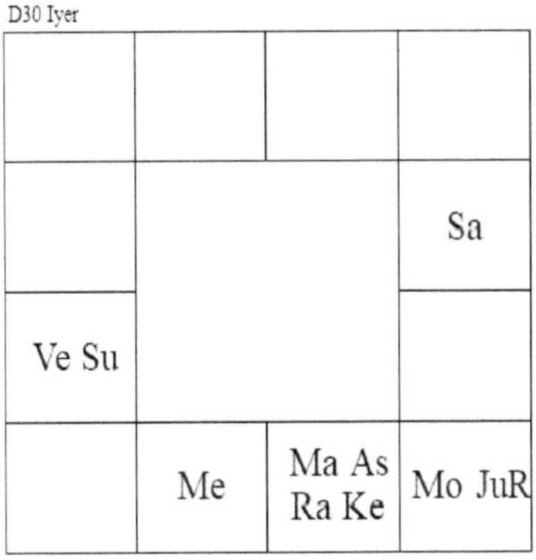

Birth horoscope – Lagan is aspected by Saturn.

Parashar Trishamsha – Lagan is not aspected by Saturn.

Iyer Trishamsha – Mars and Rahu are placed in lagan. Lagan lord is with Sun and is aspecting Saturn.

No single planet is related to lagan or lagan lord in three charts. Early affair or marriage is seen.

Example 3 – DOB 24 October 1959, TOB 2.00, POB PATNA BIHAR

Birth Chart

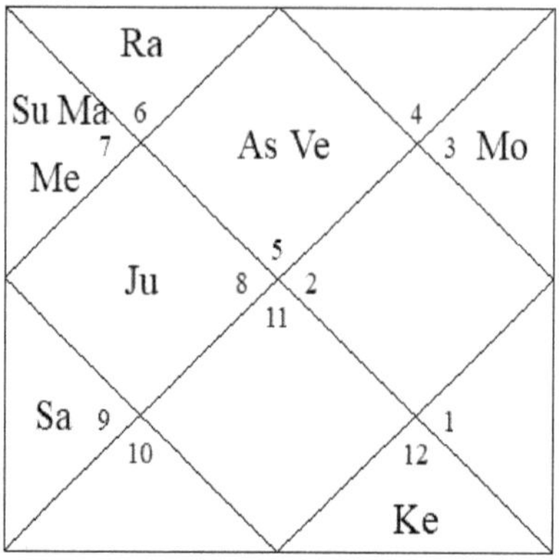

Birth Chart

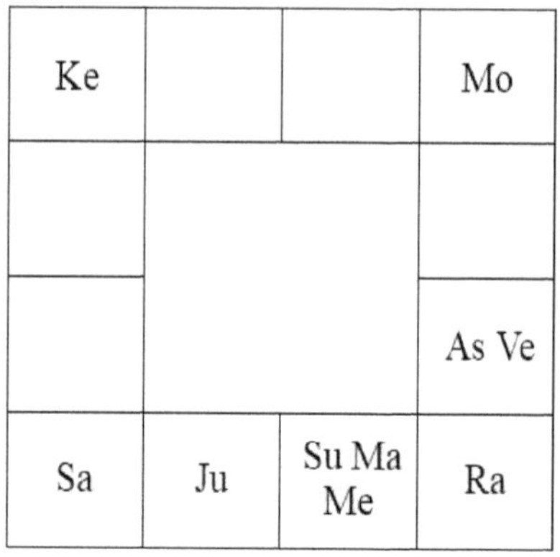

D30

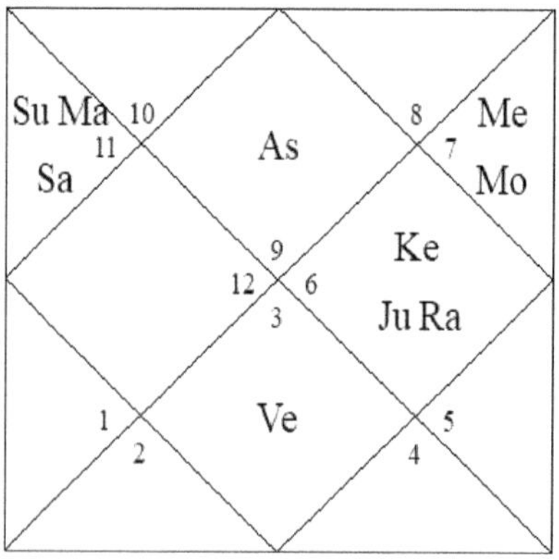

D30

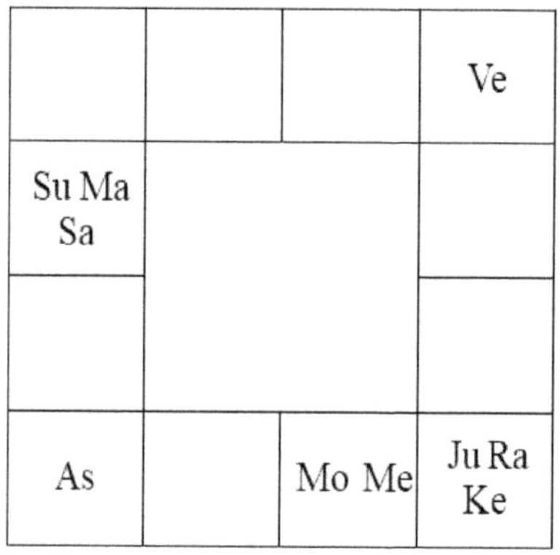

D30 Iyer

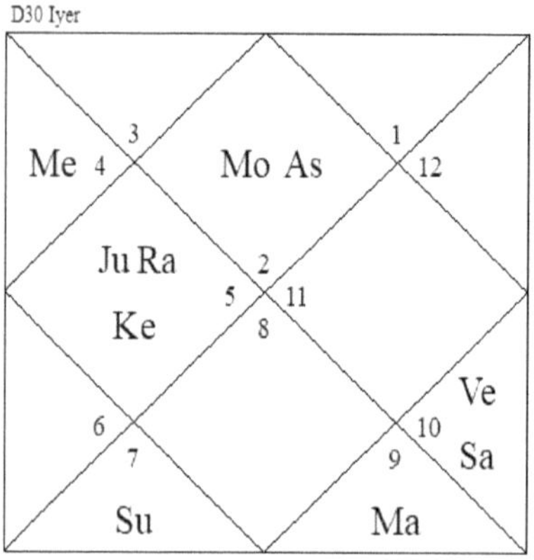

D30 Iyer

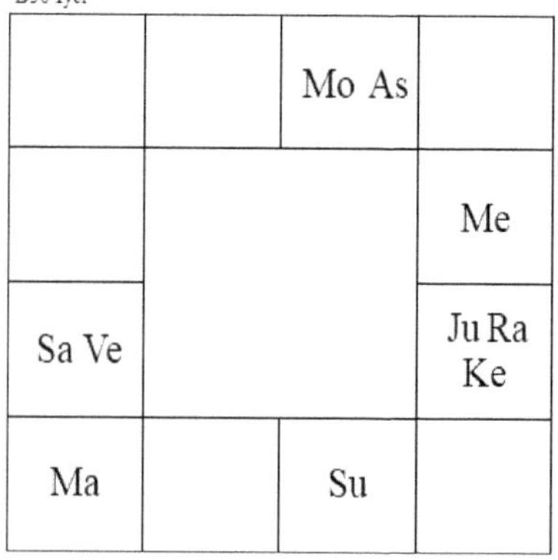

Birth horoscope – Venus is placed in lagan. Sun is with Mars and Mercury.

Parashar Trishamsha – Venus is aspecting lagan from seventh house. Jupiter is with Rahu.

Iyer Trishamsha – Venus is not connected with lagan of this Trishamsha but is lord of lagan. Venus is with Saturn and is aspecting Mercury.

This way Venus is connected to lagan of birth horoscope and in Parashar Trishamsha charts. Venus is connected with lagan of Iyer Trishamsha. This person had number of affairs in youth. The Parashar Trishamsha is giving better result in this analysis of early marriage.

Example 4 – DOB 12 November 1979, TOB 7.37, POB DELHI

Birth Chart

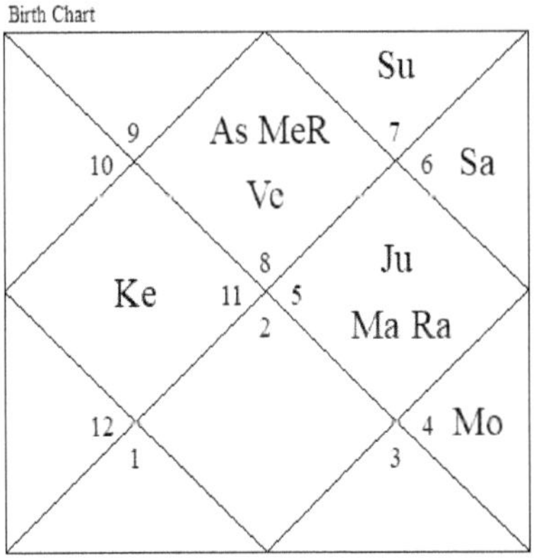

Birth Chart

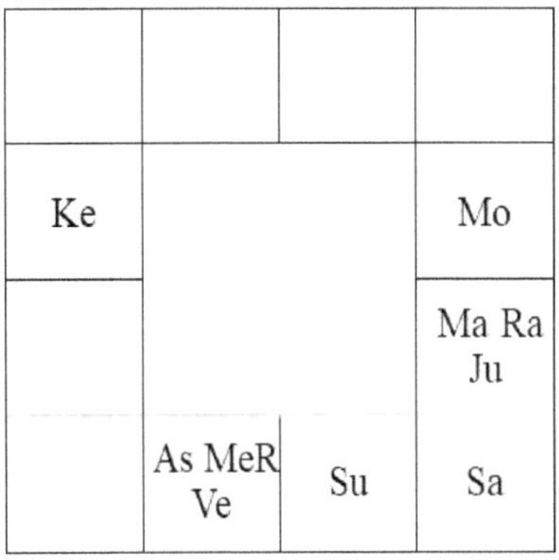

D30

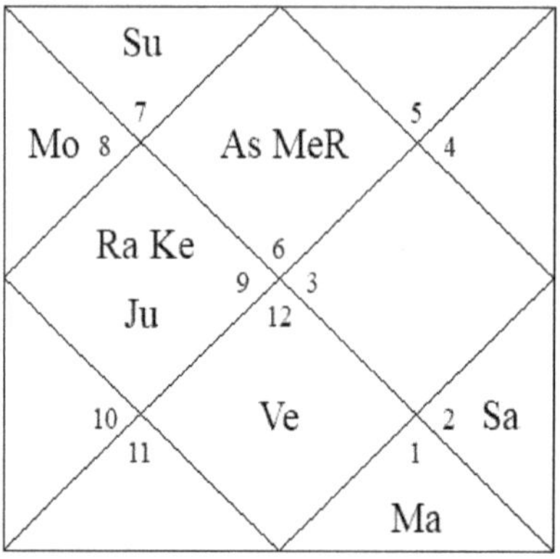

D30

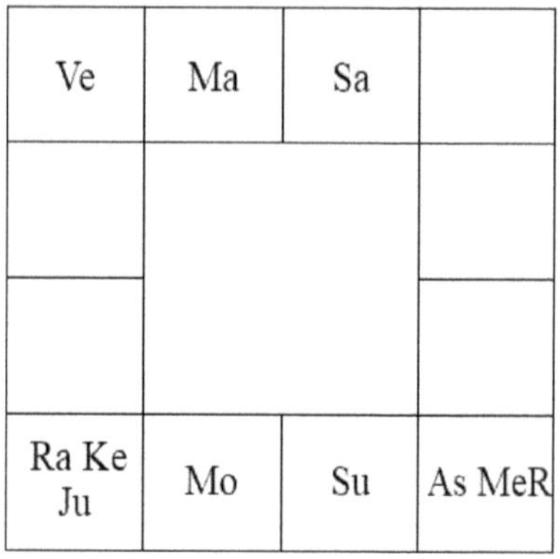

D30 Iyer

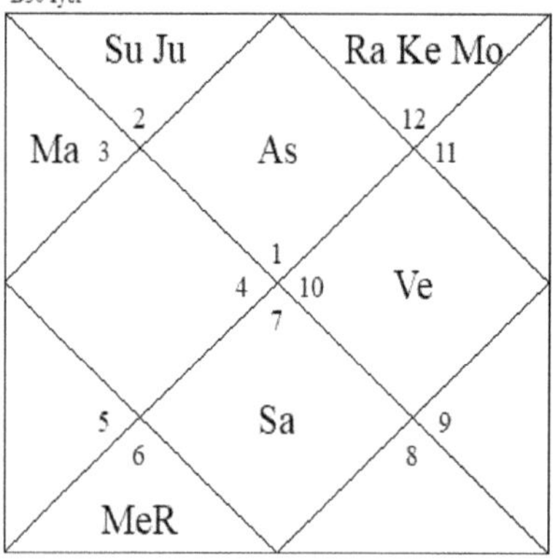

D30 Iyer

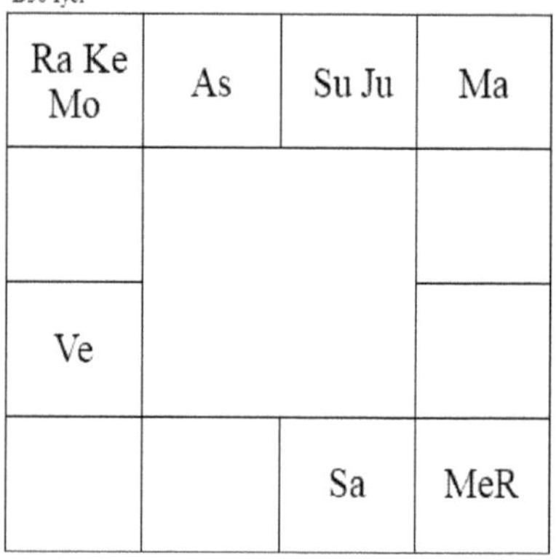

Birth horoscope – Mercury and Venus are placed in lagan. Lagan is aspected by Saturn and Mars.

Parashar Trishamsha – Venus is aspecting lagan from seventh house and Mercury is in lagan and is lagan lord. Venus is exalted.

Iyer Trishamsha – Saturn is aspecting lagan. Mars is aspecting Venus.

This way Venus is connected to lagan or lagan lord of all charts. This person had number of affairs in youth. He is the only and youngest son of his parents.

Example 5 – DOB 17 July 1977, TOB 17.20, POB DELHI

Birth Chart

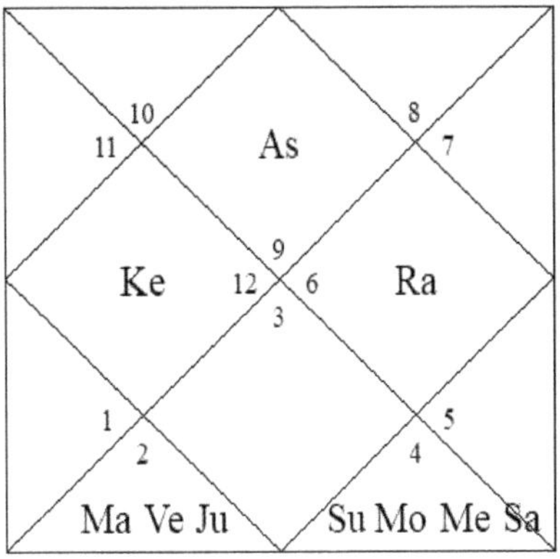

Birth Chart

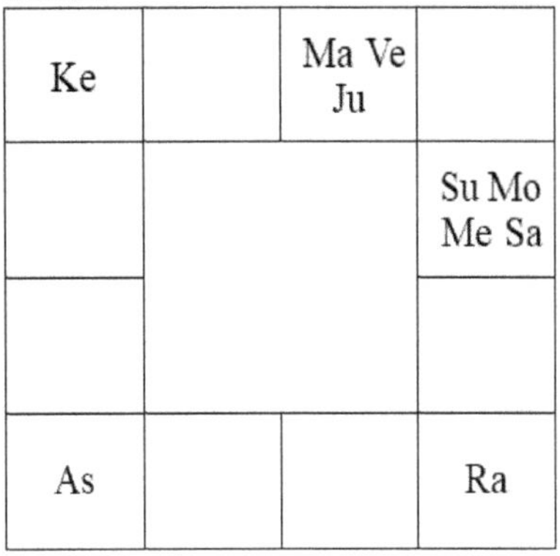

D30

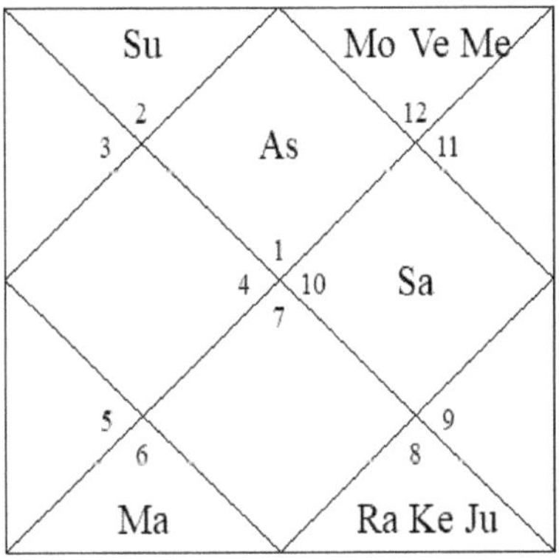

D30

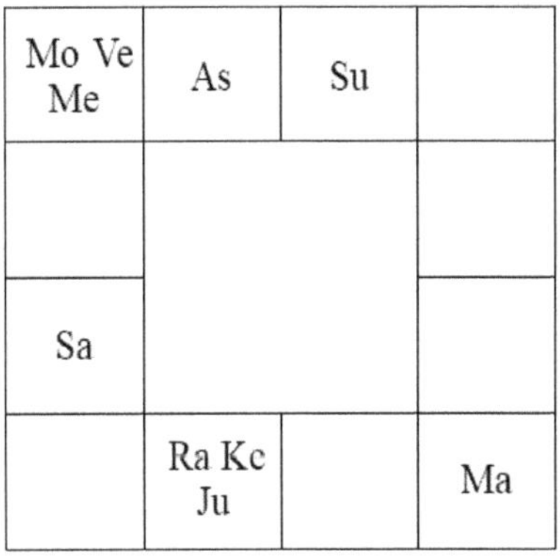

D30 Iyer

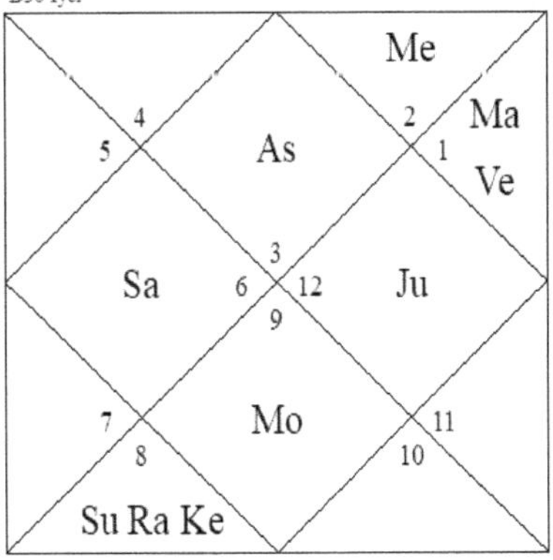

D30 Iyer

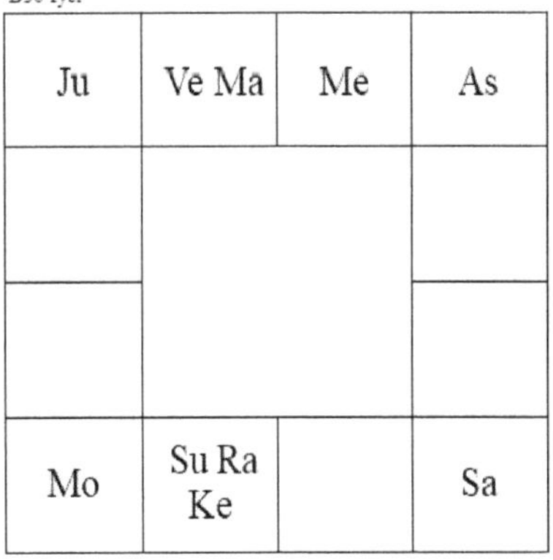

Birth horoscope – Only Mars is aspecting lagan. Jupiter is with Mars and Venus and is aspecting Rahu.

Parashar Trishamsha – Mars is aspecting lagan from sixth house. Mars is lagan lord and is aspecting Moon, Venus and Mercury.

Iyer Trishamsha – In this Trishamsha Mars is not related to lagan. Moon is aspecting lagan. Mercury is with Ketu and is aspecting Sun.

The Parashar Trishamsha is confirming it. She is an Indian girl but a USA citizen. She had an affair at a young age and got married to same person. The marriage resulted in divorce. Parashar Trishamsha gives better result for early marriage.

2. Happy or unhappy marriage.

The houses to be considered for deciding the quality of marriage are seventh and eighth house. These houses are checked in Navamsha and Trishamsha. The verdict of Trishamsha is final.

1. We must remember that seventh house is the house of marriage and eighth house is the longevity of marriage or Manglya. The lord is the manager of the house.
2. First, we check the Navamsha. It should promise marriage. Malefic relation with seventh house/ lord normally gives unhappy marriage provided he is not aspected by any benefic or the house lord.
3. The fourth house of Navamsha is the house of happiness. Malefic relation with fourth house does not give happiness. Fourth lord is manager of fourth house. When fourth house is afflicted but fourth lord has only benefic relation the person will try to find happiness even in unhappy marriage. We should weigh the benefic or malefic influence and decide which is stronger.

4. Next, we see rules for Trishamsha.
e. The lagan rising in Trishamsha belongs to a sign of Saturn, Mars or Sun. Sun sign cannot rise in Parashar Trishamsha. It is possible only in Iyer Trishamsha.
f. This lagan lord of Trishamsha is influencing the birth lagan.
g. When this lagan lord of Trishamsha is also influencing the lagan of Trishamsha the malefic effect is manifold.
h. Benefic aspect on lagan will provide protection.

Example 1 – DOB 1 JULY 1961, TOB 19.45, POB Sandringham UK

Birth Chart

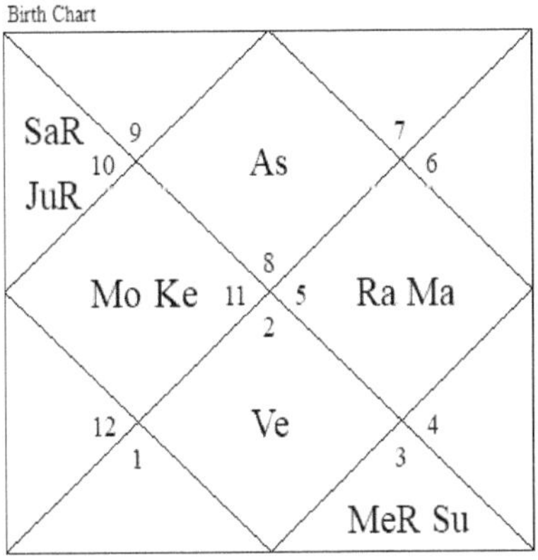

Birth Chart

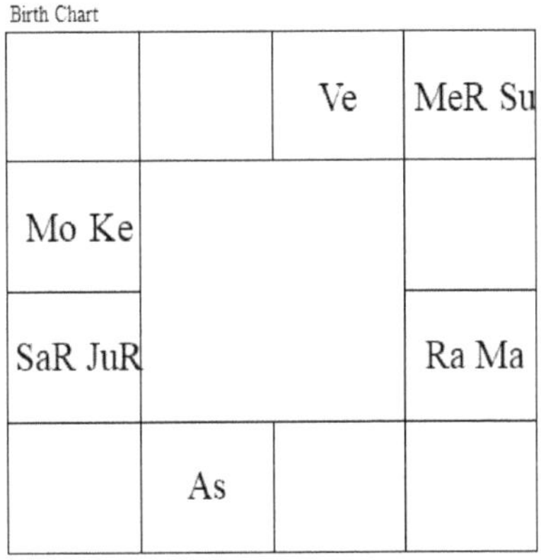

D9

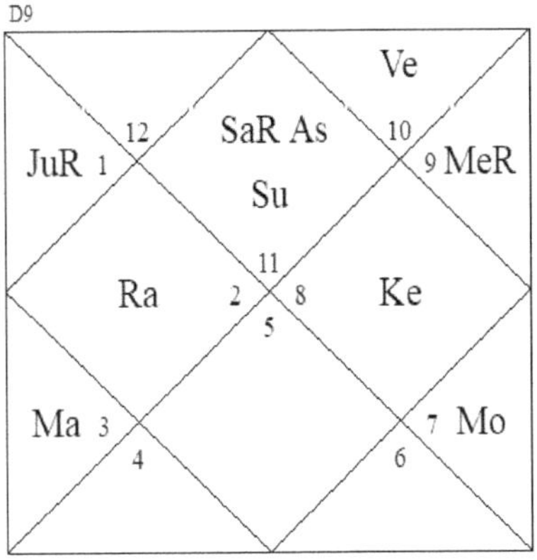

D9

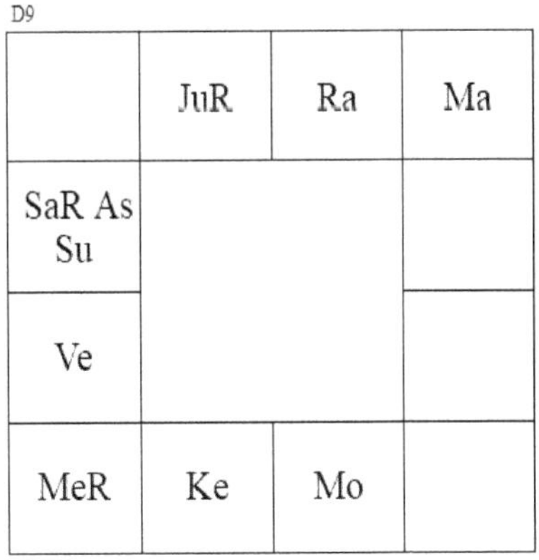

D30

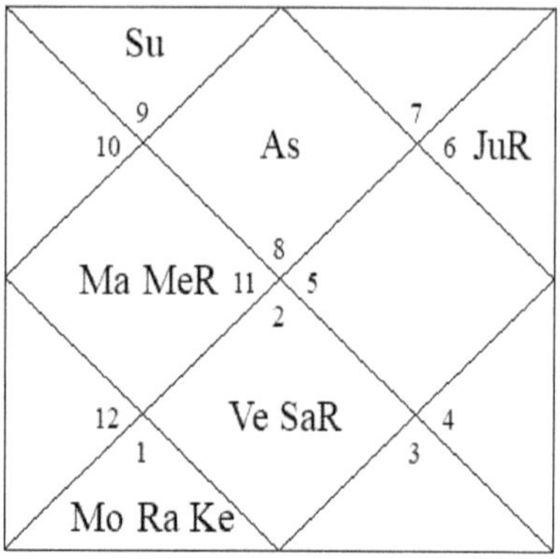

D30

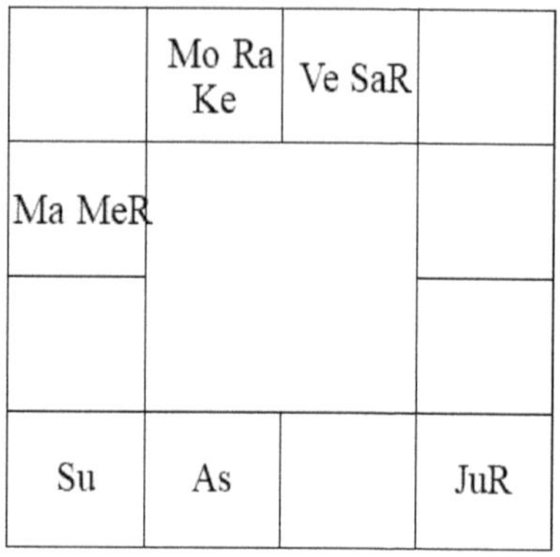

D30 Iyer

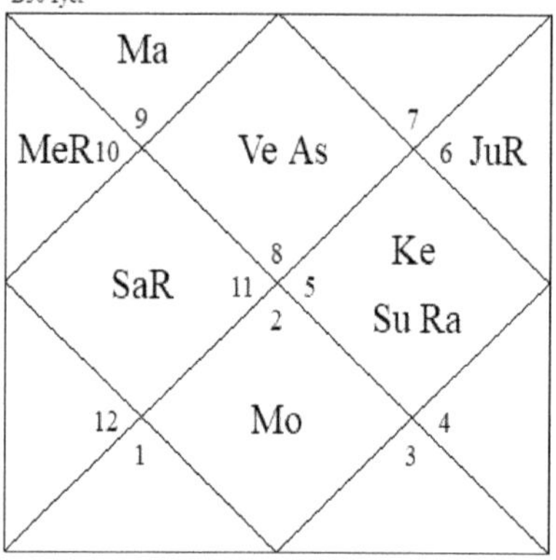

D30 Iyer

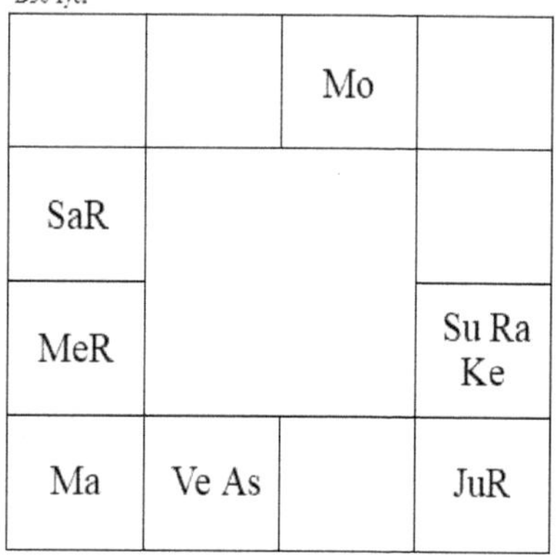

Navamsha

Lagan of Navamsha is occupied by Saturn and Sun. Saturn is lagan lord and Sun is seventh lord. It has no benefic relation. Desire for marriage is present. Saturn gives age difference. Fourth house has Rahu and not aspected any planet. It is not a good situation. Eighth house vacant and is aspected by Mars. Eighth lord is also aspected by Mars.

1. Parashar Trishamsha

Sign of Mars is rising in this Trishamsha. Mars is the lagan lord of birth and is afflicted in birth chart. Mars is not aspecting the Trishamsha lagan.

2. Iyer Trishamsha

Scorpio is rising in lagan. Venus is in lagan and is aspected by Saturn and Moon. Only Venus is related to birth lagan. This shows a mix of happiness and unhappiness in marriage.

She was unhappy in marriage but carried the marriage till her death. Fourth house of Trishamsha is afflicted.

Example 2 – DOB 28 NOVEMBER 1978, TOB 22.54, POB KANPUR

Birth Chart

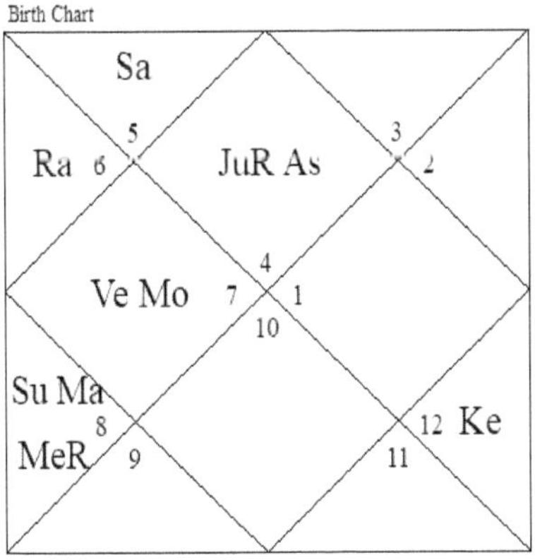

Birth Chart

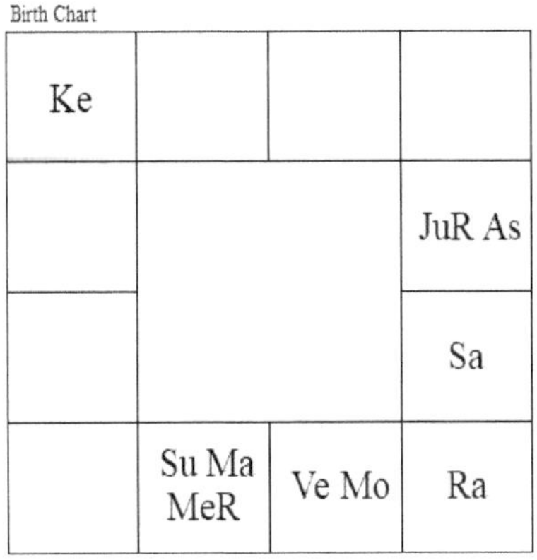

D9

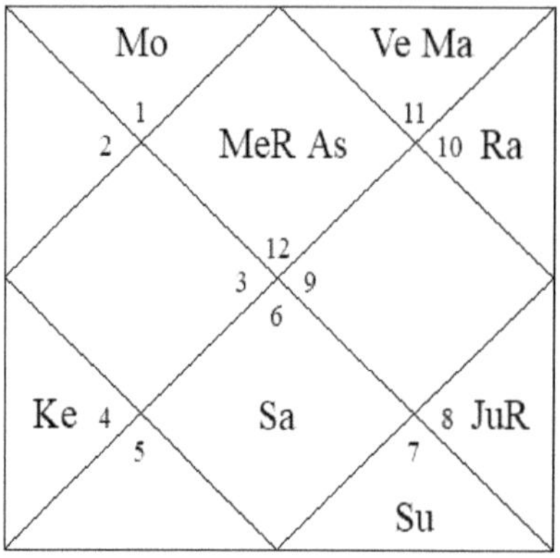

D9

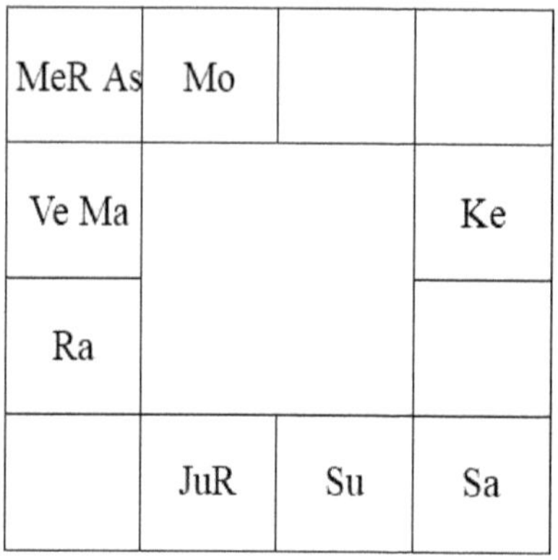

D30

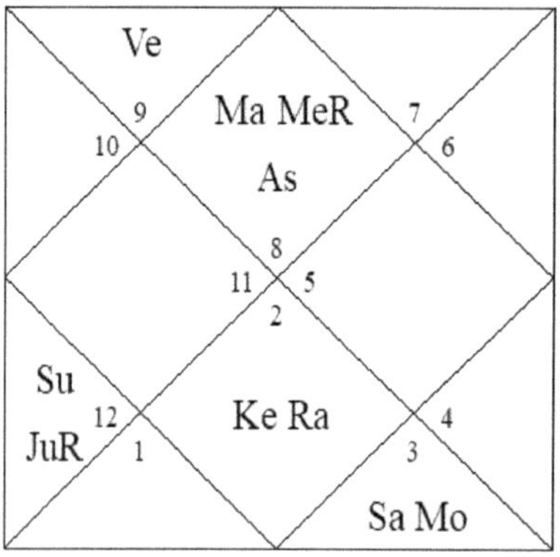

D30

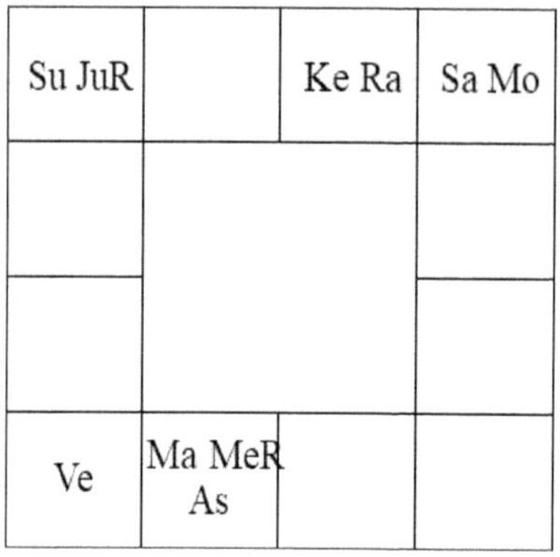

D30 Iyer

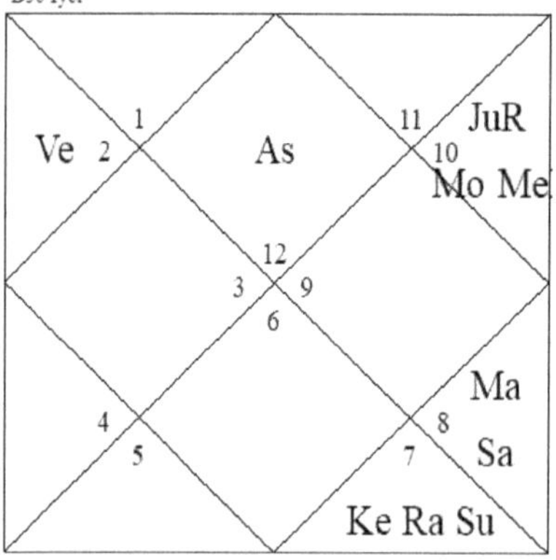

D30 Iyer

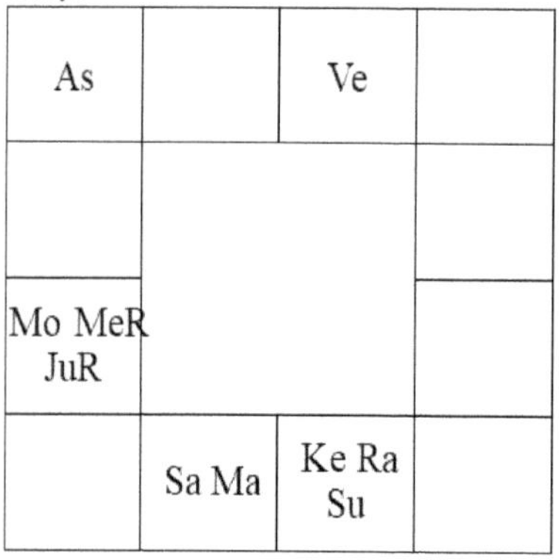

1. **Navamsha**

   Lagan of Navamsha is Pisces. It is occupied by Mercury and is aspected by Jupiter and Saturn. Desire of marriage is present. Fourth house and lord are aspected by Saturn to indicate unhappy marriage. Aspect of Jupiter on seventh lord Mercury is the saving grace.

2. **Parashar Trishamsha**

   Sign of Mars is rising in this Trishamsha. The lagan is in RKA with Mercury. It is aspected by Jupiter. Jupiter is placed in birth lagan. Mars is not aspecting lagan in birth chart but is placed in lagan of Trishamsha.

3. **Iyer Trishamsha**

   Pisces is rising in lagan. It is not aspected by any planet. The problem is eighth house. It has debilitated Sun and Rahu. The Manglya is not present.

   He was married on 1 May 2014. His wife left him on 6 May 2014 and filed number of cases against him.

Example 3 – DOB 30 APRIL 1945, TOB 10.27 (WAR TIME), POB Delhi

Birth Chart

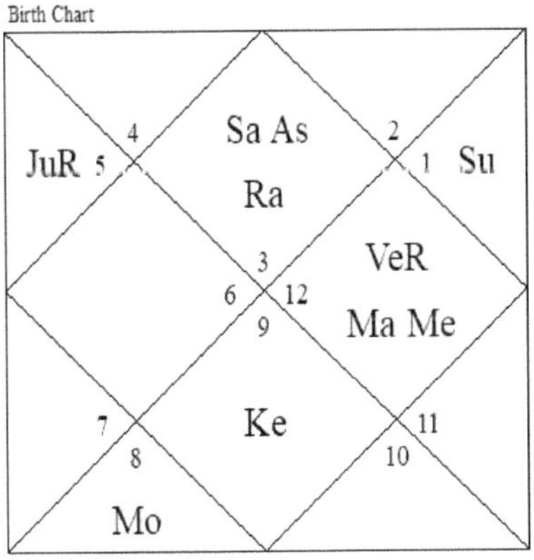

Birth Chart

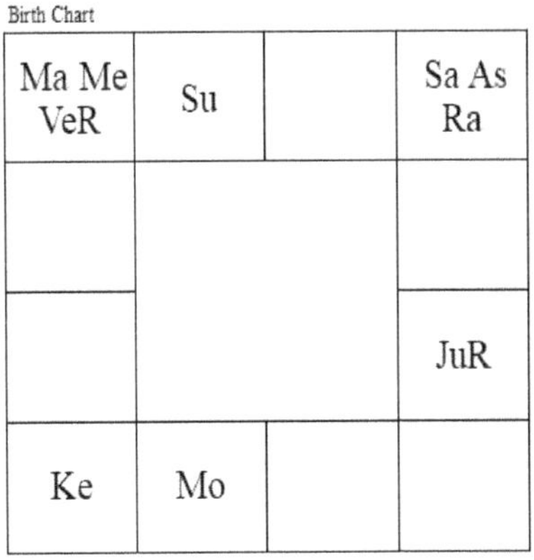

D9

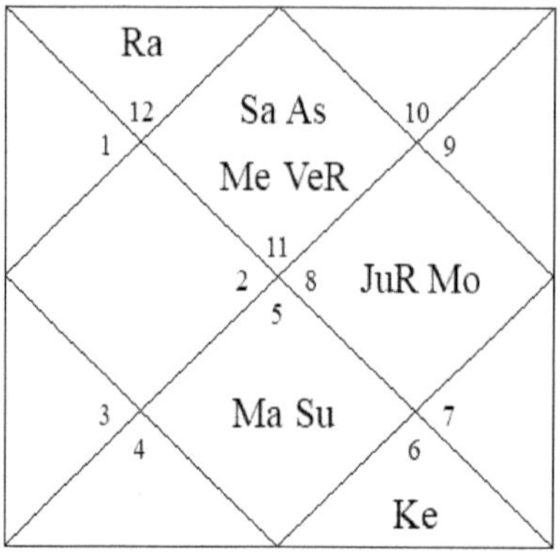

D9

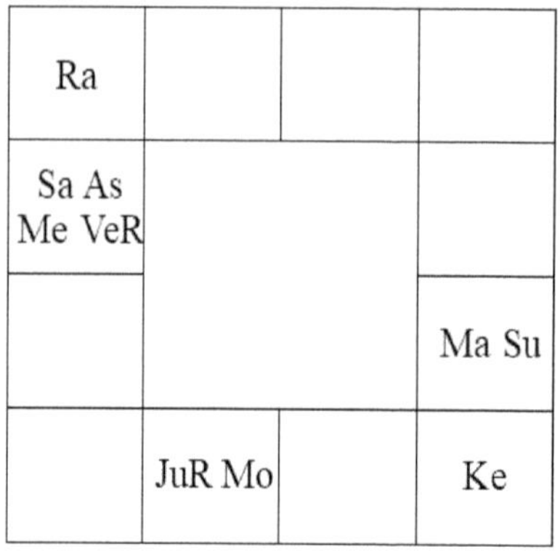

Parashar Trishamsha

D30

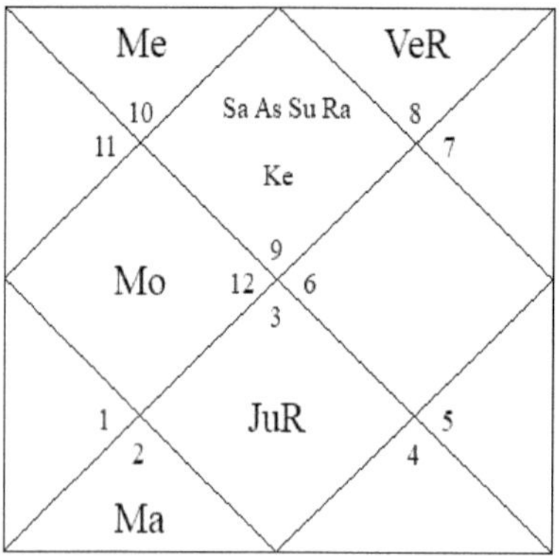

D30

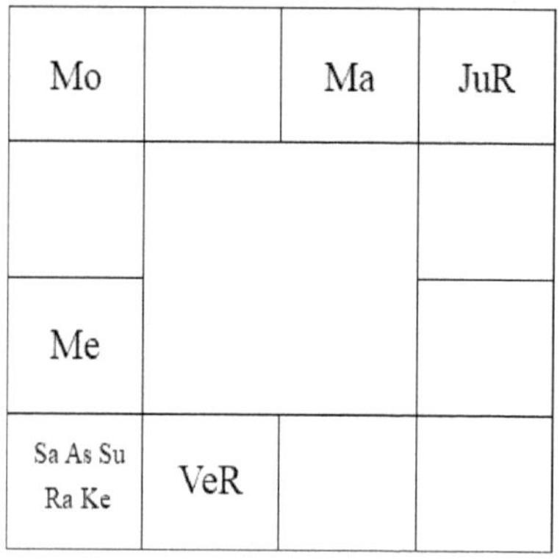

Iyer Trishamsha

D30 Iyer

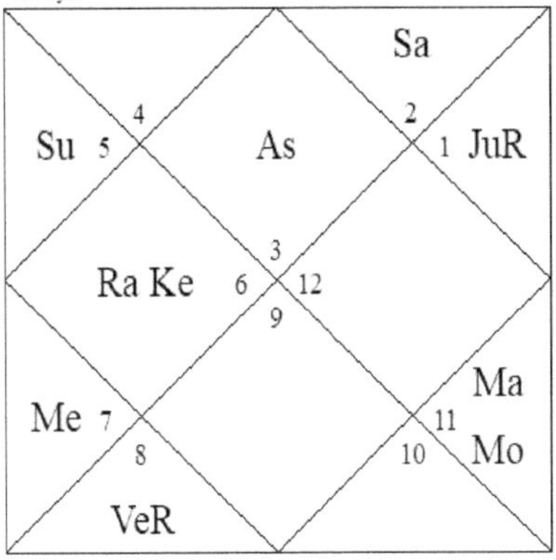

D30 Iyer

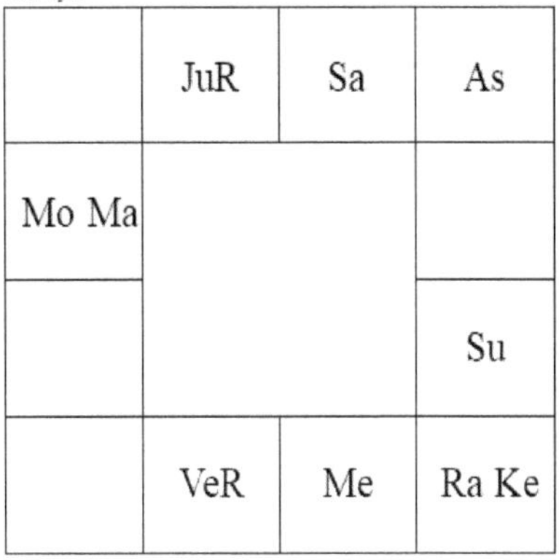

This chart is for happy marriage. The marriage has lasted for 52 years and is still continuing.

1. **Navamsha**
   Lagan of Navamsha is Aquarius. It is occupied by Saturn, Venus and Mercury. The desire of marriage is present. The fourth house is aspected by Jupiter and Moon. The marriage is happy.

2. **Parashar Trishamsha**
   Sign of Jupiter is rising in this Trishamsha. Saturn, Sun and Rahu are in lagan. Lagan is in Subh Kartari. It is aspected by Jupiter. Saturn is placed in birth lagan. Saturn is the only trouble maker. Eighth house is under benefic aspect.

3. **Iyer Trishamsha**
   Gemini is rising in lagan. It is not aspected by any planet. The eighth house is not related to any planet. The Manglya is present.

Example 4 – DOB 7 JULY 1981, TOB 11.15, POB RANCHI

This example is of happy marriage.

Birth Chart

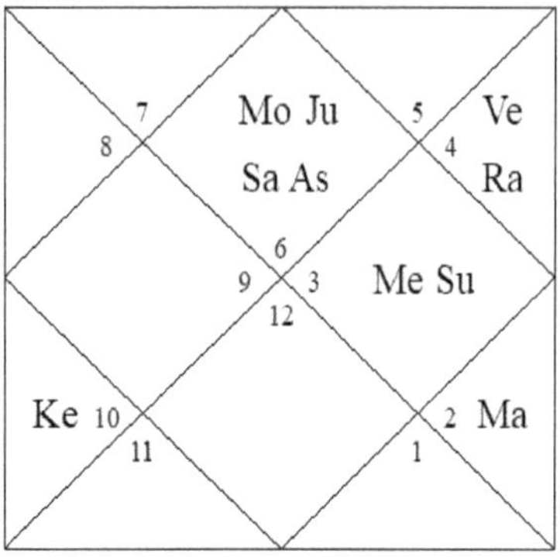

Birth Chart

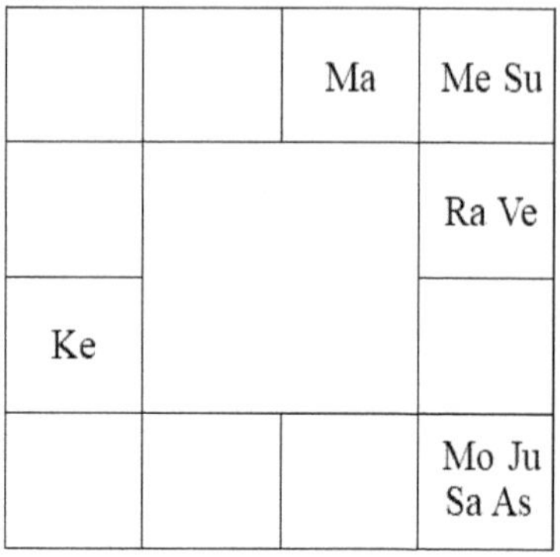

D9

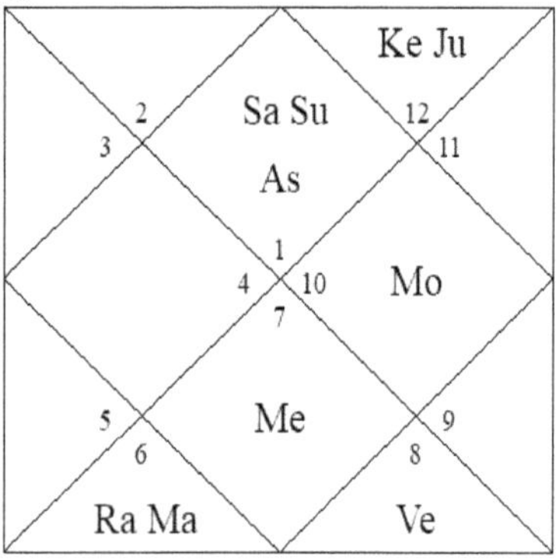

D9

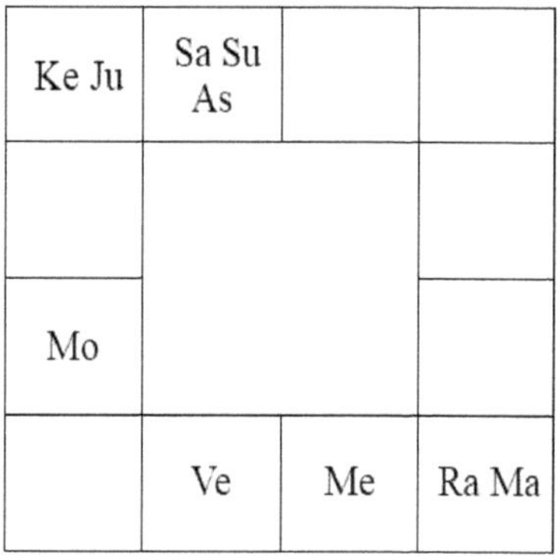

D30

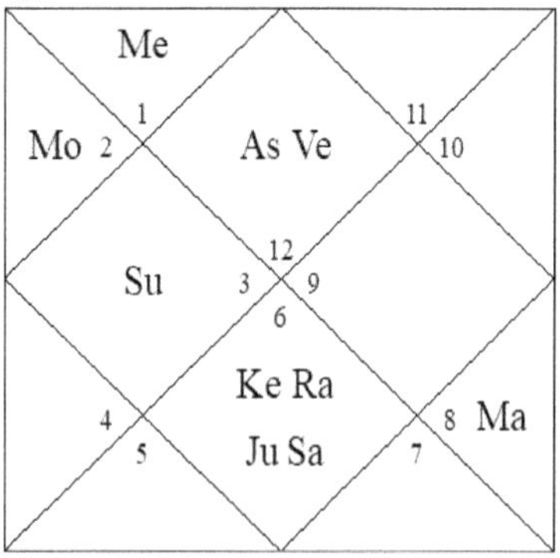

D30

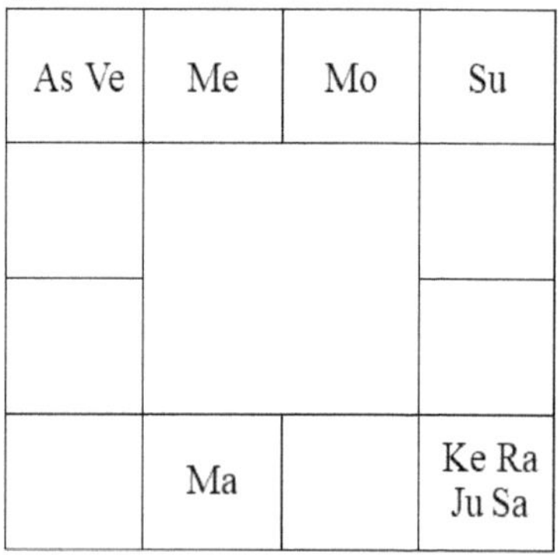

D30 Iyer

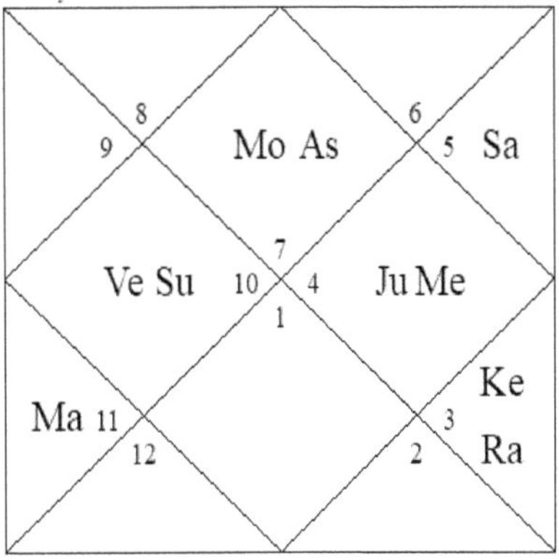

D30 Iyer

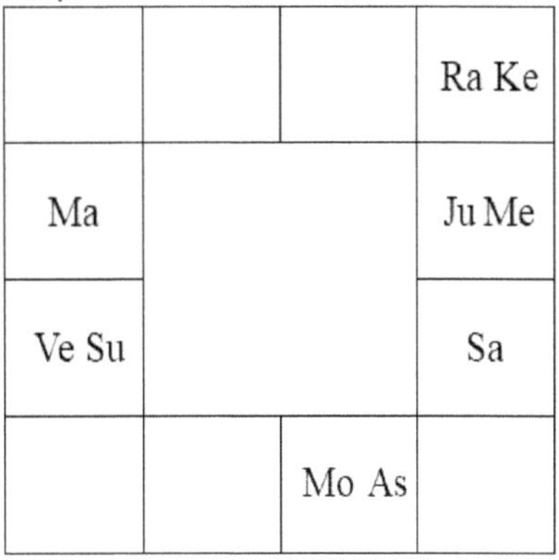

1. **Navamsha**
   Exalted Sun and debilitated Saturn are present in lagan. Lagan is aspected by its lord Mars and by Mercury. The desire of marriage is present. The fourth house is aspected by Jupiter and Moon. Moon is lord of fourth house. The marriage is happy.
2. **Parashar Trishamsha**
   Sign of Jupiter is rising in this Trishamsha. Exalted Venus and Ketu are in lagan. It is aspected by Jupiter and Saturn. Eighth house is aspected by Mercury. Manglya is present.
3. **Iyer Trishamsha**
   Libra is rising in lagan. Moon is in lagan and aspected by Saturn. The eighth house is aspected by Mars and Saturn. This not showing happy situation.

Example 5 – DOB 27 MARCH 1968, TOB 11.32, POB PUNE

This example is of an unhappy marriage. He was married on 17 February 2002. His wife left him after 27 days of marriage.

Birth Chart

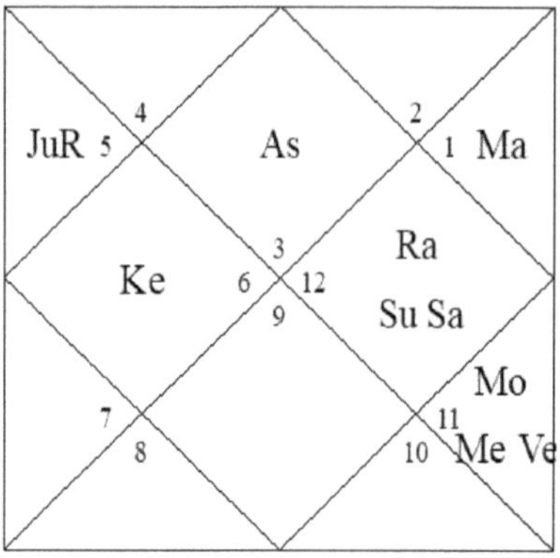

Birth Chart

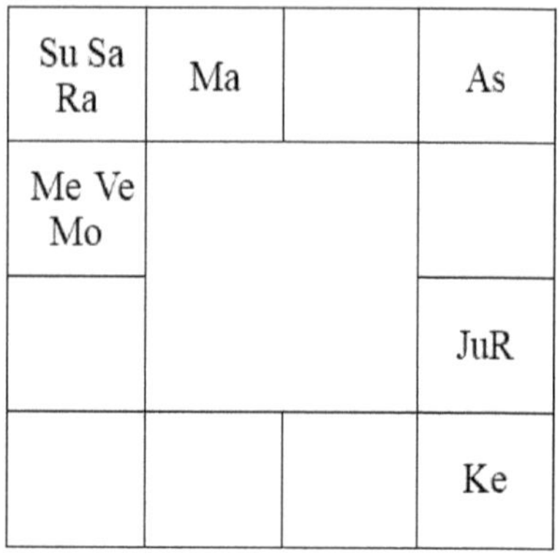

D9

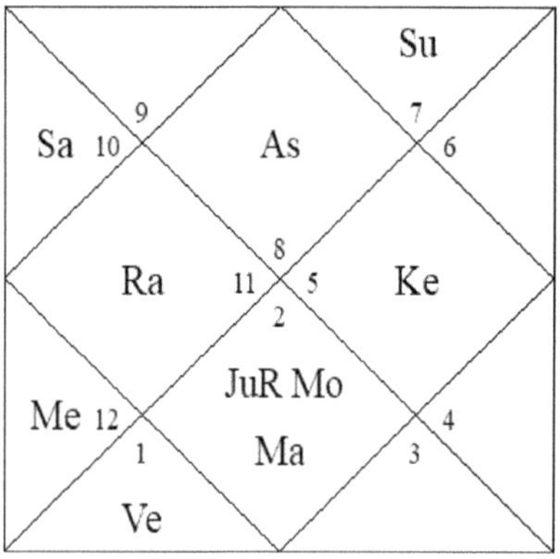

D9

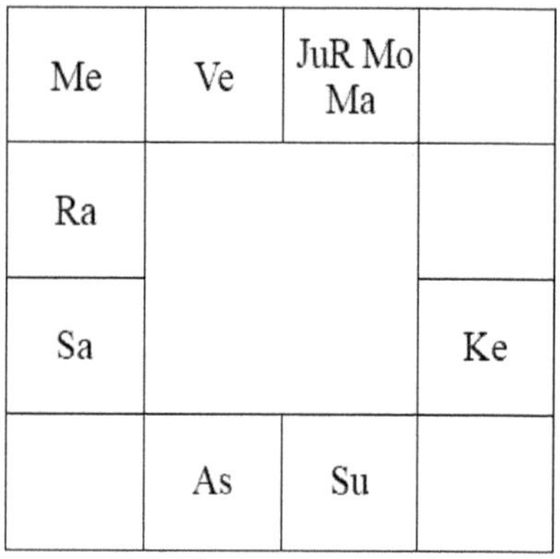

D30

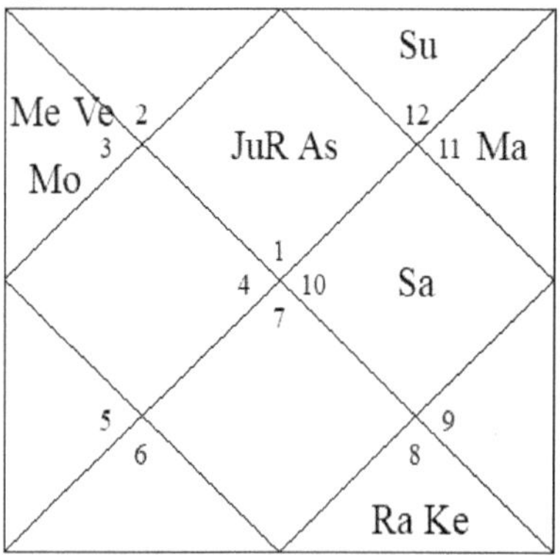

D30

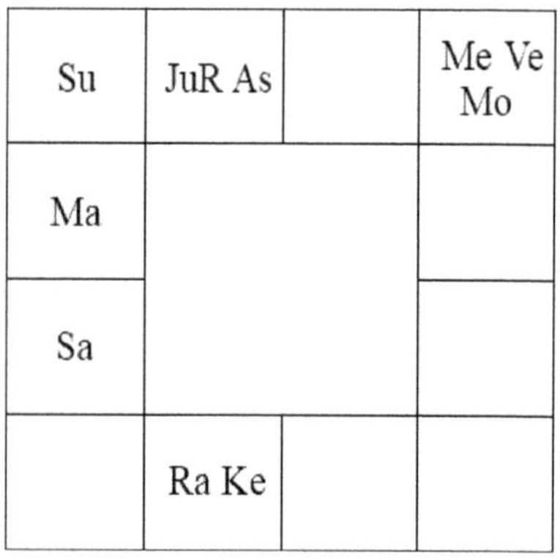

D30 Iyer

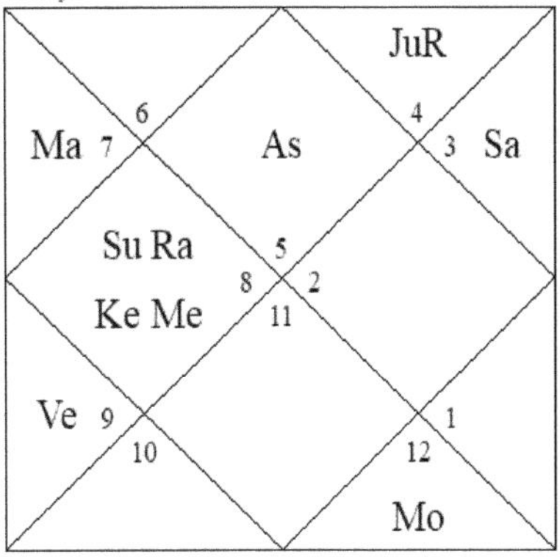

D30 Iyer

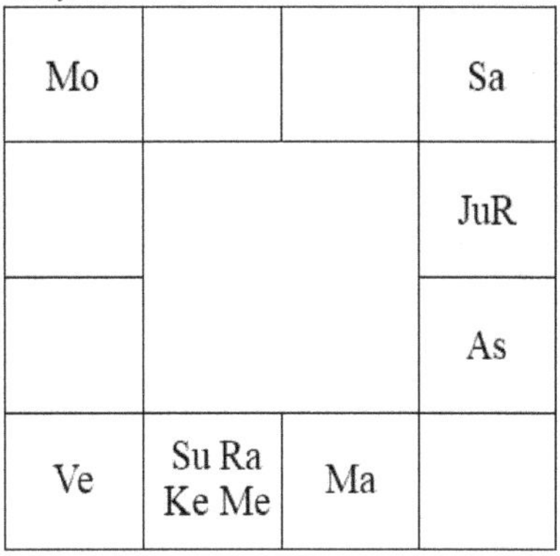

1. **Navamsha**
   Lagan is aspected by Jupiter, Moon and Mars. Mars is lord of lagan. He wants to marry. Fourth house has Rahu and is not having any aspect. The marriage is not happy.
2. **Parashar Trishamsha**
   Sign of Mars is rising in this Trishamsha. Jupiter is in lagan. Mars is not related to birth lagan. Presence of benefic gives some relief. Eighth house ha Rahu with no relief.
3. **Iyer Trishamsha**
   Sign of Sun is rising in lagan. It is aspected by Saturn. This gives unhappy marriage.

To decide the quality of marriage, fourth house of Navamsha is the primary factor. The confirmation is from lagan and eighth house of Trishamsha.

3. Death or separation in marriage._

This topic deals with end of marriage. The end of marriage can happen in three ways.

a. Separation or divorce.
b. Death of spouse.
c. Your own death.

For this analysis we have to look in the eighth house of Trishamsha. Eighth house is the house of Manglya. When eighth house is connected to only benefic then the Manglya is not broken. This means that you die as Suhagan, whether it is a male or female horoscope. Only malefic relation with eighth house shortens the life of Manglya and this can become a chart of separation, divorce or even death of your spouse. A benefic influence on eighth house along with malefic will prolong the longevity of marriage. This depends on the strength of benefic.

Seventh house is the house of marriage in Navamsha. Affliction to seventh house/ lord will break the marriage. In such cases if eighth house is benefic then spouse will not die but marriage will break.

Example 1 – DOB 14 JULY 1941, TOB, 10.12 POB SAHARANPUR

His wife died after a long-married life of approximately 45 years.

Birth Chart

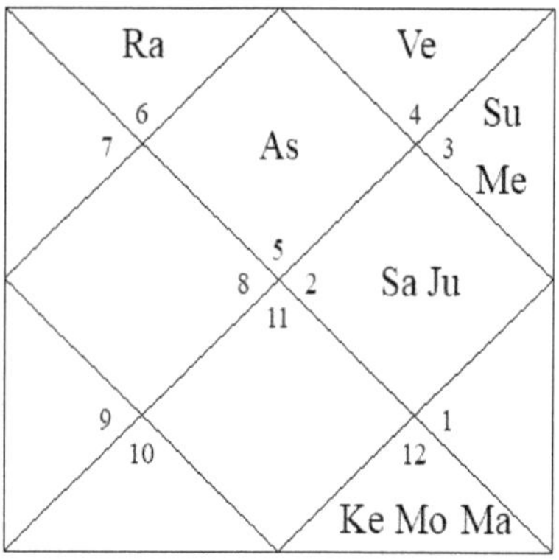

Birth Chart

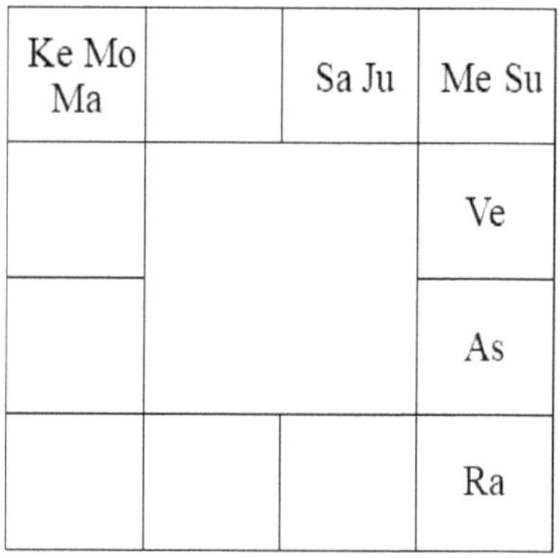

D9

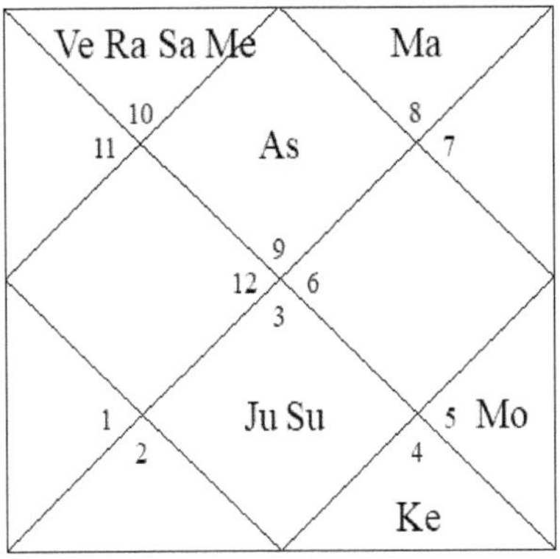

D9

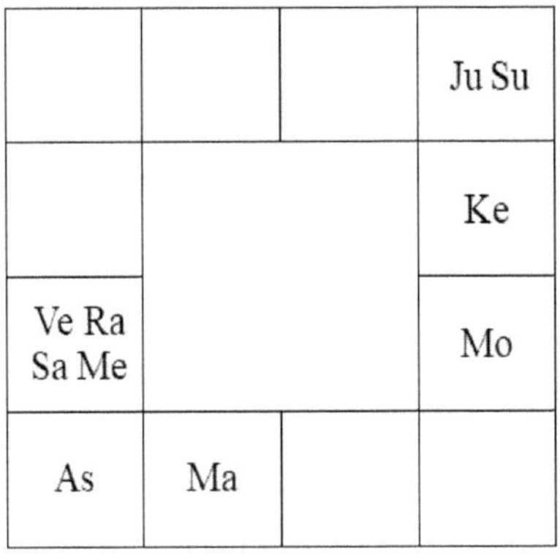

D30

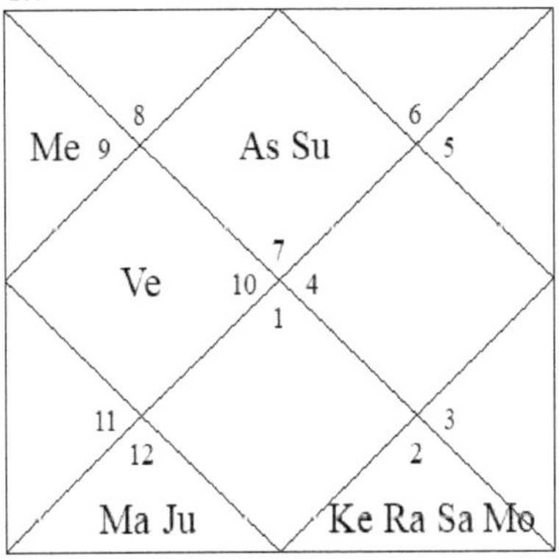

D30

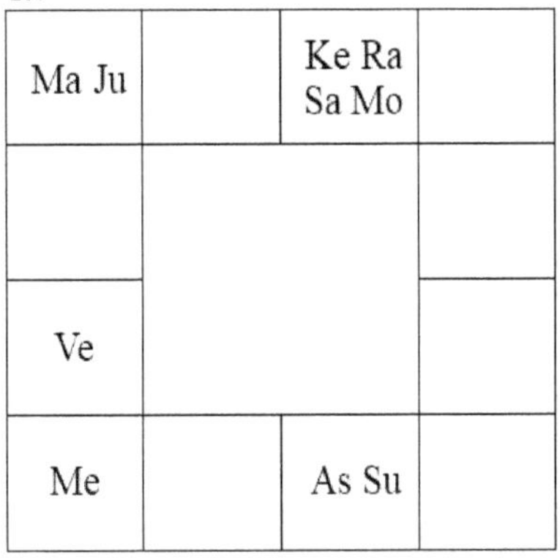

D30 Iyer

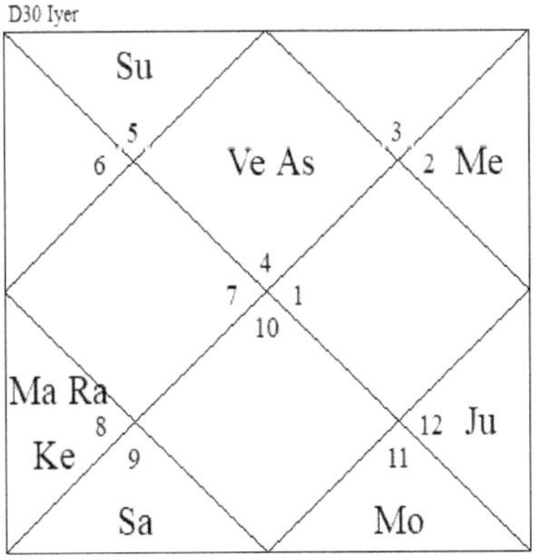

D30 Iyer

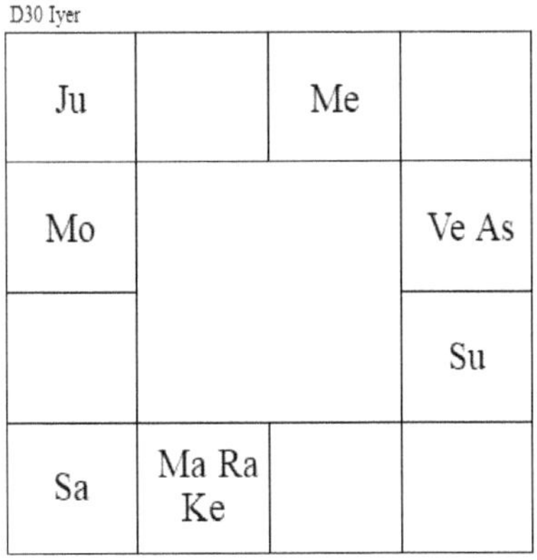

1. Navamsha

Eighth house has Ketu and is aspected by Venus, Mercury and Saturn. Long life of marriage is seen. The seventh house has Jupiter and Sun but aspected by Mars. His Maglaya is there but the partner will die.

2. Parashar Trishamsha

Rahu, Saturn and Moon are placed in eighth house. Moon is exalted. Rahu acts as Moon, Saturn and Venus. Venus and Saturn have exchanged sign. Presence of malefic gave death to spouse but benefic gave long married life. Sun is aspecting seventh house.

3. Iyer Trishamsha

Moon is placed in eighth house. It is aspected by Saturn, Mars and Sun. Saturn is lord of eighth house thus gives strength to it. Seventh house is aspected by Venus. It is not a break in marriage.

Example 2 – DOB 14 December 1946, TOB, 9.24.44 POB Delhi

He was married on 23 December 1974. He was died on 23 June 1980 in plane crash.

Birth Chart

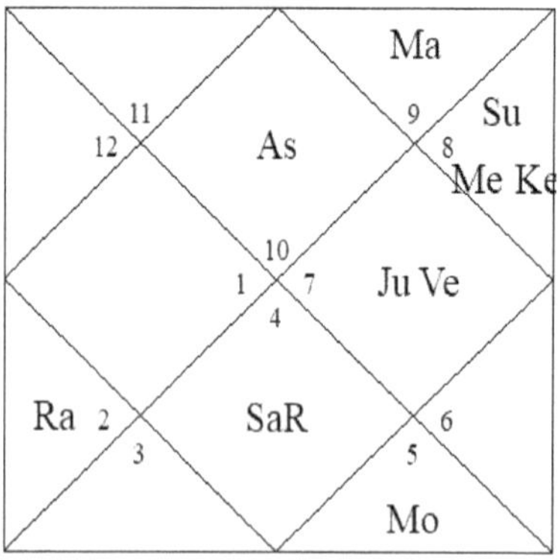

Birth Chart

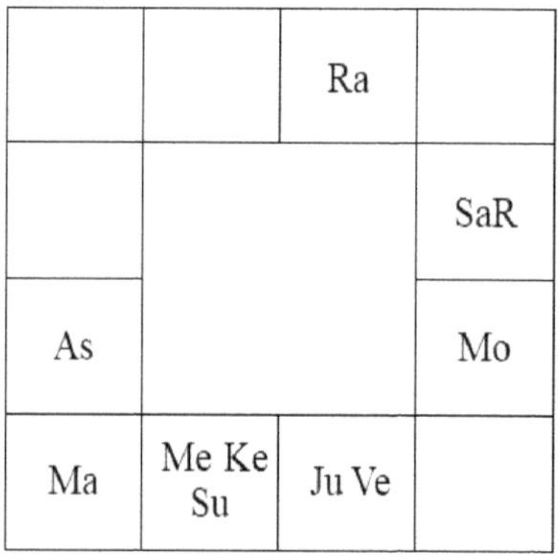

D9

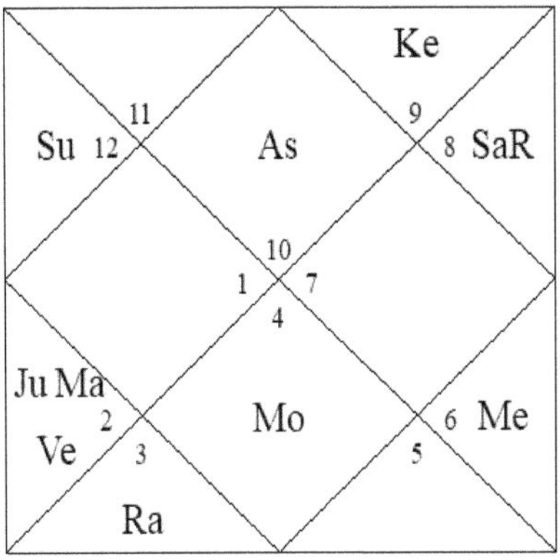

D9

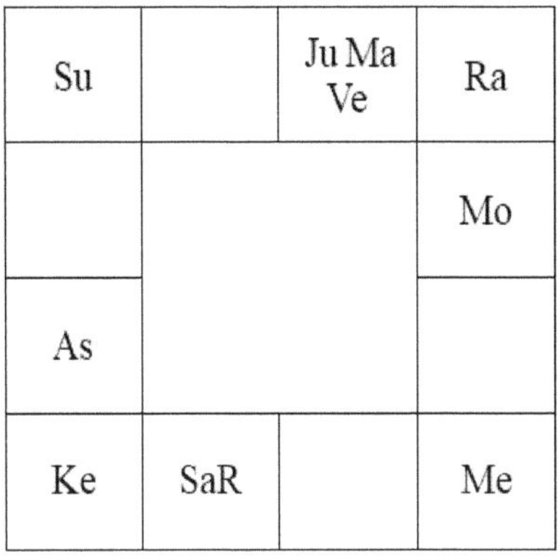

D30

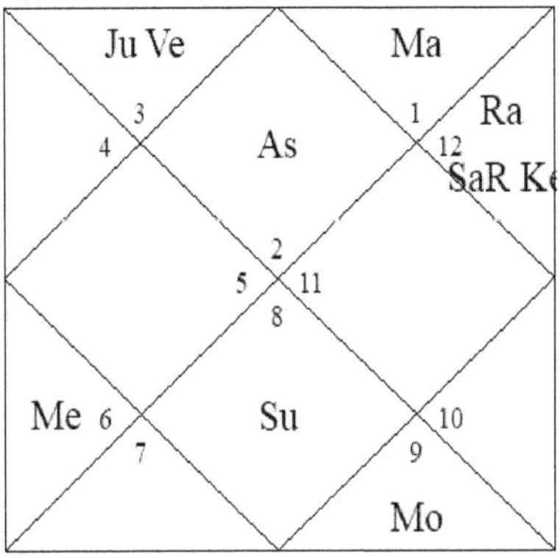

D30

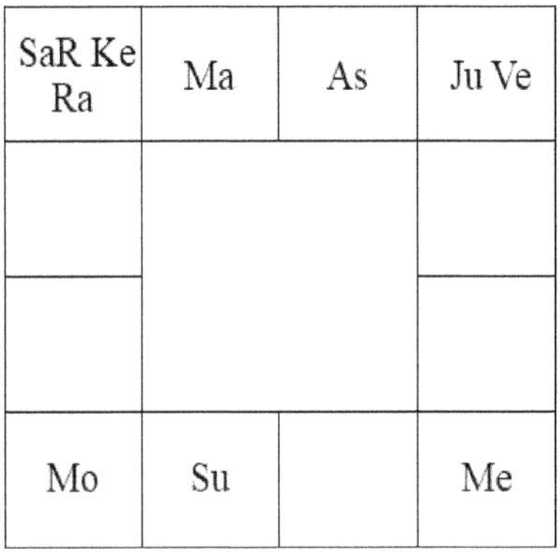

D30 Iyer

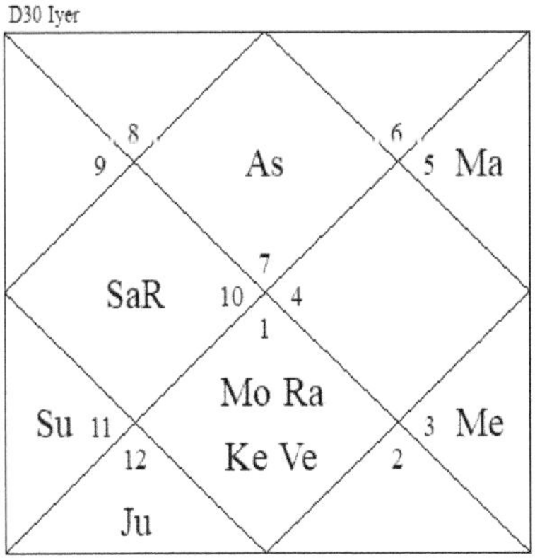

D30 Iyer

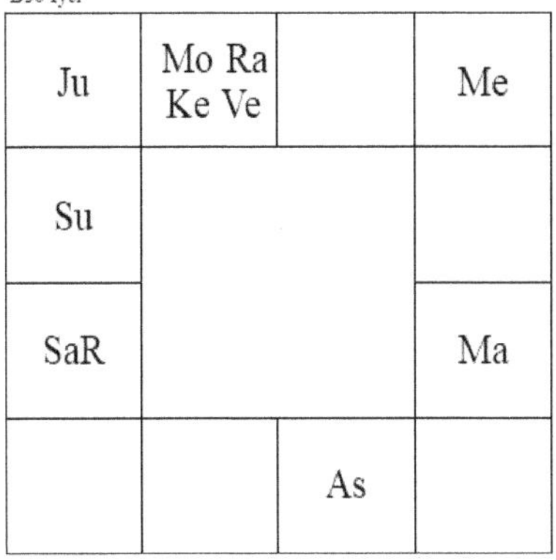

1. Navamsha

Eighth house is aspected by Saturn and Mars. The married life is short. Moon is placed in seventh house in his own sign. The partner will not die and this gives end of Maglaya by his death or separation.

2. Parashar Trishamsha

Saturn, Jupiter and Venus are aspecting eighth house. Saturn is badly afflicted. seventh house is afflicted by Sun and Mars. The end of Magalya should be separation from partner. This Trishamsha is not showing true picture.

3. Iyer Trishamsha

Eighth house is vacant and has no aspect. Seventh house has Rahu and two benefic. The partner is safe.

Iyer Trishamsha is giving true analysis. We must have correct time of birth to apply this chart.

Example 3 – DOB 13 DECEMBER 1964, TOB, 12.50 POB DELHI

Her husband died when she was 53 years of age.

Birth Chart

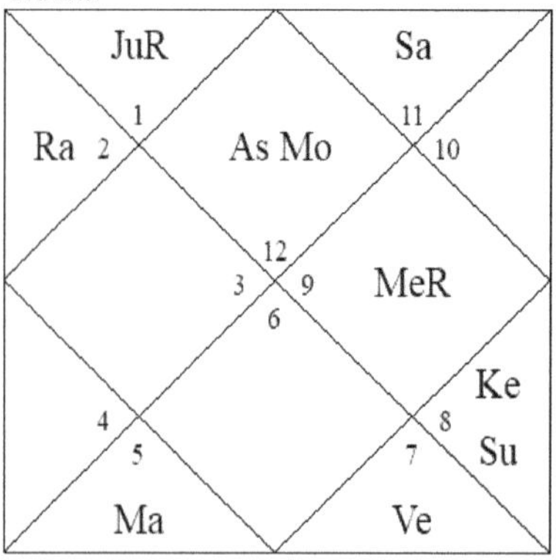

Birth Chart

As Mo	JuR	Ra	
Sa			
			Ma
MeR	Su Ke	Ve	

D9

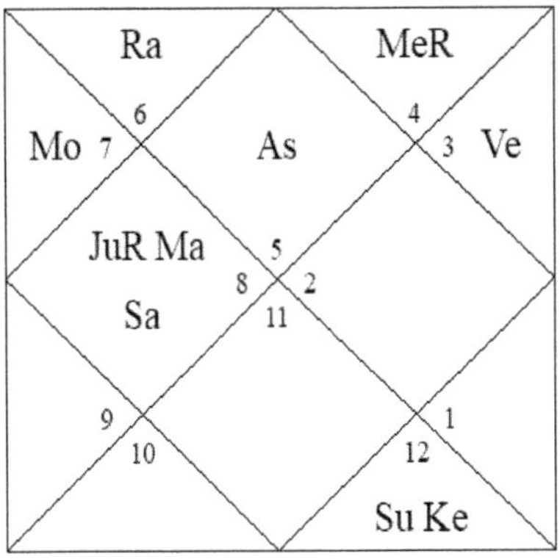

D9

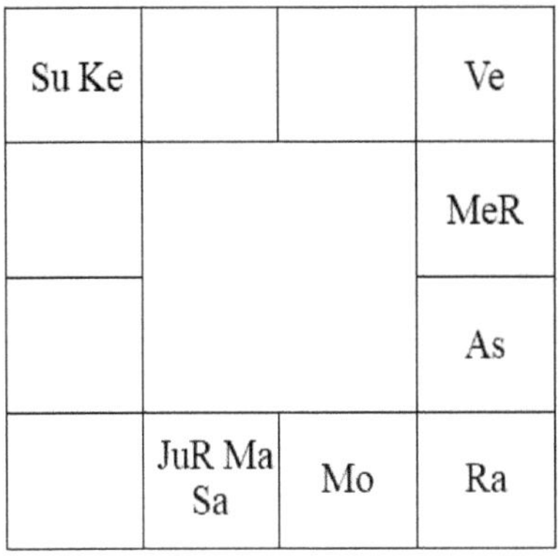

D30

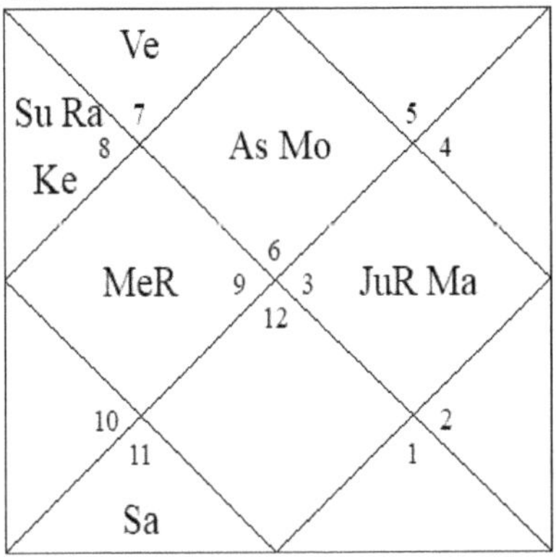

D30

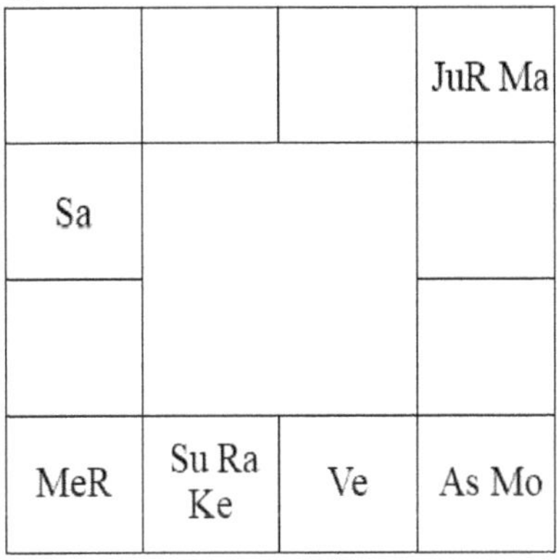

D30 Iyer

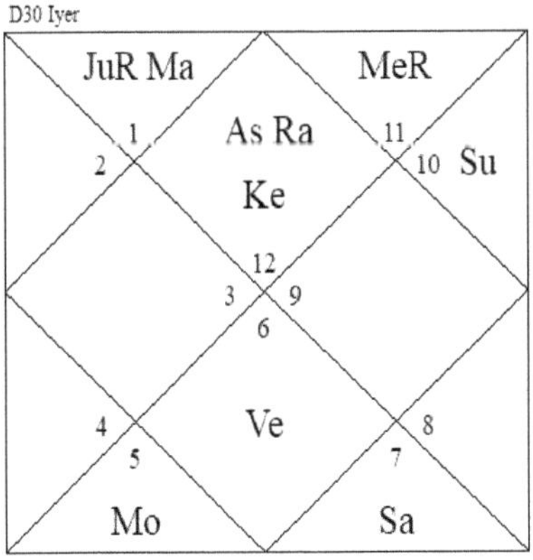

D30 Iyer

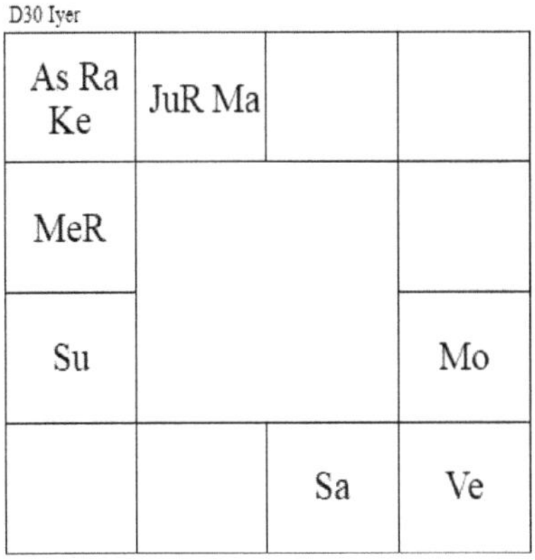

1. Navamsha

Ketu and Sun are placed in eighth house and are aspected by Jupiter. This gives long marriage life. The seventh house is aspected by Mars and has no benefic relation. The partner will go first.

2. Parashar Trishamsha

Eighth house is aspected by Venus and Saturn. Both are in their own mooltrikona sign. It shows the happiness and separation. The seventh house is not afflicted.

3. Iyer Trishamsha

In this Trishamsha malefic influence is more. Mars is in own sign and Saturn is exalted. Her husband died at an early age. Seventh house has Venus which is not allowing separation.

Example 4 – DOB 30 OCTOBER 1972, TOB 17.07, POB DELHI

This is a case of divorce.

Birth Chart

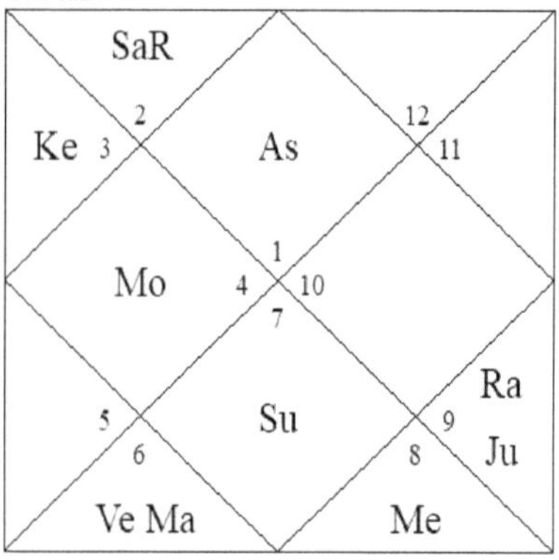

Birth Chart

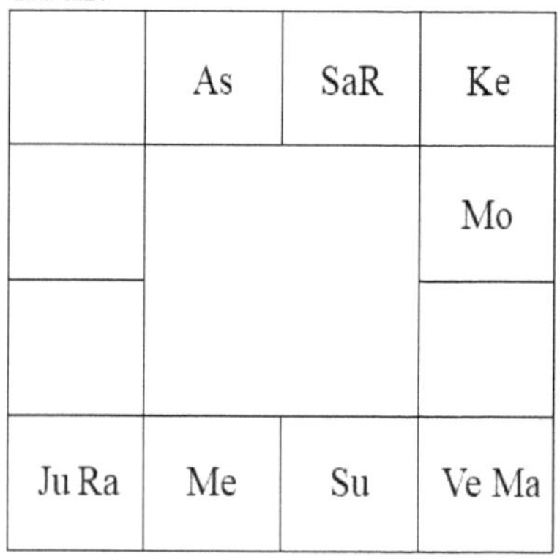

D9

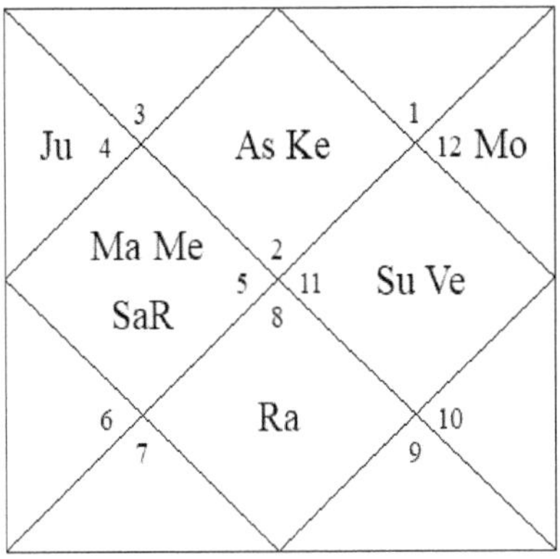

D9

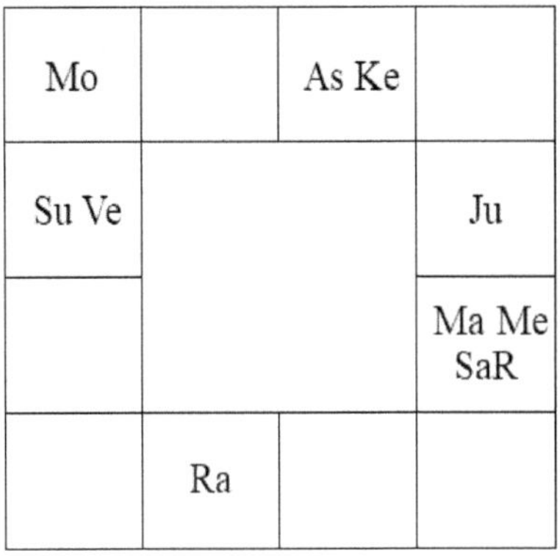

D30

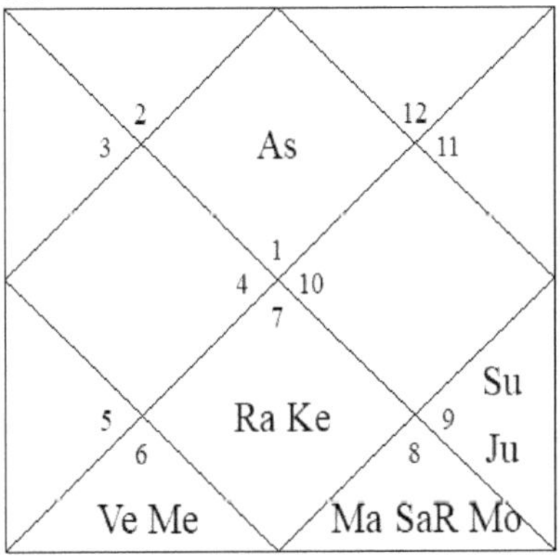

D30

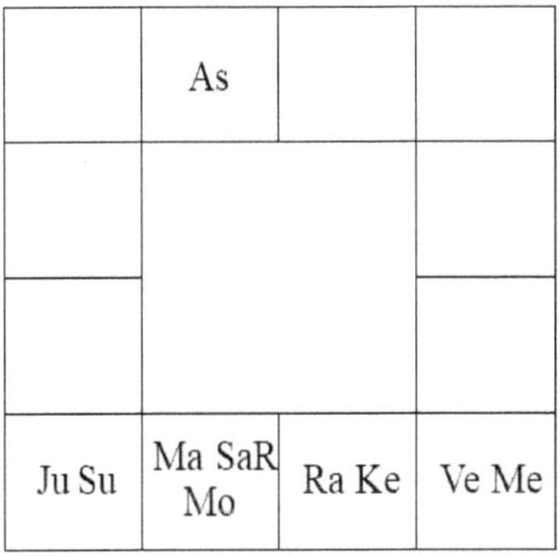

D30 Iyer

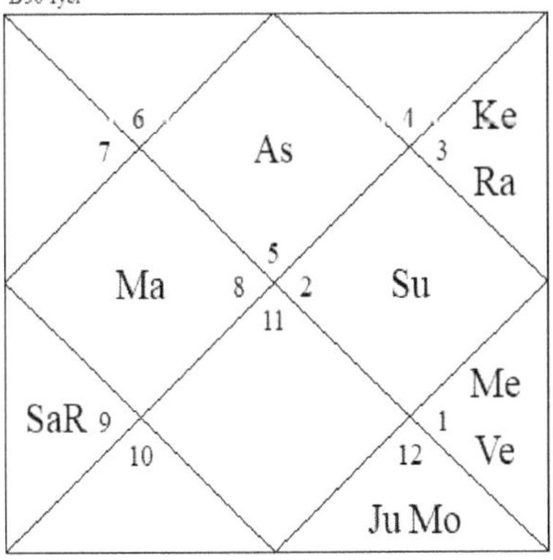

D30 Iyer

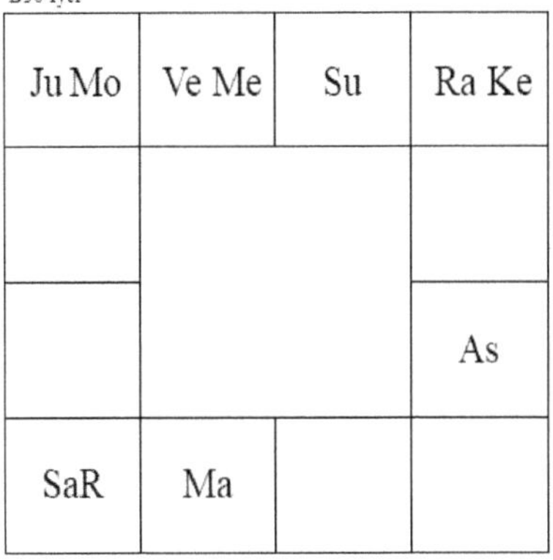

1. Navamsha

Eighth house is not occupied or aspected. Seventh house has Rahu and is aspected by Mars and Jupiter. Jupiter is eighth and eleventh lord. The malefic influence on seventh house is more.

2. Parashar Trishamsha

Eighth house has Mars, Moon and Saturn. Mars is in Scorpio. The maglaya will finish after some years. This may mean death of spouse. The seventh house has Rahu and as such it will be loss of maglaya by divorce.

3. Iyer Trishamsha

This gives better analysis. Eighth house has two benefic. Seventh house is aspected by Mars and Saturn. Divorce came after about seven years of marriage.

Example 5 – DOB 8 JUNE 1944, TOB 20.12, POB ALLEPPEY

Birth Chart

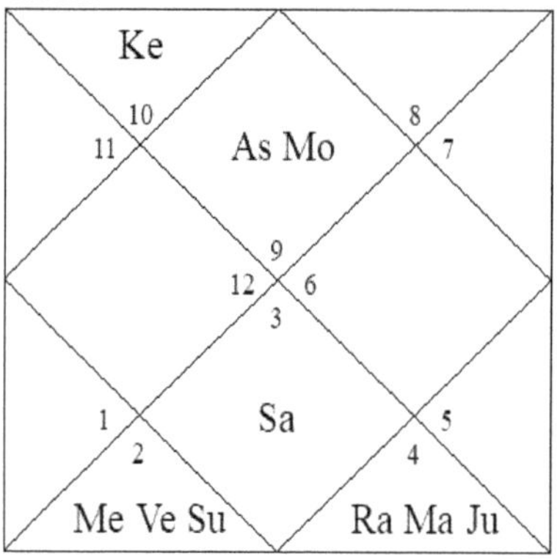

Birth Chart

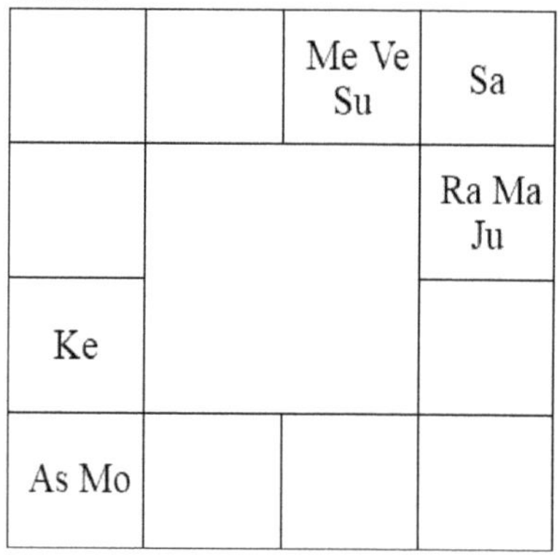

D9

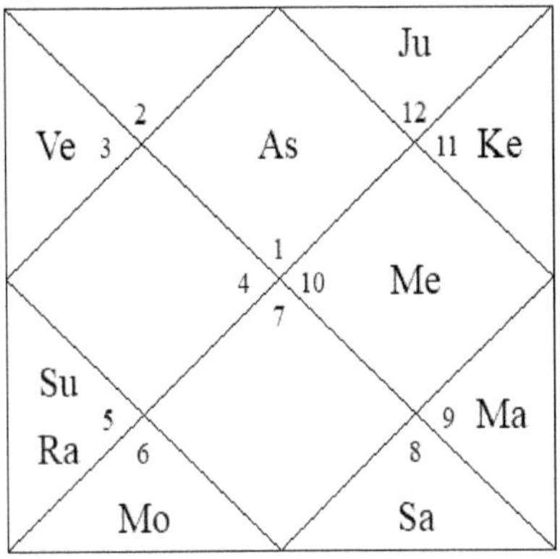

D9

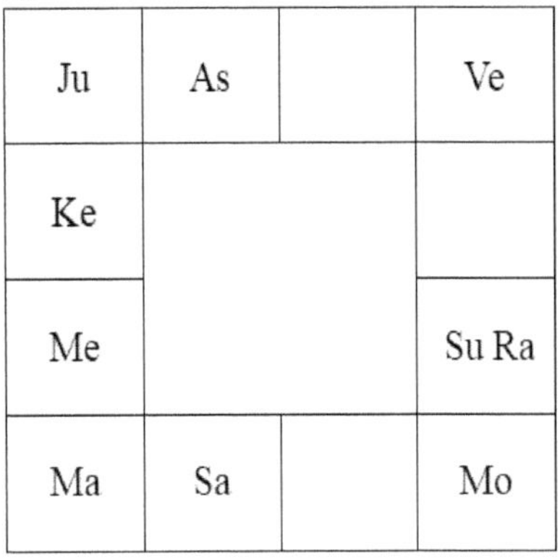

D30

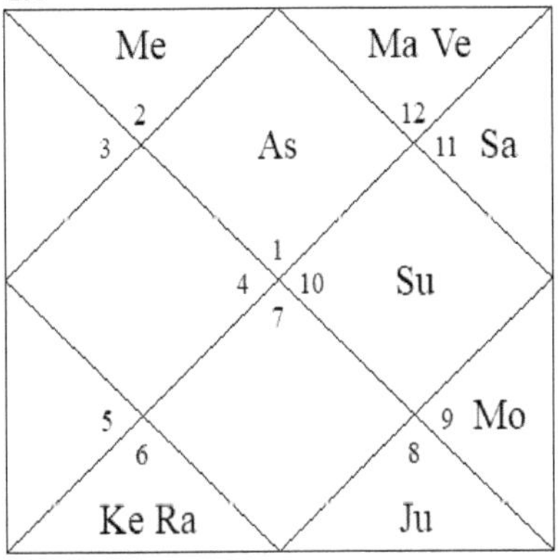

D30

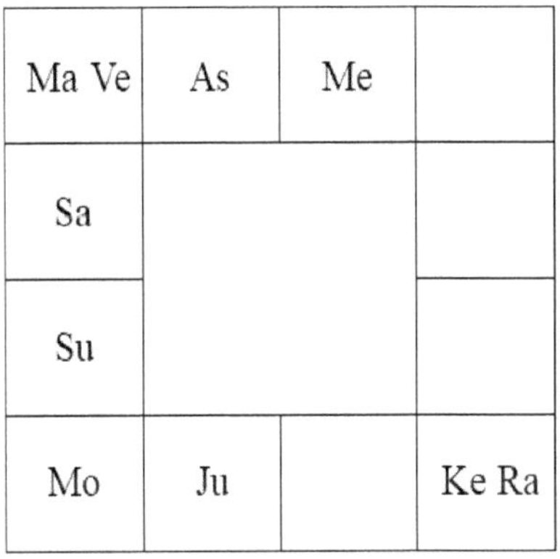

D30 Iyer

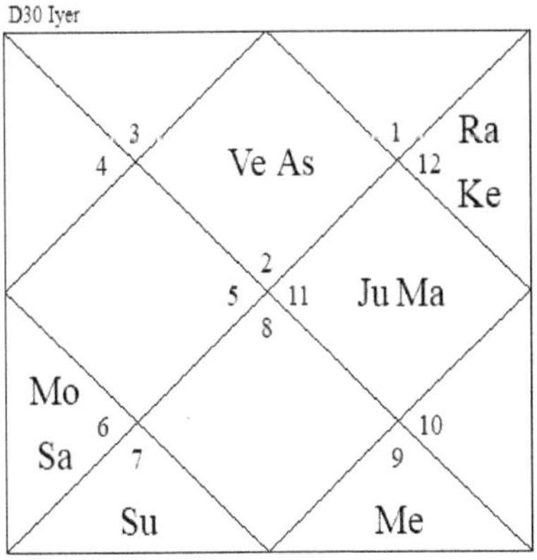

D30 Iyer

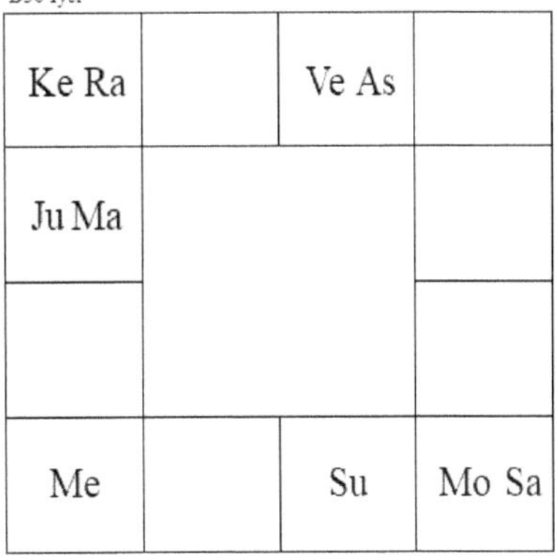

1. **Navamsha**
2. Eighth house has Saturn and is aspected by Jupiter. Seventh house has no relation. Saturn in eighth house signals end of Maglaya due to his death.
3. **Parashar Trishamsha**

   Jupiter is placed in eighth house and is aspected by Saturn and Mercury. The benefic influence is more. The spouse should die first. It is not so.
4. **Iyer Trishamsha**

   Mercury is placed in eighth house and has no malefic influence. The seventh house has aspect of Mars and Saturn. Mars is lord of seventh house and makes it strong. Since eighth house has only benefic relation he died first. There is no break of marriage.

Denial of marriage

Here also Trishamsha plays a big role. The main chart of marriage is Navamsha but Trishamsha gives confirmation.

The rule of denial of marriage emerges from our discussions we had in this chapter.

1. Navamsha chart is seen first. The seventh house is the house of marriage. The Navamsha should show no marriage. Some rules to decide this are given;

a. The karaka of marriage is placed in lagan. There is no association of benefic with lagan. The karaka of marriage is Jupiter for female and Venus for male.

b. The seventh house is afflicted by malefic. The malefic influence should be more than benefic influence.

c. A benefic relation with seventh house can indicate marriage. But if Trishamsha shows denial than this remains an affair only.

d. I have discussed this topic in my book "Predict with Navamsha" and can be referred.

2. Now Trishamsha chart is seen. The eighth house of Trishamsha should have malefic influence. This gives confirmation of denial of marriage.
3. Any relation of eighth lord with seventh house or lord can give denial or break in marriage.

We will check this on example charts.

Example 1 – DOB 4 JULY 1974, TOB 9.53, POB CUTTACK

Birth Chart

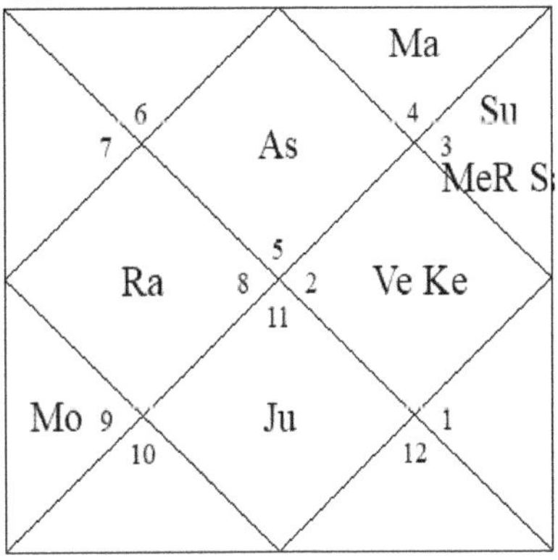

Birth Chart

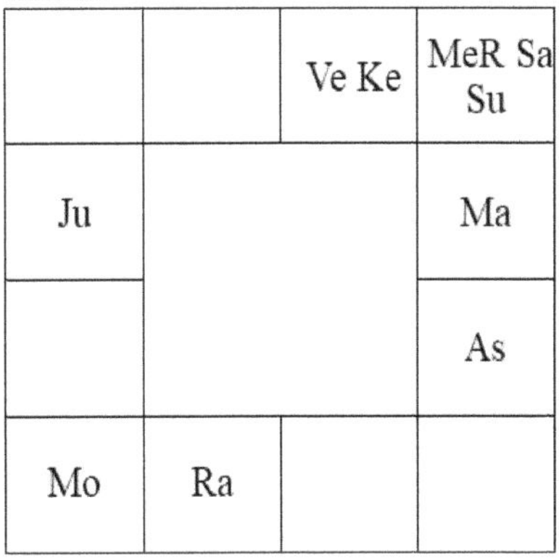

D9

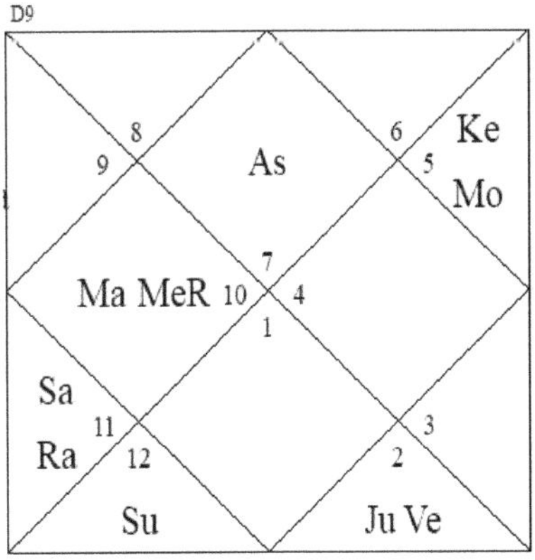

D9

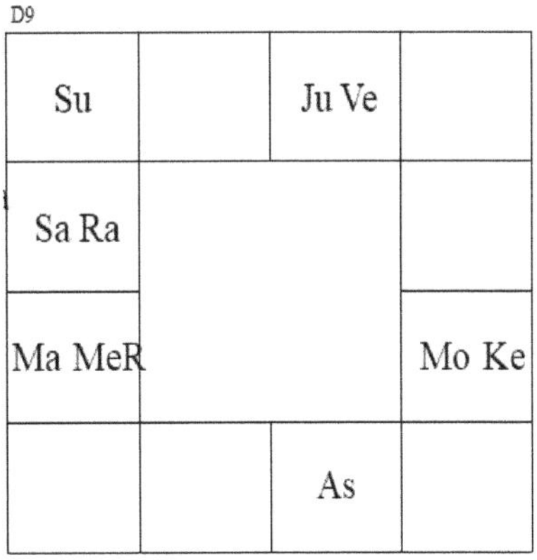

D30

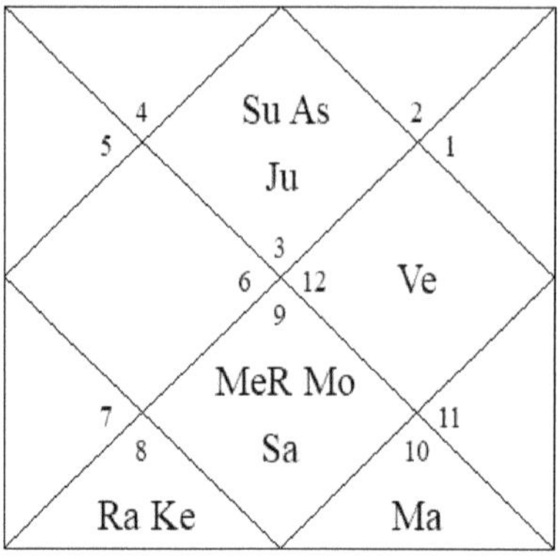

D30

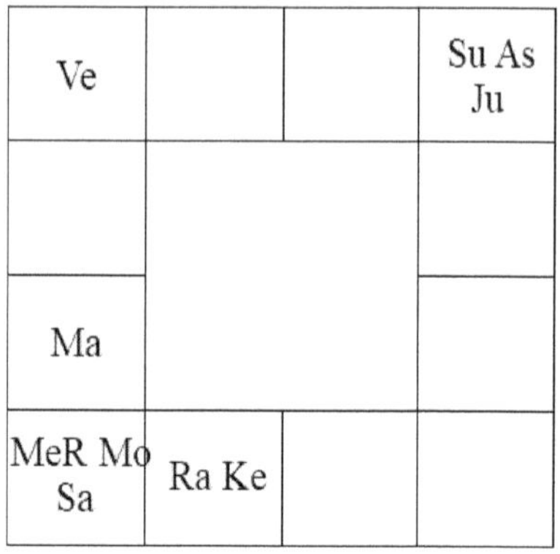

D30 Iyer

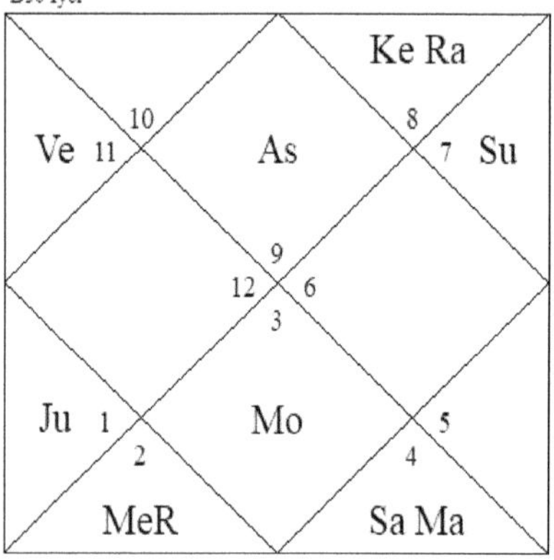

D30 Iyer

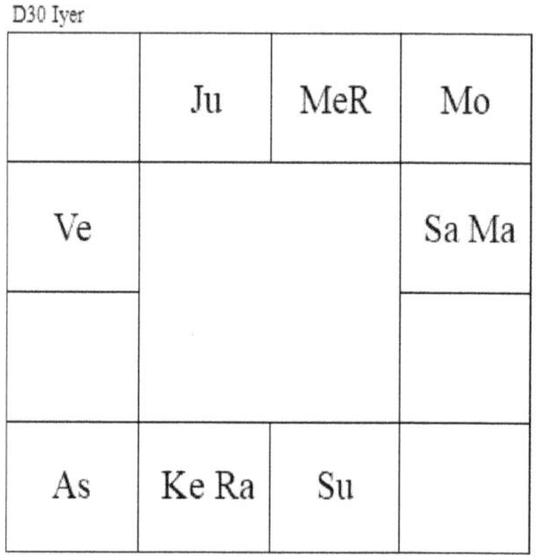

He is an engineer from IIT Kharagpur and is well placed in life. He is not married till 2019. He is learning astrology in my classes.

1. **Navamsha**
   Seventh house is aspected by Mars and Saturn. Mars is seventh lord also. There is no benefic aspect. Navamsha indicates marriage.

2. **Parashar Trishamsha**
   Eighth house is occupied by Mars and has no benefic aspects on it. This is a confirmation. Eighth lord is in seventh house.

3. **Iyer Trishamsha**
   Saturn and Mars are placed in eighth house without any benefic relation. Eighth lord is in seventh house. This shows denial of marriage.

Example 2 – DOB 19 JUNE 1970, TOB 14.38, POB DELHI

Birth Chart

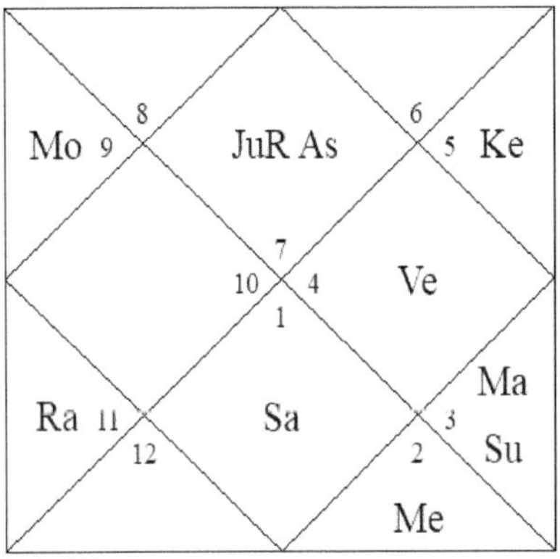

Birth Chart

	Sa	Me	Su Ma
Ra			Ve
			Ke
Mo		JuR As	

D9

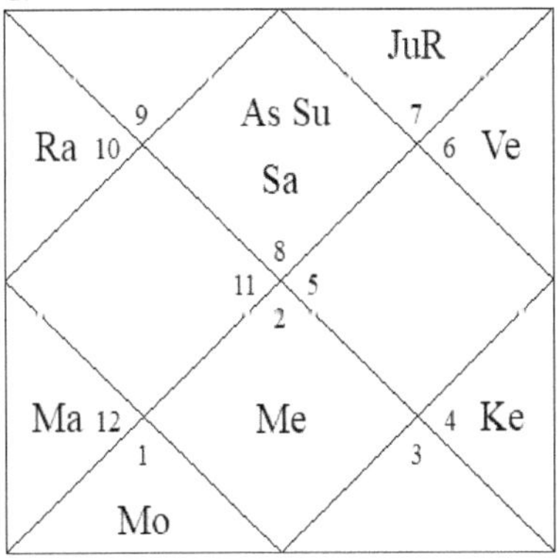

D9

Ma	Mo	Me	
			Ke
Ra			
	As Su Sa	JuR	Ve

D30

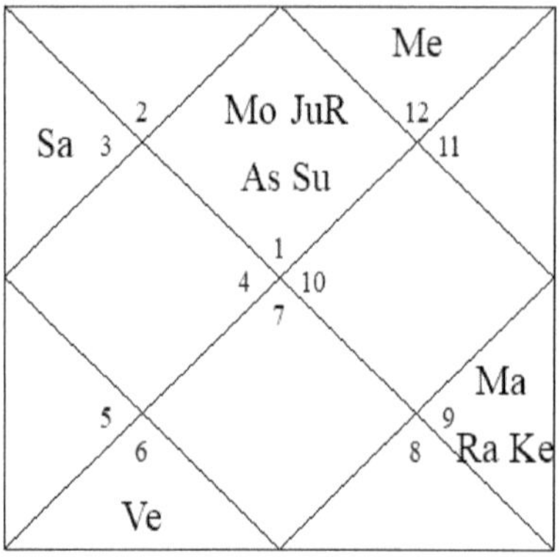

D30

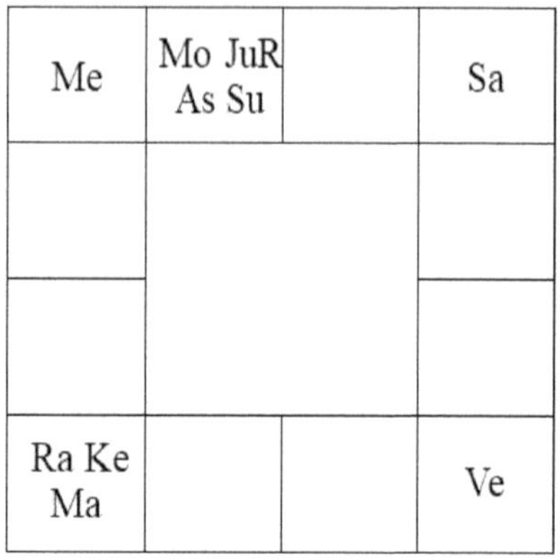

D30 Iyer

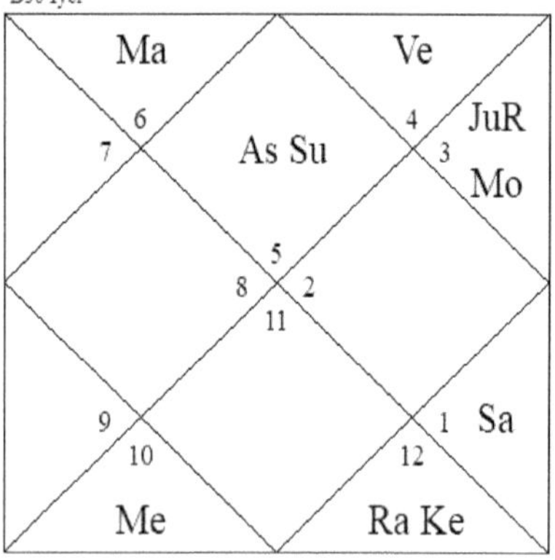

D30 Iyer

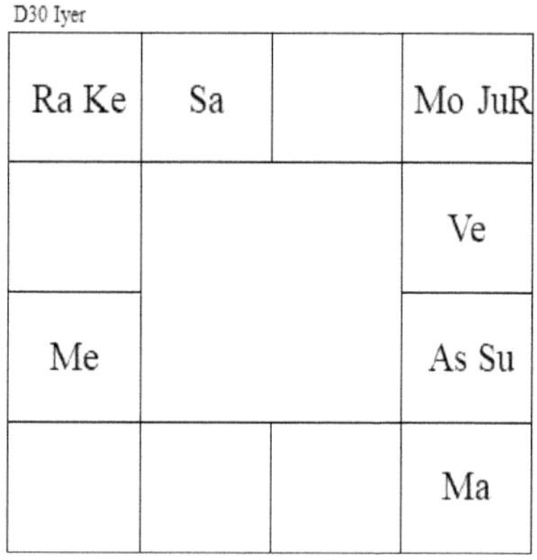

1. **Navamsha**
   Mercury is placed in seventh house. He is aspected by Sun and Saturn. The malefic influence is more.
2. **Parashar Trishamsha**
   Eighth house no influence.
3. **Iyer Trishamsha**
   In this chart, Rahu is in eighth house. Mars is aspecting this house. Eighth lord is aspecting seventh house. Now the denial is confirmed.

Example 3 – DOB 3 DECEMBER 1928, TOB 11.20, POB KARNAL

She is an authority in plant bio chemistry and was nominated for noble prize. She never married.

Birth Chart

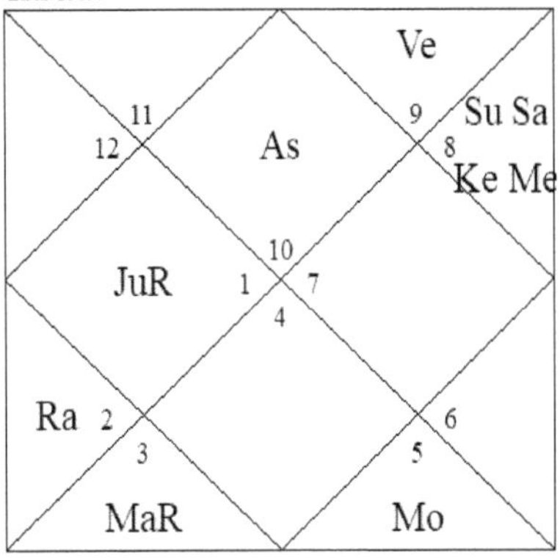

Birth Chart

	JuR	Ra	MaR
As			Mo
Ve	Ke Me Su Sa		

D9

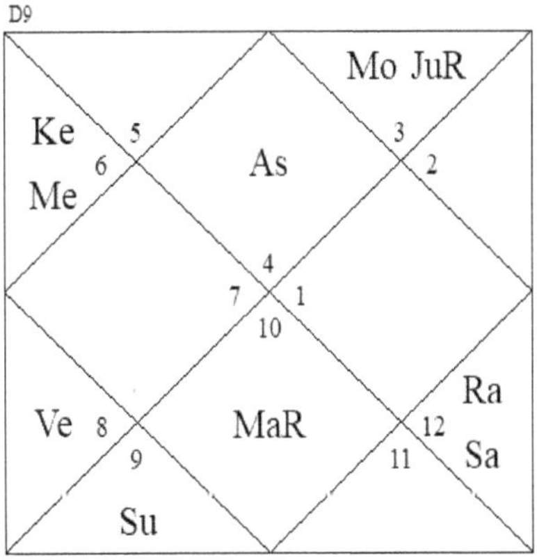

D9

Sa Ra			Mo JuR
			As
MaR			
Su	Ve		Ke Me

D30

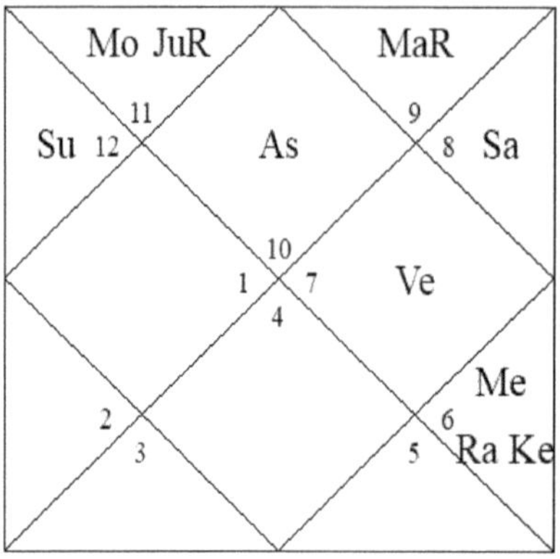

D30

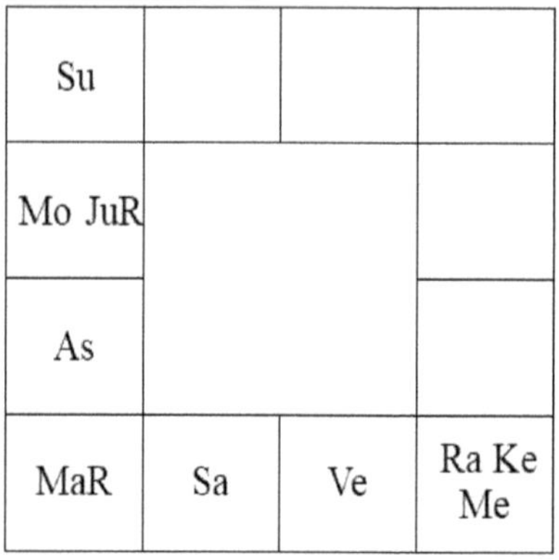

D30 Iyer

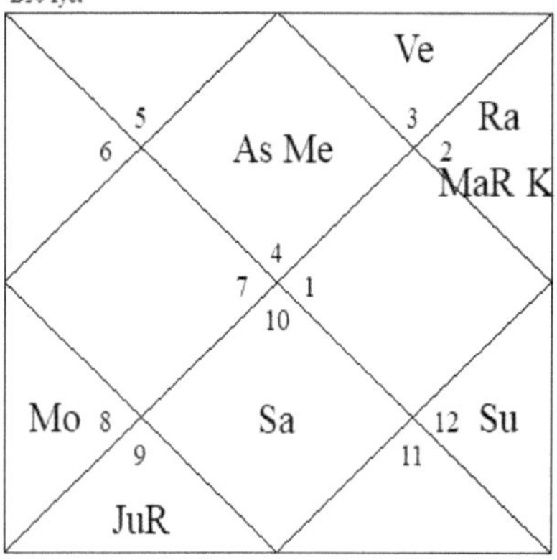

D30 Iyer

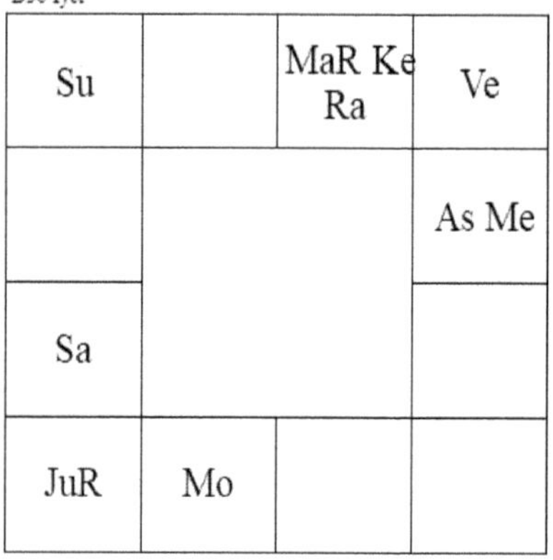

1. **Navamsha**
   Mars is placed in seventh house and has no other relation. Navamsha shows no marriage.

2. **Parashar Trishamsha**
   Eighth house is aspected by Saturn, Moon and Jupiter. Benefic effect is more. This is not showing denial of marriage.

3. **Iyer Trishamsha**
   No planet is placed or is aspecting eighth house. Eighth house is in papa Kartari. The eighth lord is in seventh house and confirms denial of marriage.

Example 4 – DOB 20 APRIL 1963, TOB 13.26, POB DELHI

She is a senior advocate and a translator. She is not married.

Birth Chart

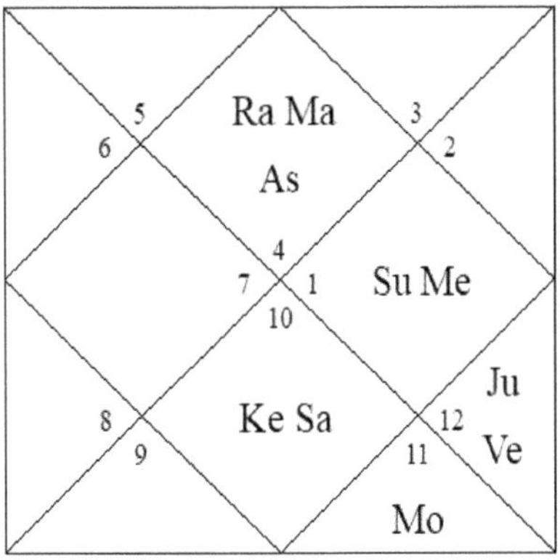

Birth Chart

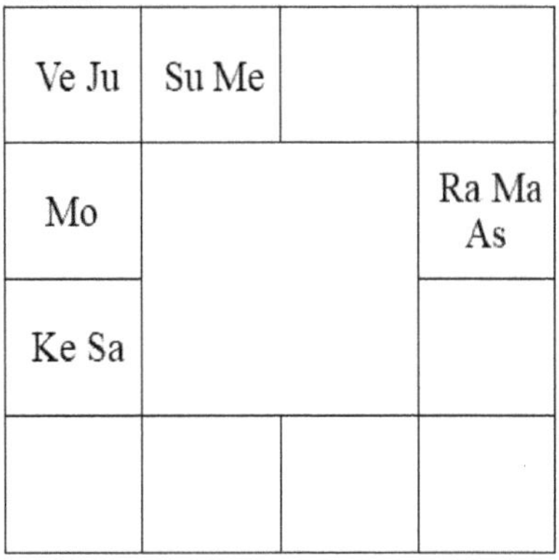

D9

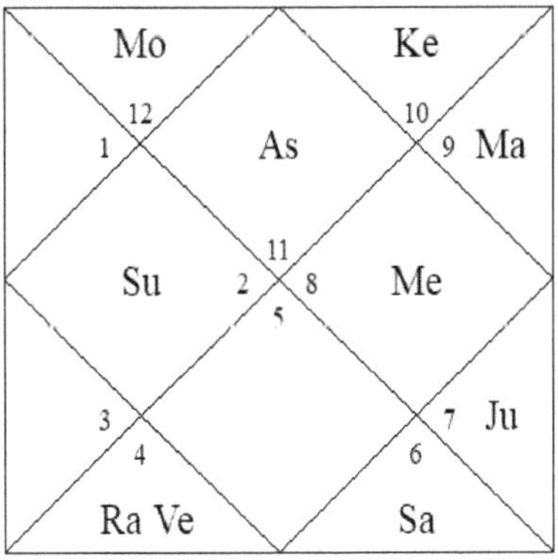

D9

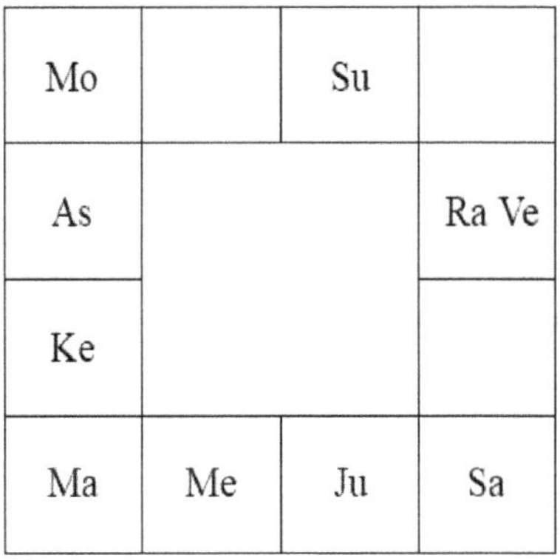

D30

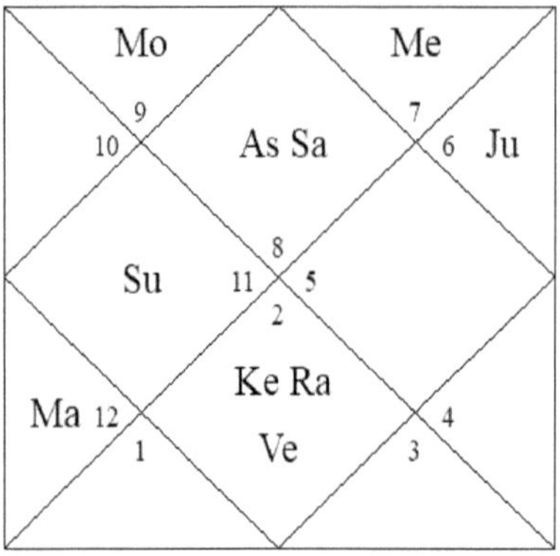

D30

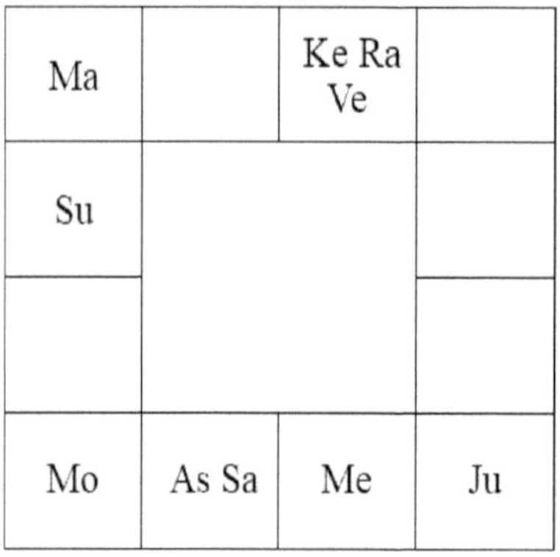

D30 Iyer

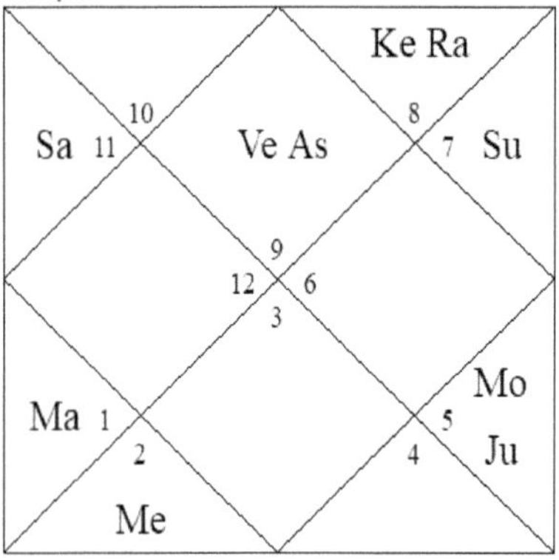

D30 Iyer

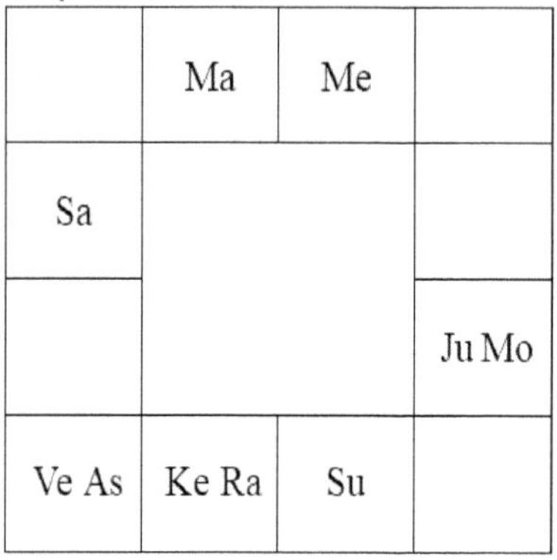

1. **Navamsha**
   Seventh house is vacant and has no aspect. We can say that it is in papa Kartari. Venus is in sixth house also.

2. **Parashar Trishamsha**
   Eighth house is aspected by Moon and Mars. Aspect of Mars is not confirming.

3. **Iyer Trishamsha**
   Here also the eighth house has no planet. It is aspected by Mars only. There is no benefic relation. This gives confirmation of no marriage.

Example 5 – DOB 21 FEBRUARY 1967 10.51, TOB, POB DELHI

Birth Chart

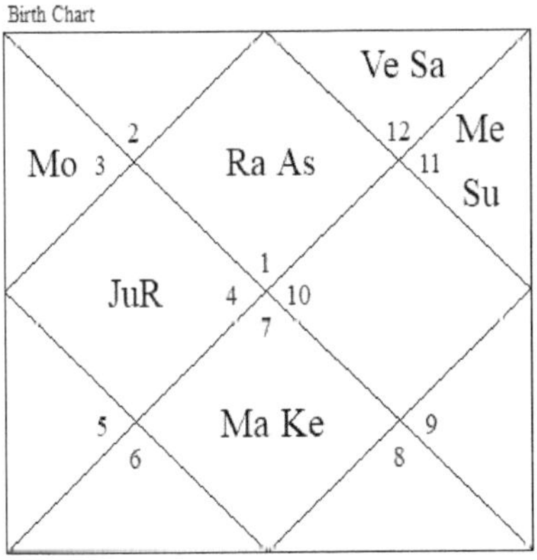

Birth Chart

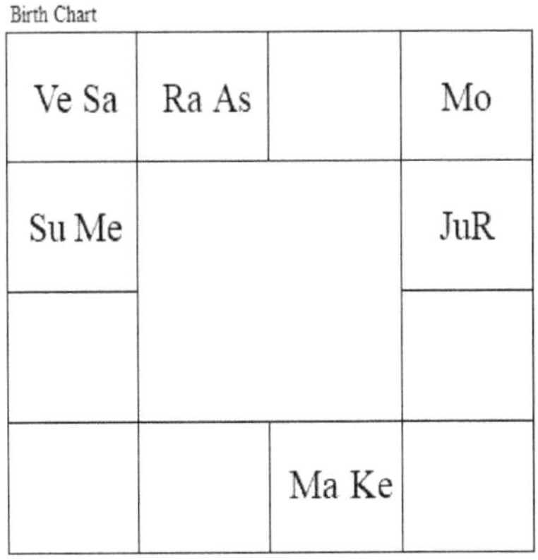

D9

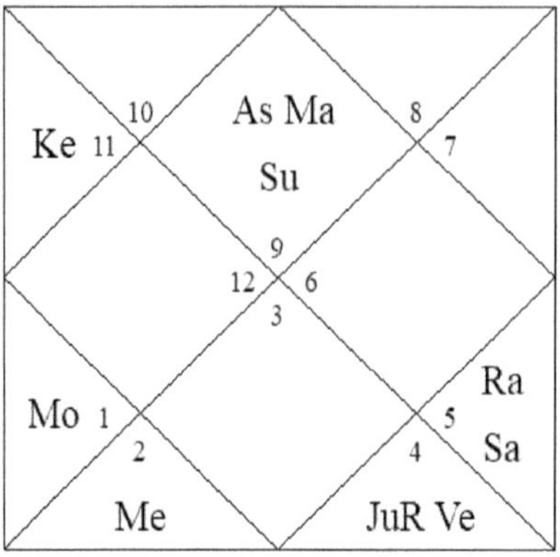

D9

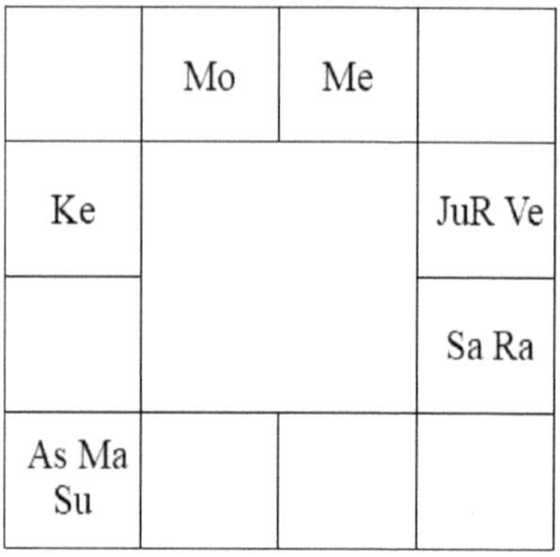

D30

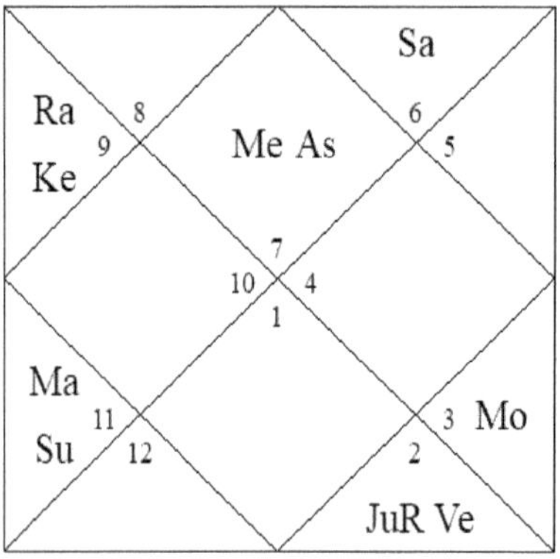

D30

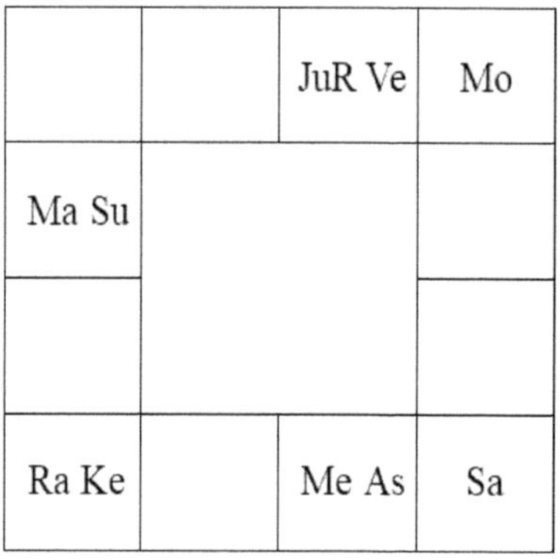

D30 Iyer

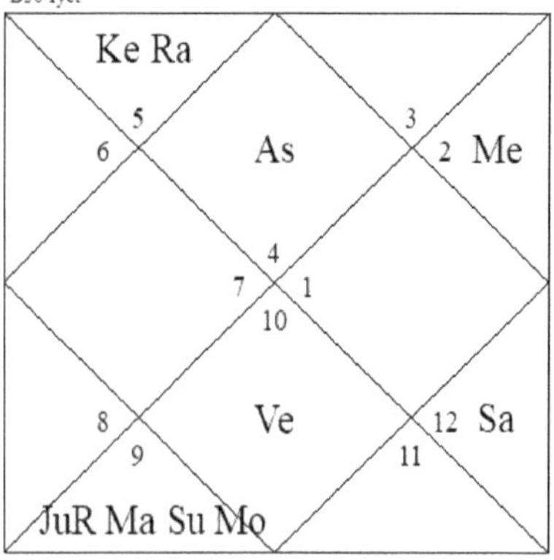

D30 Iyer

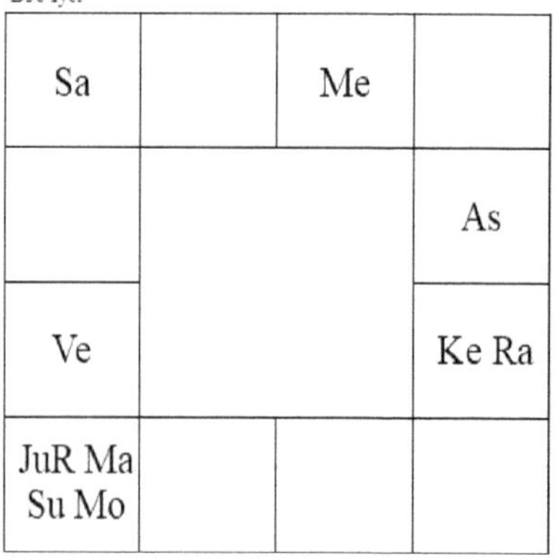

1. **Navamsha**
   Seventh house is aspected by Sun and Mars. It is in Subh Kartari and gives hope of marriage.
2. **Parashar Trishamsha**
   Jupiter and Venus are in eighth house and are aspected by Mars. This is not denial of marriage.
3. **Iyer Trishamsha**
   Eighth house is in Rahu Ketu axis. It has no other aspect. This confirms denial of marriage.

Normally we predict marriage from Navamsha chart. It is suggested that Trishamsha must be taken in consideration before deciding the final verdict.

Chapter 6
Dasha and Transit

A senior astrologer once mentioned that Trishamsha chart should never be ignored when analyzing Dasha and Transit. I have been trying to check this for number of years. The findings are given.

1. Always first see the Dasha. The Dasha considered is Vimshottary Dasha.
2. The Antar Dasha is the executive and gives the results. We must establish the relation of Maha Dasha and Antar Dasha. The Antar Dasha can be good or bad from Maha Dasha. This is checked from the normal tools available for Dasha analysis.
3. The next step is to check the Antar Dasha lord in Iyer/ Parashar Trishamsha. This check is to see whether the AD lord is favorable or not. In Parashar Trishamsha the Tatva is checked. This is explained in first chapter of this book.
4. Analyze the Pratyantar Dasha from Antar Dasha.
5. Workout the Sooksham Dasha. Examine SD for its capability to give result.
6. Now the transit is applied to fix the time of event.
7. This time frame is reduced with the help of transit of Moon.

We will some examples to understand the method.

Example 1 – DOB 17 SEPTEMBER 1950, TOB 10.10, POB VADNAGAR

Birth Chart

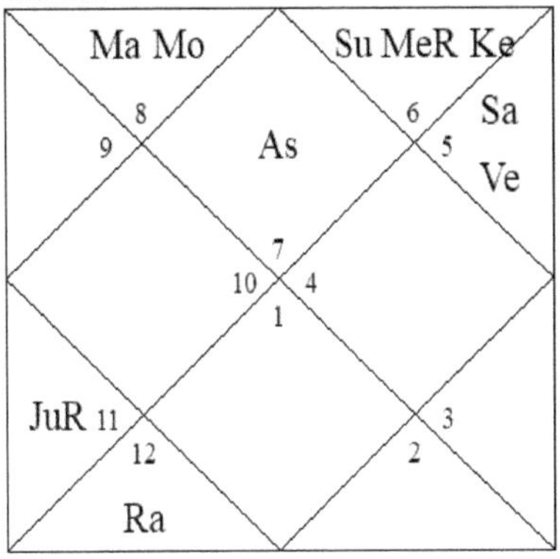

Birth Chart

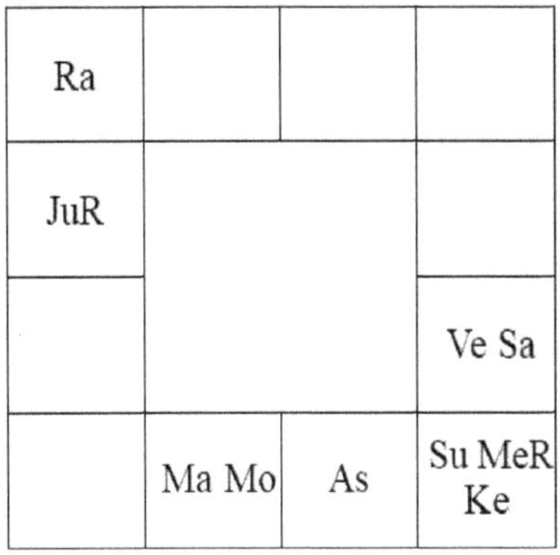

D30

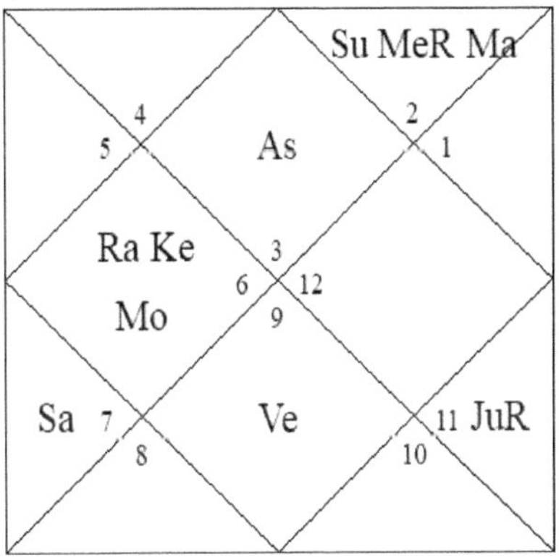

D30

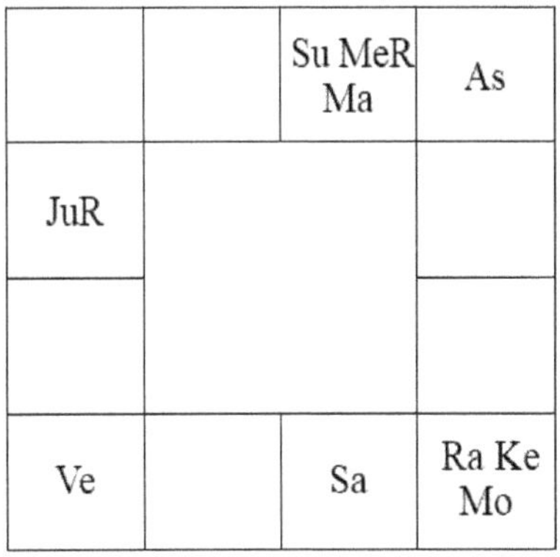

D30 Iyer

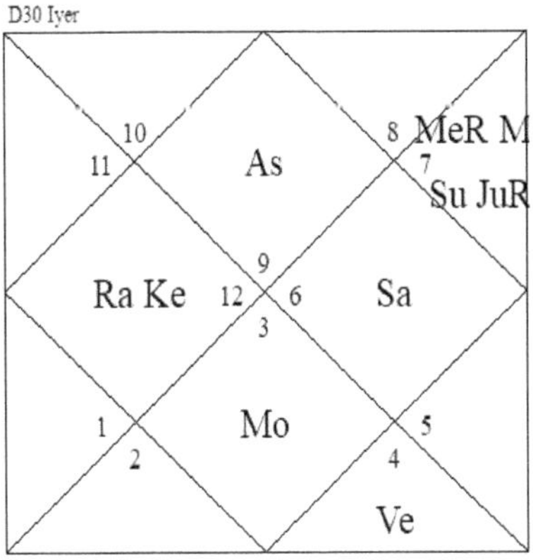

D30 Iyer

He assumed charge of office of Prime Minister of India on 26 May 2014. The Vimshottary Dasha was Moon/ Rahu/ Saturn/ Saturn. The transit position of planets on 26 May 2014 at Delhi was as under.

Transit chart of 26 May 2014

Birth Chart

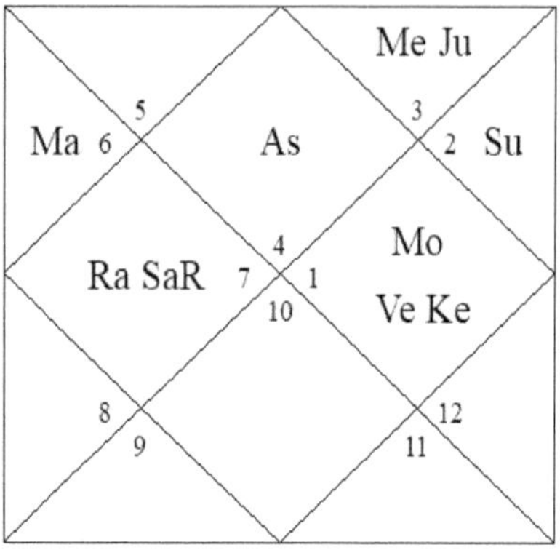

Birth Chart

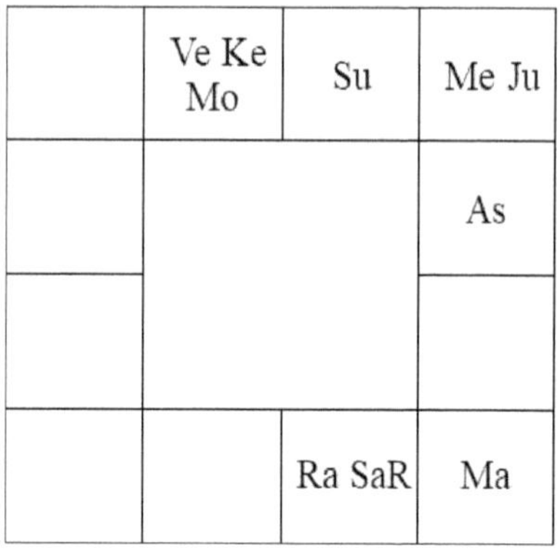

We give step by step analysis of Dasha and transit for the event.

1. The Vimshottary maha Dasha was of Moon. Moon is tenth lord of birth and is placed in second house. He is with second lord Mars and the debilitation of Moon is cancelled. The Antar Dasha was of Rahu. Rahu is in sixth house and gives victory over enemies. It is aspected by exalted Mercury and eleventh lord Sun. Thus, Dasha is favorable.
2. Now we check Rahu in Trishamsha.

a. Parashar Trishamsha – Rahu is in Kendra with Moon. Rahu will act as Mercury and Moon. The PD and SD lord Saturn is exalted in Trishamsha.

b. Iyer Trishamsha – Rahu is in Kendra and is aspected by Saturn from tenth house. In this Trishamsha raj yoga is present in eleventh house.

3. The Sooksham Dasha is of Saturn. Saturn is yoga karaka of birth.
4. Saturn is transiting Libra on this day along with Rahu. This is activating the raj yoga. The tenth lord, ninth lord and lagan lord are also involved.
5. Moon is in Aries. It is aspecting Libra.

Example 2 – DOB 14 OCTOBER 1951, TOB 13.00, POB BROOKLINE MA

He won 50 million dollars in lottery on 19 March 2004. His Iyer Trishamsha chart is amazing. Dasha on the date of winning was Mars/ Jupiter/ Saturn/ Moon.

Birth Chart

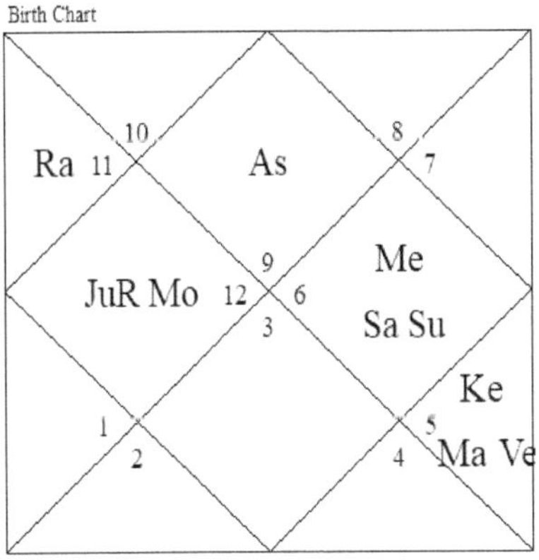

Birth Chart

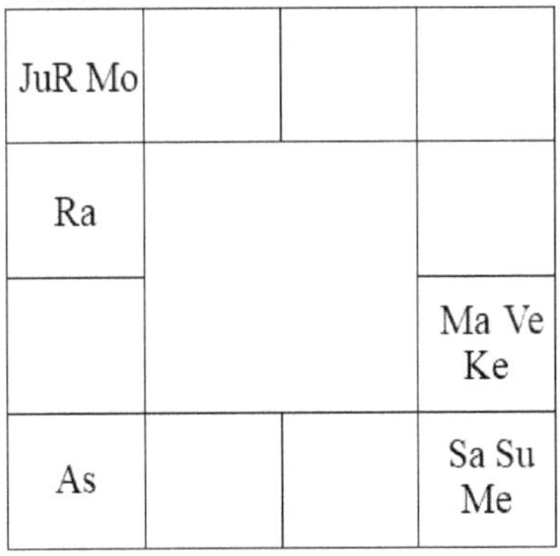

D30

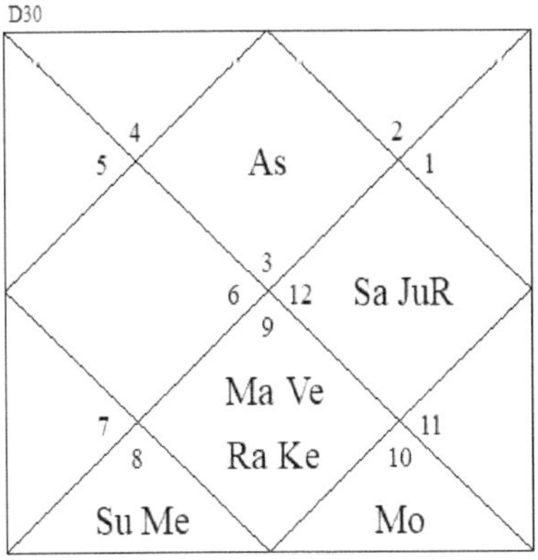

D30

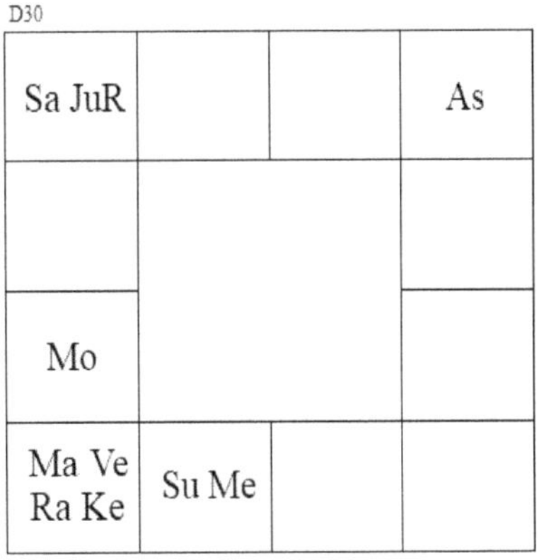

D30 Iyer

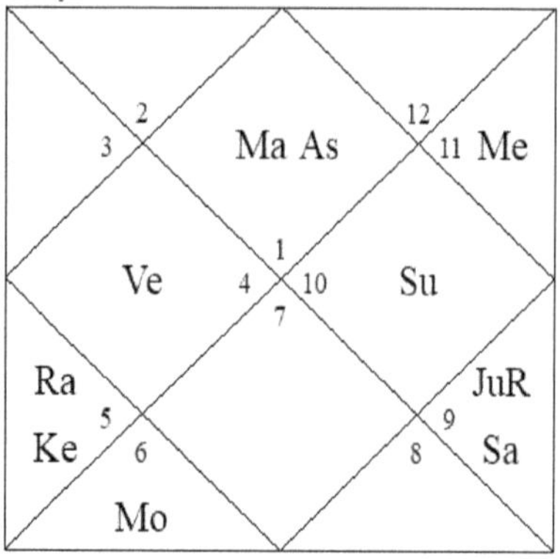

D30 Iyer

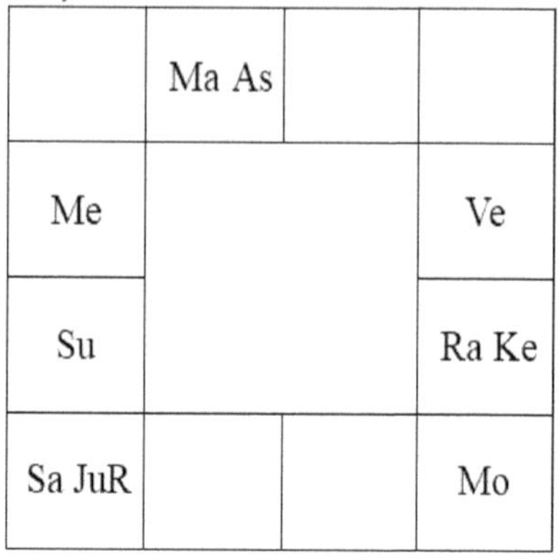

The transit chart on 19 March 2004 is as under.

Birth Chart

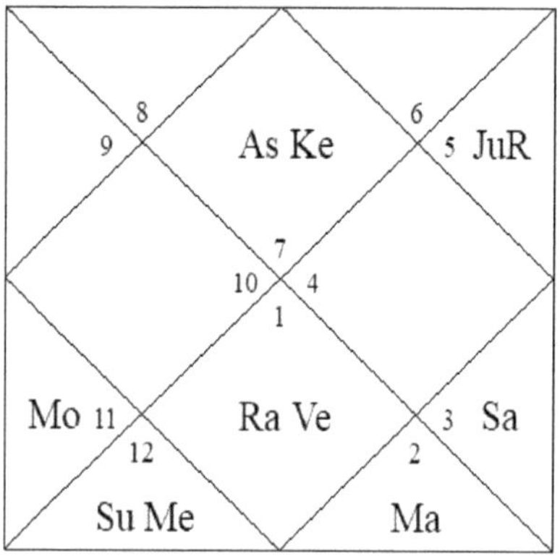

Birth Chart

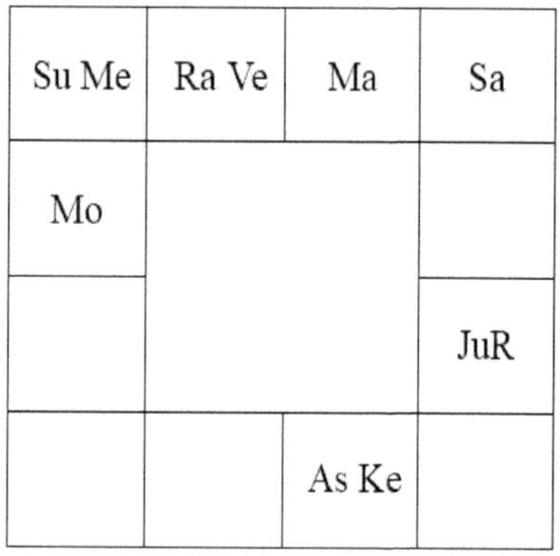

1. The Vimshottary maha Dasha was of Mars. Mars is the fifth lord of speculation and is placed in ninth house. In Iyer Trishamsha he is in lagan in Aries and is aspected by ninth lord Jupiter. Thus, Dasha is favorable.
2. Now we check Jupiter in Trishamsha.

a. Parashar Trishamsha – Jupiter is in Kendra with Saturn. Jupiter and Saturn are in raj yoga in tenth house.

b. Iyer Trishamsha – Jupiter is in ninth house of luck. Jupiter is with tenth lord Saturn causing raj yoga. The Antar Dasha of Saturn is in raj yoga.

3. The Sooksham Dasha is of Moon.
4. Saturn is transiting Gemini and activates raj yoga in Sagittarius.
5. Moon is in Aquarius. Aquarius is eleventh house of Iyer Trishamsha. Jupiter was transiting in Leo.

Example 3 – DOB 26 DECEMBER 1936, TOB 3.25.12, POB GULBARGA

He had to resign from the post of Chief Minister of a state on 25 January 2006. The Dasha was Saturn/ Jupiter/ Moon/ Saturn.

Birth Chart

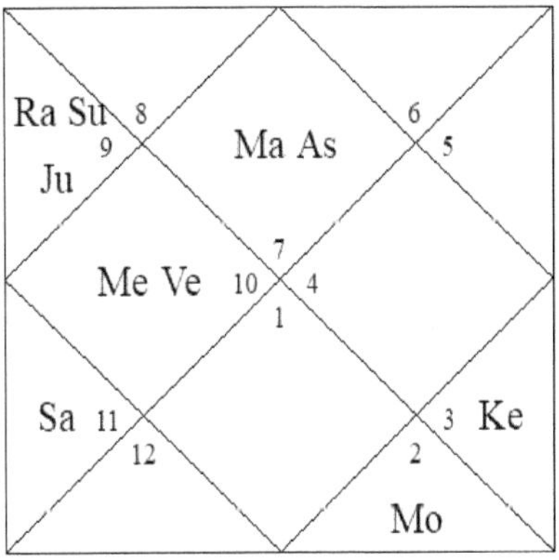

Birth Chart

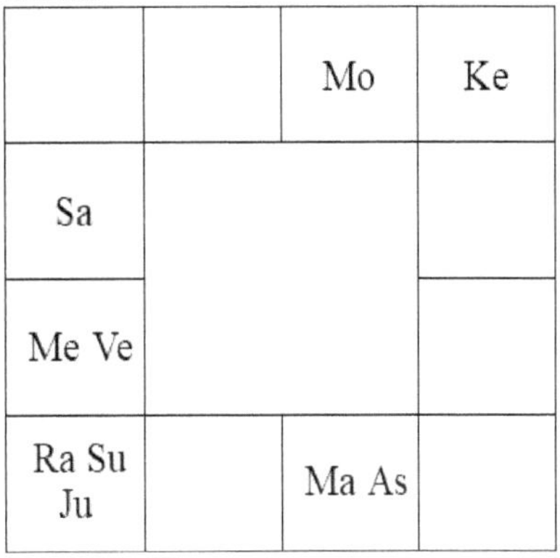

D30

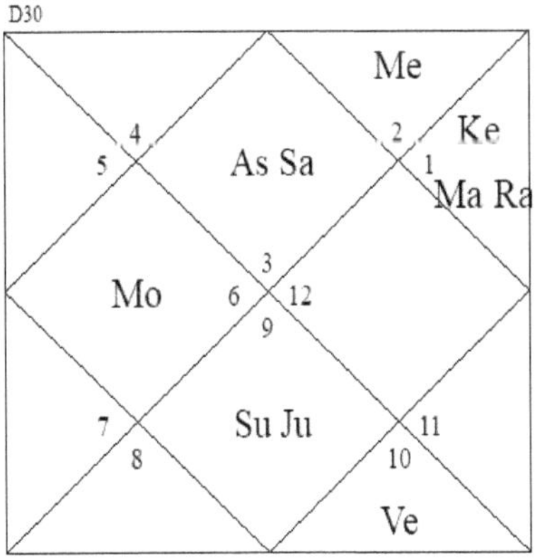

D30

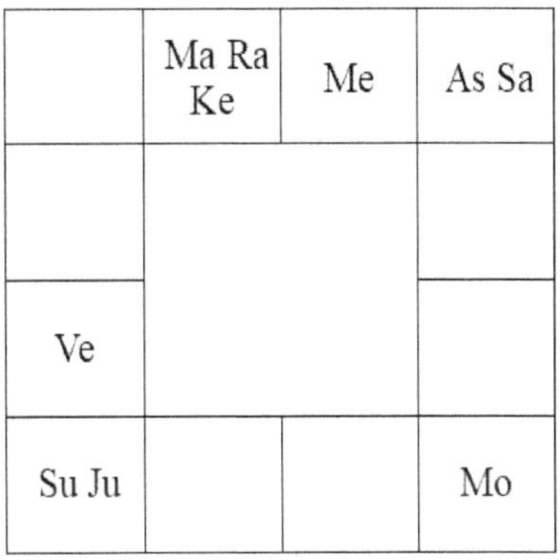

D30 Iyer

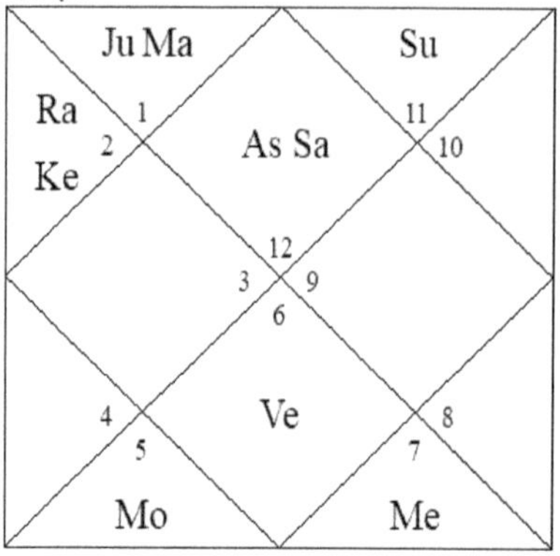

D30 Iyer

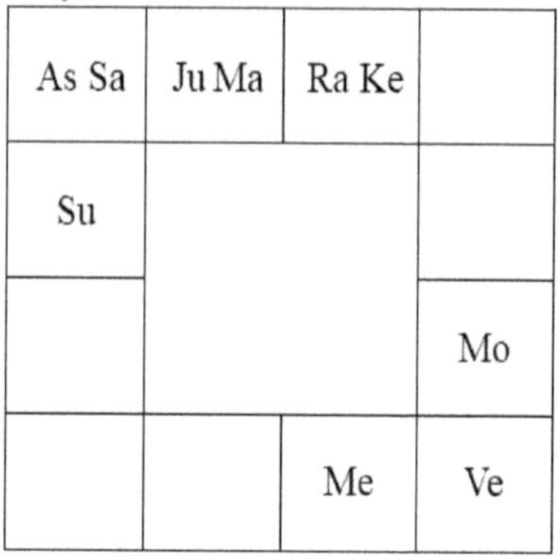

Transit on 25 January 2006

Birth Chart

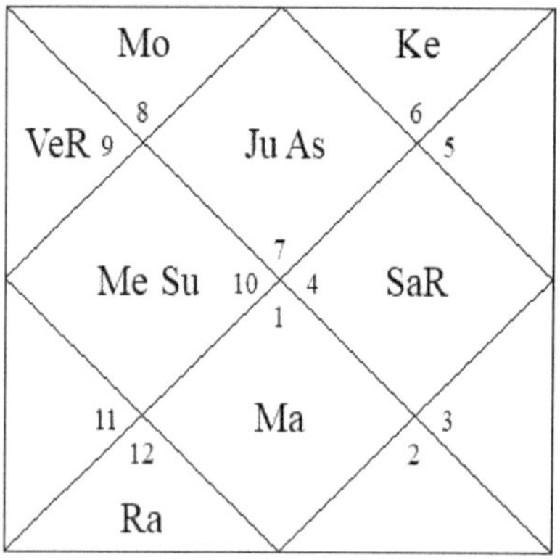

Birth Chart

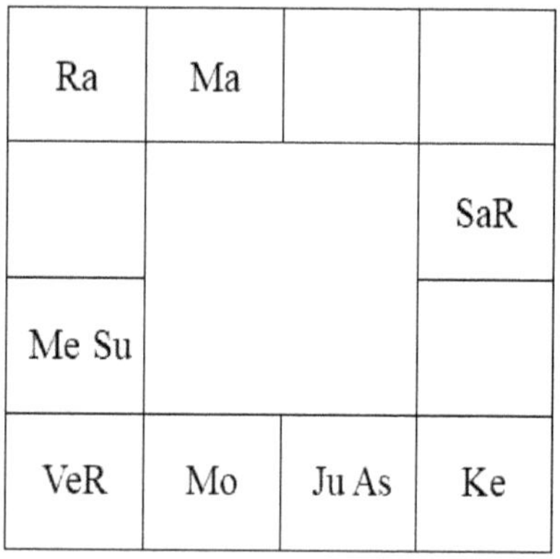

The Vimshottary maha Dasha was of Saturn. In birth chart Saturn is yoga karaka and is in Aquarius in fifth house. He has no other relation. This maha Dasha made him chief minister also. In Iyer Trishamsha Saturn is lord of twelfth house also. In Parashar Trishamsha he is eighth lord. Saturn is in lagan in both Trishamsha. He aspects tenth house. The AD is of Jupiter.

1. Now we check Jupiter in Trishamsha.

b. Parashar Trishamsha – Jupiter is in Kendra with Sun and aspected by Saturn. Jupiter and Saturn are in great raj yoga. Sun is third lord.

c. Iyer Trishamsha – Jupiter is in second house with second lord Mars. Jupiter is in papa Kartari and is with a malefic. This is not a good position for Jupiter. PD lord Moon is in sixth house and is aspected by sixth lord Sun.

2. The Sooksham Dasha is of Saturn.
3. Saturn is transiting Cancer and activates tenth lord Jupiter by tenth aspect in Iyer Trishamsha.
4. Moon is in Scorpio in transit. Scorpio is in RKA in Iyer Trishamsha. It is ninth house and is the house of loss of profession.

Example 4 – DOB 22 DECEMBER 1966, TOB 00.24, POB INDORE

This chart belongs to a student in my class. She met with a serious accident on 29 May 1992 and had three fractures. The Dasha was Venus/ Saturn/ Venus/ Venus. The Sooksham of Venus started on 29 May 1992, the date of accident.

Birth Chart

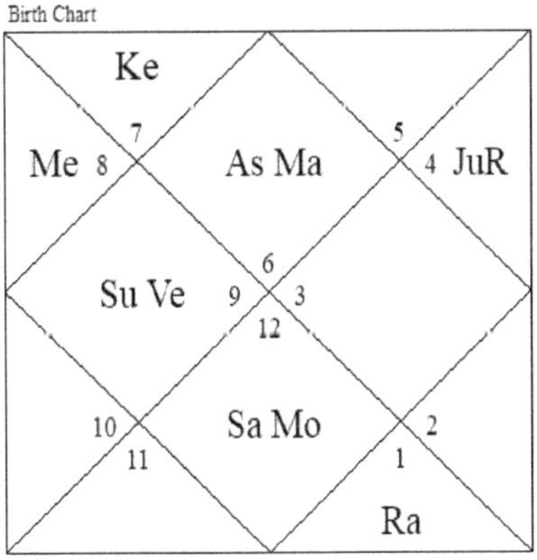

Birth Chart

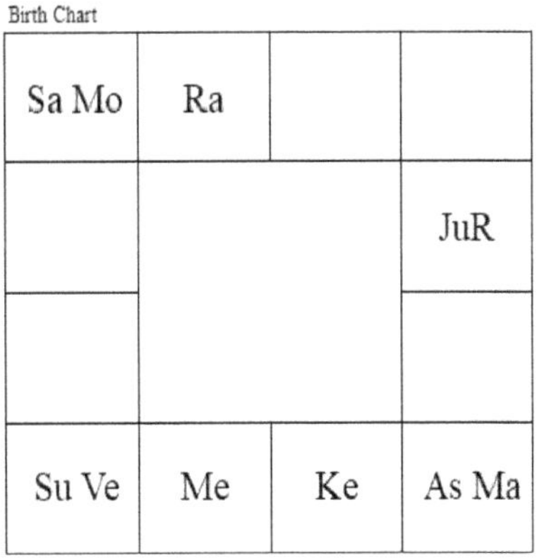

D30

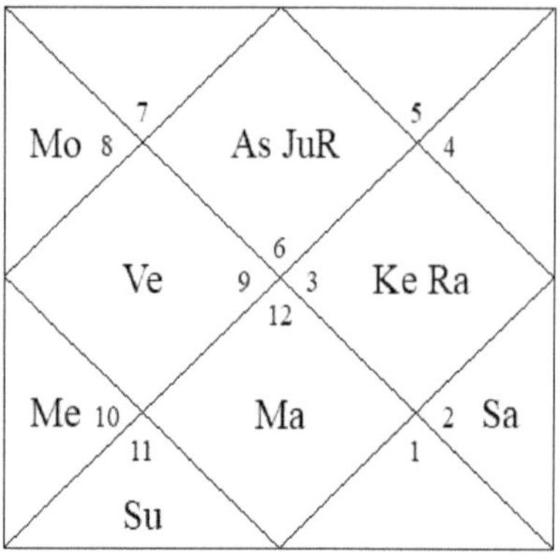

D30

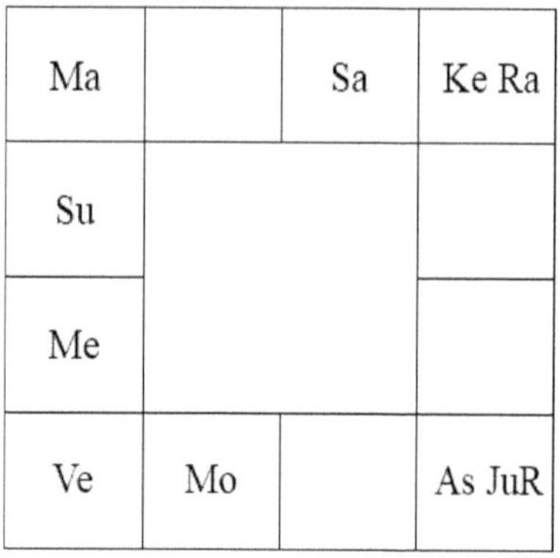

D30 Iyer

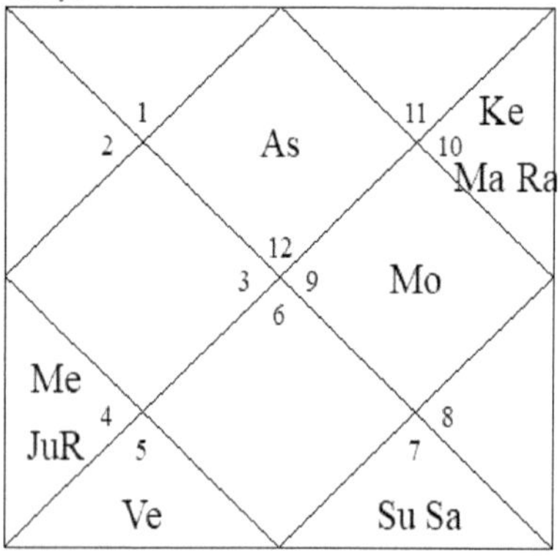

D30 Iyer

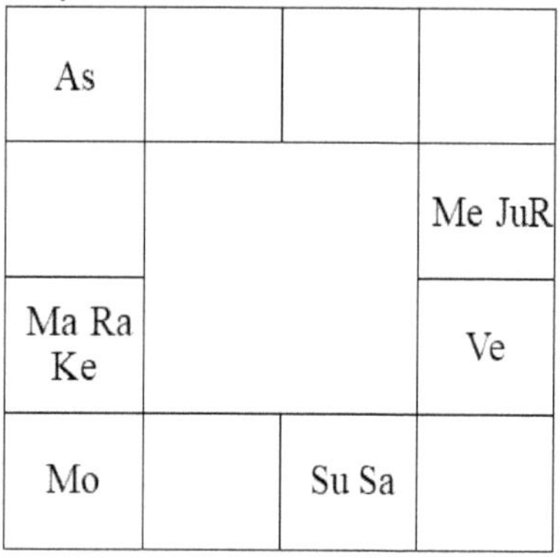

The transit on 29 May 1992 was as under.

Birth Chart

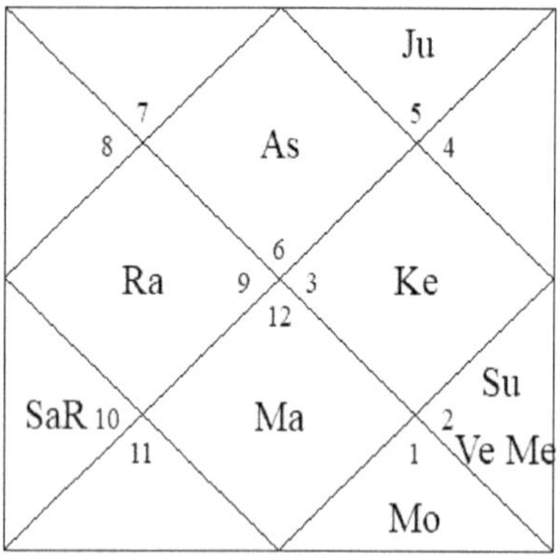

Birth Chart

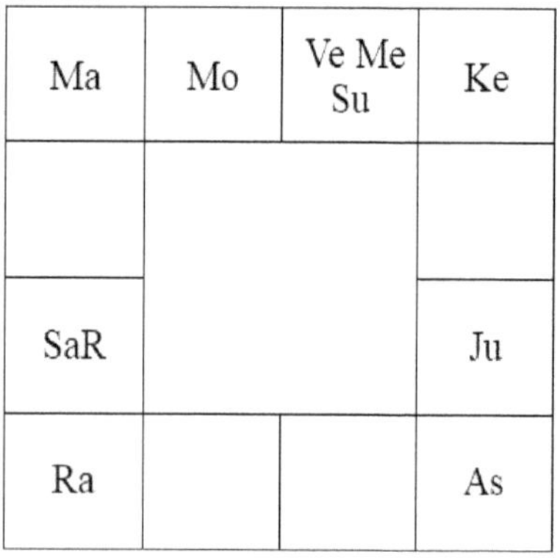

1. The Vimshottary maha Dasha was of Venus. In birth chart Venus is in fourth house with twelfth lord Sun and is aspected by sixth lord Saturn. Saturn is the AD. In Iyer Trishamsha Venus is in sixth house and is aspected by Mars. In Parashar Trishamsha it is in fourth house.
2. Now we check Saturn in Trishamsha.

a. Parashar Trishamsha – Saturn is in ninth house.

b. Iyer Trishamsha – Saturn is in eighth house with debilitated sixth lord Sun. Thus, AD lord is not in good position. The PD was of Venus. Venus is in sixth house aspected by afflicted Mars. This PD can give problems.

3. The Sooksham Dasha is of Venus again.
4. Saturn is transiting Capricorn and activates eighth house. With eighth house the lords of sixth and twelfth are also activated in Iyer Trishamsha.
5. Moon is in Aries in transit. In Iyer Trishamsha Moon is opposite to Saturn and Sun.

Example 5 – DOB 21 JANUARY 1980, TOB 18.05, POB DELHI

Birth Chart

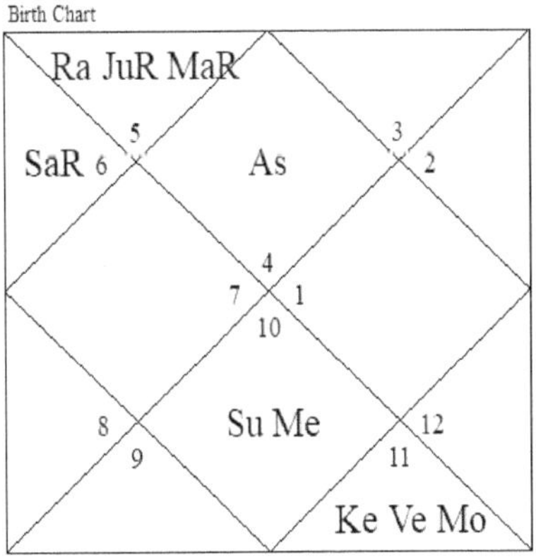

Birth Chart

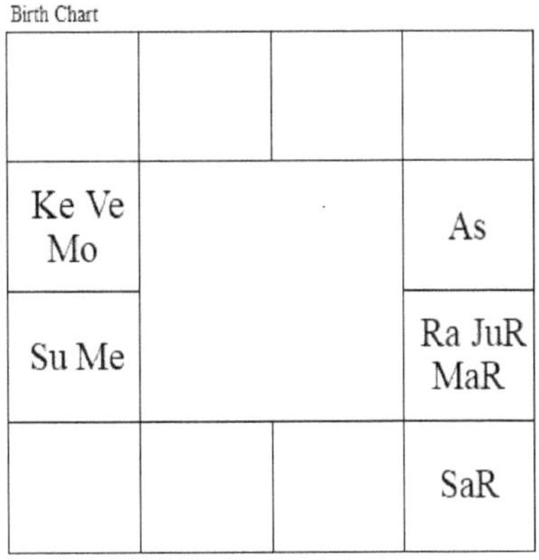

D30

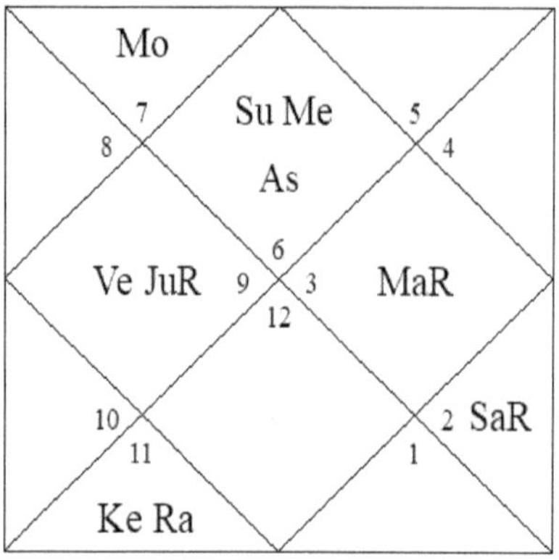

D30

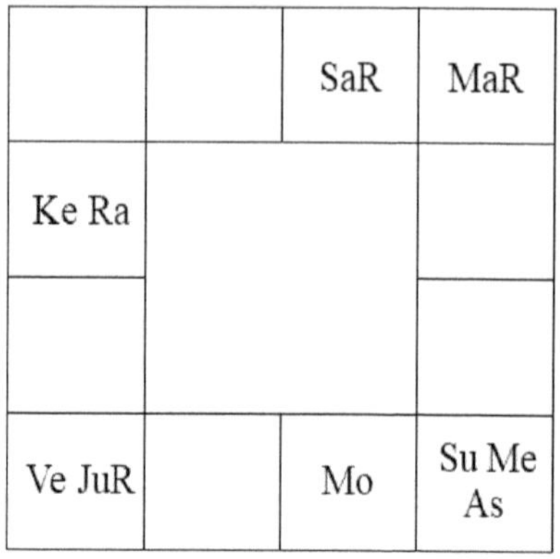

D30 Iyer

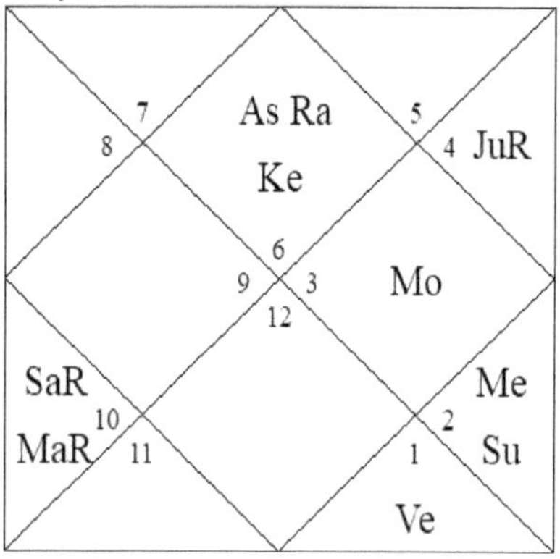

D30 Iyer

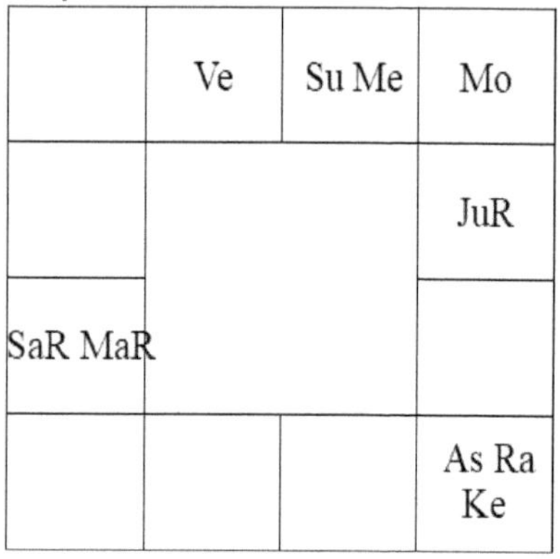

This example is taken to confirm the Dasha at the time of marriage. He was married on 20 April 2007. Vimshottary Dasha was Mercury/ Mercury/ Mercury/ Moon.

In birth chart Mercury is in seventh house and is lord of twelfth and third house. In Navamsha he is in sixth house and has no relation with seventh house or lord. In Parashar Trishamsha, Mercury is exalted in lagan.

In Iyer Trishamsha Mercury is lagan lord and is in Subh Kartari.

Transit on 20 April 2007

Birth Chart

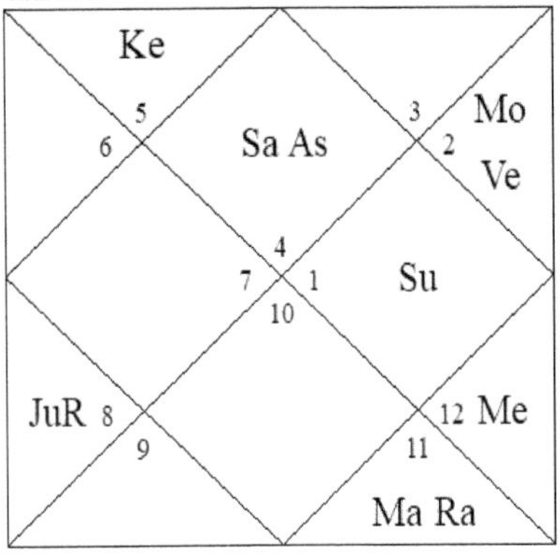

Birth Chart

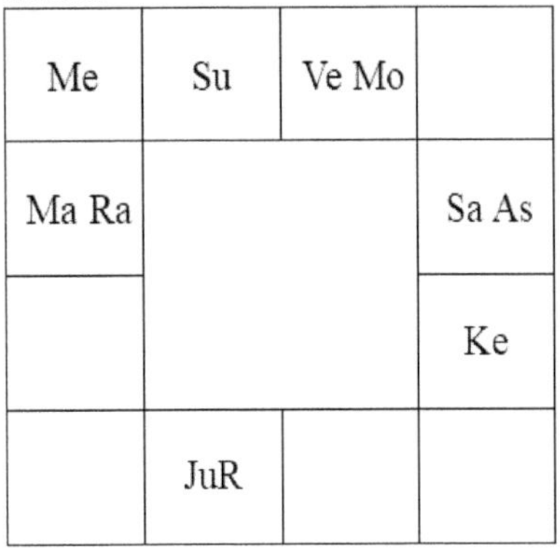

On the day of marriage Mercury was transiting the seventh house of Trishamsha.

www.ingramcontent.com/pod-product-compliance
Ingram Content Group UK Ltd.
Pitfield, Milton Keynes, MK11 3LW, UK
UKHW021402190726
13845UKWH00028B/819

9 788198 213433